To Bha~
w

D0215776

INEQUALITY REEXAMINED

INEQUALITY REEXAMINED

AMARTYA SEN

RUSSELL SAGE FOUNDATION · NEW YORK
CLARENDON PRESS · OXFORD
1992

Oxford University Press, Walton Street, Oxford OX2 6DP
Oxford   New York   Toronto
Delhi   Bombay   Calcutta   Madras   Karachi
Petaling Jaya   Singapore   Hong Kong   Tokyo
Nairobi   Dar es Salaam   Cape Town
Melbourne   Auckland
and associated companies in
Berlin   Ibadan

Oxford is a trade mark of Oxford University Press

British Library Cataloguing in Publication Data
Data available

Library of Congress Cataloging-in-Publication Data
Sen, Amartya Kumar.
Inequality reexamined/Amartya Sen.
Includes bibliographical references and indexes.
1. Equality.   2. Liberty.   3. Welfare economics.   I. Title.
JC575.S45 1992b 320'.01'1—dc20 92-10364
ISBN 0–19–828334–2

Typeset by BP Integraphics Ltd., Bath, Avon
Printed and bound in
Great Britain by Biddles Ltd.
Guildford & King's Lynn

To

Indrani and Kabir

Contents

Preface

THIS monograph, as the title indicates, is about re-examining inequality. But it is also about the evaluation and assessment of social arrangements in general. The former depends on the latter.

Equality of What?

The central question in the analysis and assessment of equality is, I argue here, 'equality of *what*?' I also argue that a common characteristic of virtually all the approaches to the ethics of social arrangements that have stood the test of time is to want equality of *something*—something that has an important place in the particular theory. Not only do income-egalitarians (if I may call them that) demand equal incomes, and welfare-egalitarians ask for equal welfare levels, but also classical utilitarians insist on equal weights on the utilities of all, and pure libertarians demand equality with respect to an entire class of rights and liberties. They are all 'egalitarians' in some essential way—arguing resolutely for equality of something which everyone should have and which is quite crucial to their own particular approach. To see the battle as one between those 'in favour of' and those 'against' equality (as the problem is often posed in the literature) is to miss something central to the subject.

I also argue that this common feature of being egalitarian in some significant way relates to the need to have equal concern, at some level, for all the persons involved—the absence of which would tend to make a proposal lack social plausibility.

Central Equality and Entailed Inequality

The crucial role of the question 'equality of what?' suggests that we can see the disputes between different schools of thought in terms of what they respectively take to be the central social exercise in which equality is to be demanded. These demands would then qualify the nature of the other social decisions. The demand for equality in terms of one variable entails that the theory concerned may have to be non-egalitarian with respect to another variable, since the two perspectives can, quite possibly, conflict.

For example, a libertarian demanding equal rights over a class of entitlements cannot, consistently with that, also insist on equality of incomes. Or, a utilitarian demanding equal weight on every unit of utility cannot, consistently with that, also require equality of freedoms or rights (and, for that matter, cannot insist even on equating *total levels* of utilities enjoyed by different persons). Wanting equality in what is taken to be the 'central' social exercise goes with accepting inequality in the remoter 'peripheries'. The disputes reside ultimately in locating the central social arrangement.

Invariant Demands and Contingent Characteristics

Indeed, the answers that are given to the question 'equality of what?' can serve as the basis of classifying different ethical theories of social arrangements. This classificatory principle brings out in each case what the invariant properties are and what are merely conditional or incidental connections. For example, a libertarian who sees the central exercise as including the requirement that a class of individual liberties be shared equally by all, need not object—as a libertarian—to the equality of incomes if, because of particular circumstances, this were also to come about. But if the circumstances were different, it is the equality of liberties that would be preserved, not the circumstantial equality of incomes.

In this connection, Willard Quine has recently suggested to me that I should explore the comparison between (1) this classificatory principle for the ethics of social arrangements based on the equalities that are preserved (when factual relations are transformed), and (2) the classificatory principles used in Felix Klein's attempted synthesis of geometry (in his *Erlanger Programm*) in terms of the properties of a space that are invariant with respect to a given group of transformations. I think there is an important general connection here, which can prove to be quite illuminating, though I have not probed this relationship in the present monograph.

Human Diversity and Disparate Equalities

At the practical level, the importance of the question 'equality of *what?*' derives from the actual diversity of human beings, so that demanding equality in terms of one variable tends to clash—*in fact* and not just *in theory*—with wanting equality in terms of another. We are deeply diverse in our internal characteristics (such as age, gender, general abilities, particular talents, proneness to illnesses, and so on) as well as in external circumstances (such as ownership of assets, social backgrounds, environmental predicaments, and so on). It is precisely because of such diversity that the insistence on egalitarianism in one field requires the rejection of egalitarianism in another.

The *substantive* importance of the question 'equality of what?' relates, thus, to the empirical fact of pervasive human diversity. Investigations of equality—theoretical as well as practical—that proceed with the assumption of antecedent uniformity (including the presumption that 'all men are created equal') thus miss out on a major aspect of the problem. Human diversity is no secondary complication (to be ignored, or to be introduced 'later on'); it is a fundamental aspect of our interest in equality.

Focusing on Freedoms and Capabilities

The monograph begins with these arguments, the reasons for presenting them, and the general implications they have (these issues are taken up in Chapter 1). The rest of the book follows on this line of analysis, and I move gradually from discussing the general nature of equality to exploring one particular way of answering the question 'equality of what?'

The chosen approach concentrates on our capability to achieve valuable functionings that make up our lives, and more generally, our freedom to promote objectives we have reasons to value. (Indeed, at one stage the monograph was even called 'Equality and Freedom'.) I distinguish this approach from other ways of answering the central question, discussing a whole class of theories varying from utilitarianism and libertarianism to the Rawlsian theory of 'justice as fairness'. Indeed, my greatest intellectual debt is undoubtedly to John Rawls. I am led by his reasoning over quite a bit of the territory, and even when I go in a different direction (e.g. focusing more on the *extents* of freedoms, rather than on the *means*—what Rawls calls the 'primary goods'), that decision is, to a considerable extent, based on an explicit critique of Rawls's theory.

Methodological and Substantive Claims

So the monograph both develops a general methodological approach to dealing with issues of inequality and explores a particular substantive approach as to how social arrangements may be assessed. In the introductory section of the book ('Introduction: Questions and Themes'), I have tried to gather together the main lines of discussion presented in this monograph.

Kuznets Lectures and Other Connections

This monograph draws on the Simon Kuznets Memorial Lectures I gave at Yale University in April 1988. I am very grateful to the Economic Growth Center and to its Director, Paul Schultz, for their invitation, for their hospitality, and for the intellectual stimulation offered to me. Much of what we know of the nature of the economic world has been deeply influenced by Simon Kuznets's works, and it was a great privilege to be able to pay tribute to his memory through these lectures.

There are other connections as well. Various parts of the monograph draw on other lectures, on different but related themes, given at the Delhi School of Economics (1986), the University of Texas (1986), Cambridge University (Marshall Lectures 1988), the University of Pittsburgh (Marion O'Kellie McKay Lecture 1988), and the Center for Operations Research and Econometrics at Louvain (1989). I have also lectured on several related themes to the Royal Economic Society (Annual Lecture 1988), to the International Economic Association (Presidential Address 1989), and to the Indian Economic Association (Presidential Address 1989). I learned a good deal from the comments and criticisms that were offered in the discussions that took place on those occasions.

Acknowledgements

I am also most grateful to the Russell Sage Foundation for research support over a part of the summer of 1988, and to Dr Eric Wanner, the President of the Foundation, for his interest in, and encouragement of, this research. I have also received much good advice from Andrew Schuller of the Clarendon Press and from Aida Donald of the Harvard University Press, and to them too I am much indebted. Some of the work was done when I was visiting the London School of Economics, and I am particularly appreciative of the splendid working atmosphere at the STICERD research centre there (under the Directorship of Nicholas Stern and efficient management of Luba Mumford).

Earlier versions of this monograph were read by A. B. Atkinson, Susan Brison, Jean Drèze, James Foster, Siddiq Osmani, Derek Parfit, Douglas Rae, Gustav Ranis, John Rawls, Emma Rothschild, Paul Schultz, and Bernard Williams, and I am most deeply indebted to them for the numerous helpful suggestions they made. Parts of the monograph were also read by Wilfred Beckerman, Jos de Beus, Moshe Halbertal, Steven Hawes, Athar Hussain, Robert Keohane, Peter Lanjouw, Stephen Marglin, James Mirrlees, Martha Nussbaum, Sanjay Reddy, and Thomas Schelling, and their comments have been extremely useful. Over the years I have also had the opportunity of profiting from discussions with a number of people on these and related subjects, and I would like to acknowledge my debt to Sudhir Anand, Kenneth Arrow, Pranab Bardhan, Kaushik Basu, Peter Bauer, André Béteille, Charles Blackorby, Christopher Bliss, John Broome, James Buchanan, G. A. Cohen, Douglas Dacy, Ralf Dahrendorf, Partha Dasgupta, Claude d'Aspremont, Angus Deaton, Meghnad Desai, Bhaskar Dutta, Ronald Dworkin, Wulf Gaertner, Louis Gevers, Jonathan Glover, James Griffin, Keith Griffin, Peter Hammond, Mahbub ul Haq, Richard Hare, Albert Hirschman, Eric Hobsbawm, Lal Jayawardena, Kumari Jayawardena, Ravi Kanbur, Nanak Kakwani, John Knight, Richard Layard, Isaac Levi, John Mackie, Mukul Majumdar, John Muellbauer, Amulya Ratna Nanda, Robert Nozick, Prasanta Pattanaik, Hilary Putnam, Ruth Anna Putnam, Willard Quine, V. K. Ramachandran, Martin Ravallion, Ashok Rudra, Thomas Scanlon, A. F. Shorrocks, T. N. Srinivasan, David Starrett, Hillel Steiner, Frances Stewart, Paul Streeten, Kotaro Suzumura, Larry Temkin, Philippe Van Parijs, Patricia Williams, Bengt Christer Ysander, Stefano Zamagni, and Vera Zamagni.

I have benefited from valuable research assistance from Chitrita Banerji, Stephan Klasen, and Sanjay Reddy. I am also grateful for the organizational support I have received from Jacky Jennings and Anna Marie Svedrofsky.

Some Presentational Points

I should, finally, make a few remarks about the presentational aspects. First, the minor issue of gender and language. I refer here not to the substantive concerns of this monograph, which include questions of gender inequality in various forms, but to the appearance of inconsistency in my use of gender-specific pronouns—sometimes using the 'he', sometimes 'she', sometimes 'he or she'. The exclusive use of 'he' to refer to both women and men is open to the charge of some implicit sexism; the exclusive use of 'she' can sound somewhat self-conscious and precious (and also open to a similar charge of discrimination from the opposite direction); and using 'he or she' everywhere every time is verbose, cumbrous, and ugly. If no great symbolic significance is to be attached to the gender form of the pronoun, then the natural route to take is to use the different forms *interchangeably*, and to refuse to see any inconsistency in this. This is exactly what I have tried to do.

Second, since I have been anxious to reach a wider audience than that of formally trained economists, I have tried to use as few technical concepts and mathematical expressions as possible. This has sometimes left room for further specification, but I have also referred to other writings (including my own) in which those issues have been further discussed.

Third, I have been told that the long list of references included in the monograph may 'raise some eyebrows'. But the literature is varied and vast, and having had the benefit of profiting from it, it would be wrong not to acknowledge the presence of this vast body of writings. The monograph is *not* a synthetic contribution, and I do want to take the discussion of inequality in a somewhat different direction—away from the prevailing traditions. But to do that I have to establish the co-ordinates of past and ongoing work, if only to ascertain where a departure might be due. Many of the works cited are also disputed, but even when they are, I have often been left with residual gain from the dialectic encounter. The bibliography may also, I hope, be of some use to readers—different parts, I imagine, to different readers, since they cover distinct aspects of inequality analysis. Be that as it may, I am working on steeling myself against elevated eyebrows.

A.K.S.

Introduction
Questions and Themes

The idea of equality is confronted by two different types of diversities: (1) the basic heterogeneity of human beings, and (2) the multiplicity of variables in terms of which equality can be judged. This book is concerned with both these diversities. It is also specifically concerned with the relation between the two. The heterogeneity of people leads to divergences in the assessment of equality in terms of different variables. This adds significance to the central question: equality of *what*?

Diverse Humanity

Human beings are thoroughly diverse. We differ from each other not only in external characteristics (e.g. in inherited fortunes, in the natural and social environment in which we live), but also in our personal characteristics (e.g. age, sex, proneness to illness, physical and mental abilities). The assessment of the claims of equality has to come to terms with the existence of pervasive human diversity.

The powerful rhetoric of 'equality of man' often tends to deflect attention from these differences. Even though such rhetoric (e.g. 'all men are born equal') is typically taken to be part and parcel of egalitarianism, the effect of ignoring the interpersonal variations can, in fact, be deeply inegalitarian, in hiding the fact that equal consideration for all may demand very unequal treatment in favour of the disadvantaged. The demands of substantive equality can be particularly exacting and complex when there is a good deal of antecedent inequality to counter.

Sometimes, human diversities are left out of account not on the misconceived 'high' ground of 'equality of human beings', but on the pragmatic 'low' ground of the need for simplification. But the net result of this can also be to ignore centrally important features of demands of equality.

Diversity of Focus

Equality is judged by comparing some particular aspect of a person (such as income, or wealth, or happiness, or liberty, or opportunities, or rights, or need-fulfilments) with the same aspect of another person. Thus, the judgement and measurement of inequality is thoroughly dependent on the choice of the variable (income, wealth, happiness, etc.) in terms of which comparisons are made. I shall call it the 'focal variable'—the variable on which the analysis focuses, in comparing different people.

The chosen focal variable can, of course, have an *internal* plurality. For example, freedoms of different types may be put together as the preferred focus of attention, or the variable selected may involve a combination of freedoms and achievements. The multiple features *within* a chosen focal variable have to be distinguished from the diversity *between* the chosen focal variables. Some variables that are often taken to be elementary and uniform do, in fact, have much internal plurality (e.g. real income or happiness).[1]

To use the kind of language for which we economists are often—not unreasonably—teased, this is the question of the choice of 'space' in which different persons are to be compared. That spatial analogy, despite its demonstratively Cartesian pretensions, is a useful classificatory device, and I shall invoke it to separate out the problem of the choice of focal variables ('the choice of space') from other issues in the assessment of inequality.

Links and Disharmonies

The characteristics of inequality in different spaces (such as income, wealth, happiness, etc.) tend to diverge from each other, because of the heterogeneity of people. Equality in terms of one variable may not coincide with equality in the scale of another. For example, equal opportunities can lead to very unequal incomes. Equal incomes can go with significant differences in wealth. Equal wealth can coexist with very unequal happiness. Equal happiness can go with widely divergent fulfilment of needs. Equal fulfilment of needs can be associated with very different freedoms of choice. And so on.

If every person were much the same as every other, a major cause

---

[1] I have discussed these issues elsewhere, addressing also the problem of overall ranking and aggregate valuation of inherently plural variables (in Sen 1980–1, 1982*a*).

of these disharmonies would disappear. If the rankings of equality in different spaces coincide, it would then be less important to have a clear answer to the question: equality of what? The pervasive diversity of human beings intensifies the need to address the diversity of focus in the assessment of equality.

Diverse Egalitarianism

It is convenient to begin with the observation that the major ethical theories of social arrangement all share an endorsement of equality in terms of *some* focal variable, even though the variables that are selected are frequently very different between one theory and another. It can be shown that even those theories that are widely taken to be 'against equality' (and are often described as such by the authors themselves) turn out to be egalitarian in terms of some other focus. The *rejection* of equality in such a theory in terms of some focal variable goes hand in hand with the *endorsement* of equality in terms of another focus.

For example, a libertarian approach (such as the entitlement theory forcefully developed in Robert Nozick's *Anarchy, State and Utopia*[2]) may give priority to extensive liberties to be *equally* guaranteed to each, and this demands rejecting equality—or any 'patterning'—of end states (e.g. the distribution of incomes or happiness). What is taken—usually by implication—to be a more central focus rules the roost, and inequalities in the variables that are, in effect, treated as peripheral must, then, be accepted in order not to violate the right arrangements (including equality) at the more central level.

Plausibility and Equality

There is a reason for this apparently ubiquitous 'egalitarianism'. Ethical plausibility is hard to achieve unless everyone is given equal consideration in *some* space that is important in the particular theory (Chapter 1). While it may be too ambitious to claim (as some have done) that this is a logical necessity, or simply a part of the discipline of the language of morals,[3] it is difficult to see how an

---

[2] See Nozick (1973, 1974). For a reassessment and some revision, see Nozick (1989).

[3] See particularly Hare (1952, 1963).

ethical theory can have general social plausibility without extending equal consideration to all at *some* level.

While the question 'why equality?' is by no means dismissible, it is not the central issue that differentiates the standard theories, since they are all egalitarian in terms of some focal variable. The engaging question turns out to be 'equality of what?'

To that question—'equality of what?'—different theories give different answers. The different answers are distinguishable *in principle* and involve different conceptual approaches. But the *practical* force of these distinctions depends on the empirical importance of the relevant human heterogeneities which make equality in one space diverge from equality in another.

Achievement and Freedom

Sources of divergence between different approaches can, of course, go well beyond the identification of the space itself, and may be concerned instead with the way the space is utilized. In the standard theory of inequality measurement, these problems of 'appropriate indices' have tended to receive much attention. The analysis can fruitfully proceed on the basis of postulating—explicitly or implicitly—acceptable axioms for inequality assessment in *that* space. While the focus of this book is on the choice of space and its implications, it is not my intention to deny the practical importance of these indexing problems in a given space (this was in fact the main subject of analysis in my previous book on inequality[4]).

One of the aspects of inequality assessment that has received less attention than it deserves relates to the distinction between *achievement* and the *freedom* to achieve. The nature, reach, and relevance of that distinction between achievement and freedom are briefly discussed in Chapter 2, making use of conceptual grounds for discrimination as well as analytical procedures used in modern economics.

Functionings and Capability

The monograph then proceeds to identify, develop, and defend a particular choice of space and its use in terms of the freedom to achieve (Chapter 3). A person's capability to achieve functionings

[4] *On Economic Inequality*; Sen 1973*a* in bibliography. Since I shall have to cite it frequently (mainly to avoid having to repeat myself), I shall refer to it in a more easily recognizable form, viz. *OEI*.

that he or she has reason to value provides a general approach to the evaluation of social arrangements, and this yields a particular way of viewing the assessment of equality and inequality.

The functionings included can vary from most elementary ones, such as being well-nourished, avoiding escapable morbidity and premature mortality, etc., to quite complex and sophisticated achievements, such as having self-respect, being able to take part in the life of the community, and so on. The selection and weighting of different functionings influence the assessment of the capability to achieve various alternative functioning bundles.

The roots of this approach can be traced to Aristotelian distinctions, but its ramifications can take various different forms. The particular class of possibilities developed here is less assertive and less insistently complete than some possible alternatives. But it is also less demanding on interpersonal agreement and more tolerant of unresolved disputes.

Evaluation of Effective Freedom

The concentration on *the freedom to achieve* and not just on the level of *achievement* raises some deep questions about the connection between the appraisal of the alternative *achievements* and the value of the *freedom* to achieve them (Chapter 4). Even the freedom-based perspective must pay particular attention to the nature and value of the actual achievements, and inequalities in achievement can throw light on inequalities in the respective freedoms enjoyed. This recognition requires us to reject such proposed rules of freedom assessment as the counting of the number of alternatives in the 'range of choice'. More constructively, it suggests practical ways of using observable data regarding achievements to get a partial but significant view of the freedoms enjoyed by different persons.

In this context I also discuss the difference between well-being objectives and the other objectives a person may have. This difference not only leads to some plurality within the idea of freedom itself, it also has important implications on the divergence between the perspective of achievements and that of freedoms.

One of the related issues taken up here is the possibility that more freedom can be disadvantageous to a person, which—if generally true—can undermine the rationale of judging inequality in terms of freedoms. I argue that the real conflict is between different types of freedoms, and not between freedom *tout court* and advantages in general.

Distinctions: Capability and Utility

The focus on the space of functionings—and on the capability to achieve functionings—differs quite substantially from the more traditional approaches to equality, involving concentration on such variables as income, wealth, or happiness (Chapters 3 and 4). The fact of human diversity is closely related to substantive conflicts between focusing on different informational bases for assessing equality, efficiency, and justice.

In particular, judging equality and efficiency in terms of the capability to achieve differs from the standard utilitarian approaches as well as from other welfarist formulations. Welfarism in general and utilitarianism in particular see value, ultimately, only in individual utility, which is defined in terms of some mental characteristic, such as pleasure, happiness, or desire.[5] This is a restrictive approach to taking note of individual advantage in two distinct ways: (1) it ignores freedom and concentrates only on achievements, and (2) it ignores achievements other than those reflected in one of these mental metrics. In so far as utility is meant to stand for individual well-being, it provides a rather limited accounting of that, and it also pays no direct attention to the freedom to pursue well-being—or any other objective (Chapter 3).

This way of seeing individual advantage is particularly limiting in the presence of entrenched inequalities. In situations of persistent adversity and deprivation, the victims do not go on grieving and grumbling all the time, and may even lack the motivation to desire a radical change of circumstances. Indeed, in terms of a strategy for living, it may make a lot of sense to come to terms with an ineradic-

---

[5] There is some ambiguity in the characterization of the 'preference' view of utility, as it can be—and has been—defined in quite distinct and divergent ways. If it is defined entirely in terms of individual choice (as in Samuelson 1938), then the preference view does not give any immediate content to *interpersonal* comparisons and thus does not yield any straightforward judgements of inequality. The devised meanings that can be somewhat artificially constructed (e.g. Harsanyi's 1955 engaging proposal that we consider our preference regarding *who* we would choose to be) involve conceptual problems as well as empirical difficulties (I have discussed this issue in Sen 1982a). On the other hand, if preference is defined in terms of a person's sense of desire or satisfaction (as in Edgeworth 1881 or Hicks 1939), then the preference approach is in line with the mental-metric views considered in the text.

able adversity, to try to appreciate small breaks, and to resist pining for the impossible or the improbable. Such a person, even though thoroughly deprived and confined to a very reduced life, may not appear to be quite so badly off in terms of the mental metric of desire and its fulfilment, and in terms of the pleasure–pain calculus. The extent of a person's deprivation may be substantially muffled in the utility metric, despite the fact that he or she may lack the opportunity even to be adequately nourished, decently clothed, minimally educated, or properly sheltered.

The misleading nature of utility metrics may be particularly important in the context of stable differentiation of class, gender, caste, or community. It contrasts with the focus on capabilities, which provides a straightforward account of the lack of freedom of the deprived people to achieve those elementary functionings (Chapter 3).

Capability and Opportunities: Equality and Efficiency

The capability perspective also differs from various concepts of 'equality of opportunities' which have been championed for a long time. In a very basic sense, a person's capability to achieve does indeed stand for the opportunity to pursue his or her objectives. But the concept of 'equality of opportunities' is standardly used in the policy literature in more restrictive ways, defined in terms of the equal availability of some *particular means*, or with reference to equal applicability (or equal *non*-applicability) of some *specific barriers or constraints*.

Thus characterized, 'equality of opportunities' does not amount to anything like equality of *overall* freedoms. This is so because of (1) the fundamental diversity of human beings, and (2) the existence and importance of various means (such as income or wealth) that do not fall within the purview of standardly defined 'equality of opportunities'. In terms of the position outlined and defended in this monograph, a more adequate way of considering 'real' equality of opportunities must be through equality of capabilities (or through the elimination of unambiguous inequalities in capabilities, since capability comparisons are typically incomplete).

But equality is not the only social charge with which we have to be concerned, and there are demands of efficiency as well. An attempt to achieve equality of capabilities—without taking note of aggregative considerations—can lead to severe curtailment of the capabilities that people can altogether have. The demands of equality of capabilities has to be seen in the context of the contending claims of efficiency and, in general, of aggregative concerns. Indeed, it will be argued that the import of the concept of equality cannot even be adequately understood without paying simultaneous attention also to aggregative consideration—to the 'efficiency aspect', broadly speaking (Chapter 9).[6]

Differences with the Rawlsian Focus

A particularly important contrast is that between capability-based evaluation and Rawls's (1971) procedure of focusing on the holding of 'primary goods' (including resources such as incomes, wealth, opportunities, the social bases of self-respect, etc.). This is a part of his 'Difference Principle', which is an integral component of the Rawlsian theory of 'justice as fairness'. While my own approach is deeply influenced by Rawls's analysis,[7] I argue that the particular informational focus on which Rawls himself concentrates neglects some considerations that can be of great importance to the substantive assessment of equality—and also of efficiency.[8]

The importance of the contrast once again turns on the fundamental diversity of human beings. Two persons holding the same bundle of primary goods can have very different freedoms to pursue their respective conceptions of the good (whether or not these conceptions coincide). To judge equality—or for that matter efficiency—in the space of primary goods amounts to giving priority to the *means* of freedom over any assessment of the *extents* of freedom, and this can be a drawback in many contexts. The practical importance of the divergence can be very great indeed in dealing with

[6] In several ethical frameworks, the insufficient attention paid explicitly to efficiency considerations is combined with choice of somewhat insensitive indicators for the assessment of inequality, and thus the neglect of efficiency does not yield immediately unappealing results. But this kind of 'double limitation' does little justice either to equality or to efficiency. I argue that something of this problem is present even in the Rawlsian formulation of the Difference Principle (Ch. 9).

[7] In fact, one reason for my concentration on the difference between Rawls's analysis and what I have proposed is precisely my indebtedness to Rawls. By specifying in some detail (Chs. 5 and 9) the departures from Rawls's position, it is possible to clarify what exactly is being claimed and why.

[8] A similar remark can be made, though for somewhat different reasons, about Ronald Dworkin's (1981) arguments for 'the equality of resources' (see Ch. 5, and also Sen 1984: ch. 13).

inequalities related to gender, location, and class, and also to general variations in inherited characteristics.

Economic Inequality and Poverty

The perspective of functionings and capabilities suggests particular approaches to the evaluation of economic inequality. They differ from the standardly used informational focus in welfare economics, which tends to concentrate on incomes, wealth, and utilities (Chapter 6). They also raise some questions about the analytical procedures of inequality evaluation commonly used in economic theory.

The theory of inequality evaluation has close links with that of assessment of poverty, and the choice of space becomes a central concern in identifying the poor and in aggregating the information about the states of those identified. If poverty is seen as the deprivation of some minimum fulfilment of elementary capabilities, it becomes easier to understand why poverty has both an absolute and a relative aspect. These considerations are important in dealing with poverty in any country (rich or poor), but are particularly relevant in understanding the nature of poverty in the richer countries, such as the USA and those in Western Europe (Chapter 7). The persistence of poverty in otherwise affluent countries is an apparently puzzling phenomenon that is beginning to get serious attention in contemporary debates. The understanding and the remedying of this problem can both be helped by explicit consideration of the relation between deprivations in different spaces, especially between incomes and the capability to lead secure and worthwhile lives.

Class, Gender and Other Categories

In Chapter 8 the relevance of the capability perspective is discussed in the context of differences in class, gender, and other social features. Once again, the fact of human diversity plays a crucial part in strengthening the significance of the informational departure in moving from the spaces of incomes, opportunities, happiness, primary goods, etc., to taking direct note of the achievement of functionings and the capability to achieve them (Chapter 8).

The capability perspective is more sensitive than utility-based approaches to problems of entrenched deprivation, which can lead to defensive adjustment of desires and expectations (thereby distorting the metric of utilities). It can also be fairer in dealing directly with freedoms rather than concentrating on the means of freedoms. These differences are significant in assessing inequality and injustice across the barriers of class, gender, and other social divisions.

Equality, Efficiency and Incentives

While the last chapter does not 'summarize' the monograph (or list the main conclusions), it contains a fairly wide-ranging discussion of many of the issues covered in the book. It also tries to link the methodological arguments on equality with the substantive analysis of the capability perspective as the basis of judging equality.

In this context, it is argued that the demands of equality cannot be properly assessed without seeing them in the context of other demands, especially those of aggregative objectives and of overall efficiency. When equality is viewed isolated from other concerns, the evaluation of equality tends to get distorted because of the unnecessary load it has to carry (proxying for efficiency objectives that can be better accommodated elsewhere). This consideration has some bearing on the formulation of theories of justice, including Rawlsian theory.

In considering the conflict between aggregative and distributive objectives, the incentive problem proves to be less of a force against egalitarianism when the inequalities are generated by entrenched antecedent diversities (as they typically are in the case of class, gender, and other non-adjustable and identifiable barriers). Since the problem of inequality can be particularly serious in the presence of extensive human diversities, this question is of some relevance for economic and social policy.

Methods and Substance

This monograph is concerned with methodological as well as substantive issues. The attention is mostly concentrated on conceptual clarification in the early chapters, emphasizing the importance of the question 'equality of what?' and relating it to the fact of extensive human diversity. The substantive claims take the form of proposing a particular way of *answering* that question and suggesting various implications of that answer. The implications, I have argued, are not only of theoretical interest, they also have some practical importance.

1

EQUALITY OF WHAT?

1.1. WHY EQUALITY? WHAT EQUALITY?

Two central issues for ethical analysis of equality are: (1) Why equality? (2) Equality of what? The two questions are distinct but thoroughly interdependent. We cannot begin to defend or criticize equality without knowing what on earth we are talking about, i.e. equality of what features (e.g. incomes, wealths, opportunities, achievements, freedoms, rights)? We cannot possibly answer the first question without addressing the second. That seems obvious enough.

But if we *do* answer question (2), do we still *need* to address question (1)? If we have successfully argued in favour of equality of *x* (whatever that *x* is—some outcome, some right, some freedom, some respect, or some something else), then we have already argued for equality in *that* form, with *x* as the standard of comparison. Similarly, if we have rebutted the claim to equality of *x*, then we have already argued against equality in that form, with *x* as the standard of comparison. There is, in this view, no 'further', no 'deeper', question to be answered about why—or why not—'equality'. Question (1), in this analysis, looks very much like the poor man's question (2).

There is some sense in seeing the matter in this way, but there is also a more interesting substantive issue here. It relates to the fact that every normative theory of social arrangement that has at all stood the test of time seems to demand equality of *something*—something that is regarded as particularly important in that theory. The theories involved are diverse and frequently at war with each other, but they still seem to have that common feature. In the contemporary disputes in political philosophy, equality does, of course, figure prominently in the contributions of John Rawls (equal liberty and equality in the distribution of 'primary goods'), Ronald Dworkin ('treatment as equals', 'equality of resources'), Thomas Nagel ('economic equality'), Thomas Scanlon ('equality'), and others generally associated with a 'pro equality' view.[1] But equality in some space seems to be demanded even by those who are typically seen as having disputed the 'case for equality' or for 'distributive justice'. For example, Robert Nozick may not demand equality of utility or equality of holdings of primary goods, but he does demand equality of libertarian rights—no one has any more right to liberty than anyone else. James Buchanan builds equal legal and political treatment—indeed a great deal more—into his view of a good society.[2] In each theory, equality *is* sought in some space—a space that is seen as having a central role in that theory.[3]

But what about utilitarianism? Surely, utilitarians do not, in general, want the equality of the total utilities enjoyed by different people. The utilitarian formula requires the maximization of the sum-total of the utilities of all people *taken together*, and that is, in an obvious sense, not particularly egalitarian.[4] In fact, the equality that utilitarianism seeks takes the form of equal treatment of human beings in the space of *gains and losses of utilities*. There is an insistence on equal weights on everyone's utility gains in the utilitarian objective function.

This diagnosis of 'hidden' egalitarianism in utilitarian philosophy might well be resisted on the ground that utilitarianism really involves a sum-total maximizing approach, and it might be thought that, as a result, any egalitarian feature of utilitarianism cannot be more than accidental. But this reasoning is deceptive. The utilitarian approach is undoubtedly a *maximizing* one, but the real question is

[1] See Rawls (1971, 1988a), R. Dworkin (1978, 1981), Nagel (1979, 1986), Scanlon (1982, 1988b). The positions taken by the modern utilitarians raise a more complex question (on which more presently), but the starting-point is something like 'giving equal weight to the equal interests of all the parties' (Hare 1982: 26), or a procedure to 'always assign the same weight to all individuals' interests' (Harsanyi 1982: 47).

[2] See Nozick (1973, 1974), J. M. Buchanan (1975, 1986). See also J. M. Buchanan and Tullock (1962).

[3] This does not, obviously, apply to those critiques of equality (in some space) that do not include a proposal for something constructive instead. It is the presentation or defence of such a constructive proposal that can be expected to entail—often implicitly—the demand for equality in some *other* space. Nor is the expectation of a demand for equality in some other space likely to apply to theories that do not refer to human beings at all, e.g. proposals that advocate 'maximization of the total market value of wealth'. It is in a *constructive* proposal making use of some human condition that an implicit demand for some type of equality is likely to occur.

[4] In my earlier book on inequality (*On Economic Inequality*, Sen 1973a in the bibliography), I had discussed in some detail (see ch. 1) why utilitarianism is inegalitarian in some important respects. As indicated in the Introduction, that book is referred to in this monograph as *OEI*.

what is the nature of the objective function it maximizes. That objective function could have been quite inegalitarian, e.g. giving much more weight to the utilities of some than to those of others. Instead, utilitarianism attaches exactly the same importance to the utilities of all people in the objective function, and that feature—coupled with the maximizing format—guarantees that everyone's utility gains get the same weight in the maximizing exercise. The egalitarian foundation is, thus, quite central to the entire utilitarian exercise. Indeed, it is precisely this egalitarian feature that relates to the foundational principle of utilitarianism of 'giving equal weight to the equal interests of all the parties' (Hare 1981: 26), or to 'always assign the same weight to all individuals' interests' (Harsanyi 1982: 47).[5]

What do we conclude from this fact? One obvious conclusion is that being egalitarian (i.e. egalitarian in *some space or other* to which great importance is attached) is not really a 'uniting' feature.[6] Indeed, it is precisely because there are such substantive differences between the endorsement of different spaces in which equality is recommended by different authors that the basic similarity between them (in the form of wanting equality in *some* space that is seen as important) can be far from transparent. This is especially so when the term 'equality' is defined—typically implicitly—as equality in a *particular* space.

For example, in his interesting essay, 'The Case against Equality', with which William Letwin (1983) introduces an important collection of papers by different authors on that theme (the volume is called *Against Equality*), he argues against equal distribution of incomes (or commodities) thus: 'Inasmuch as people are unequal, it

---

[5] John Rawls (1971) has argued that 'there is a sense in which classical utilitarianism fails to take seriously the distinction between persons' (p. 187). In so far as a utilitarian theorist argues simply for the maximization of the amount of happiness, pleasure, etc., with no attention being paid to the fact that these things are features of particular persons, Rawls's claim has much force. But a utilitarian can also see utility as an irreducibly personal feature demanding attention precisely because the well-beings of the persons involved command respect and regard. On this see Bentham (1789), Mill (1861), Edgeworth (1881), Pigou (1952), Hare (1981), Harsanyi (1982), and Mirrlees (1982). This limited 'defence' of utilitarianism should not be seen as supporting it as an adequate ethical or political theory. Utilitarianism does have serious deficiencies (I have tried to discuss them elsewhere: Sen 1970*a*, 1979*b*, 1982*b*), but not taking the distinction between different persons seriously may not be a fair charge against utilitarianism in general.

[6] On this and related issues, see B. Williams (1973*a*), Suppes (1977), Sen (1980*a*), R. Dworkin (1981), Rae (1981), Béteille (1983*b*).

is rational to presume that they ought to be treated unequally—which might mean larger shares for the needy or larger shares for the worthy' ('A Theoretical Weakness of Egalitarianism', 8). But even the demand for equal satisfaction of 'needs' is a requirement of equality (in a particular space), and it has indeed been championed as such for a long time. Even though the idea of individual 'worth' is harder to characterize, the usual formulations of the demand for 'larger shares for the worthy' tend to include equal treatment for equal worth, giving to each the same reward for worth as is given to another. Thus, these critiques of egalitarianism tend to take the form of being—instead—egalitarian in some *other* space.[7] The problem again reduces to arguing, implicitly, for a different answer to the question 'equality of what?'.

Sometimes the question 'equality of what?' gets *indirectly* addressed in apparently discussing 'why equality?', with equality defined in a *specific* space. For example, Harry Frankfurt's (1987) well-reasoned paper attacking 'equality as a moral ideal' is concerned mainly with disputing the claims of *economic* egalitarianism in the form of 'the doctrine that it is desirable for everyone to have the same amounts of income and wealth (for short, "money")' (p. 21).[8] Though the language of the presentation puts 'egalitarianism' as such in the dock, this is primarily because Frankfurt uses that general term to refer specifically to a particular version of 'economic egalitarianism': 'This version of economic egalitarianism (for short, simply "egalitarianism") might also be formulated as the doctrine that there should be no inequalities in the *distribution* of money' (p. 21).

The choice of space for equality is, thus, central to Frankfurt's main thesis.[9] His arguments can be seen as disputing the specific demand for a common interpretation of economic egalitarianism by

[7] Similarly, Peter Bauer's (1981) forceful argument in favour of the same right for all to enjoy what they have 'produced' is also an egalitarian demand in that chosen space—that of receiving a reward commensurate with one's productive contribution.

[8] See also J. R. Lucas (1965, 1980). For a pointed critique of Frankfurt's thesis, see Goodin (1987).

[9] Indeed, the nature of the space is crucial to all axioms that take the form of demanding or rejecting equality. For example, the 'weak equity axiom' stated in my *OEI* indicated a preference for equality in the space or *overall well-being*. While that condition was possibly over-strong, since it incorporated a lexicographic priority of equality over aggregative considerations, some of the critiques of the condition have been misplaced in interpreting the formal requirement in *other spaces*, e.g. in the allocation of specialist medical care among persons (see J. Griffin 1981, 1986; see also Brandt 1979, and my response to his critique in Sen 1980–1).

arguing (1) that such an equality is of no great intrinsic interest, *and* (2) that it leads to the violation of intrinsically important values—values that link closely to the need for paying equal attention to all in some other—more relevant—way.

Wanting equality of *something*—something seen as *important*—is undoubtedly a similarity of some kind, but that similarity does not put the warring camps on the same side. It only shows that the battle is not, in an important sense, about 'why equality?', but about 'equality of what?'.

Since some spaces are traditionally associated with claims of 'equality' in political or social or economic philosophy, it is equality in one of those spaces (e.g. incomes, wealths, utilities) that tend to go under the heading 'egalitarianism'. I am *not* arguing against the continued use of the term 'egalitarianism' in one of those senses; there is no harm in that practice if it is understood to be a claim about equality in a specific space (and by implication, *against* equality in other spaces). But it is important to recognize the limited reach of that usage, and also the fact that demanding equality in one space—no matter how hallowed by tradition—can lead one to be anti-egalitarian in some other space, the comparative importance of which in the overall assessment has to be critically assessed.

1.2. IMPARTIALITY AND EQUALITY

The analysis in the last section pointed to the partisan character of the usual interpretations of the question 'why equality?'. That question, I have argued, has to be faced, just as much, even by those who are seen—by themselves and by others—as 'anti-egalitarian', for they too are egalitarian in *some* space that is important in their theory. But it was not, of course, argued that the question 'why equality?' was, in any sense, pointless. We may be persuaded that the basic disputations are likely to be about 'equality of what?', but it might still be asked whether there *need be* a demand for equality in *some* important space or other. Even if it turns out that every substantive theory of social arrangements in vogue *is*, in fact, egalitarian in some space—a space seen as central in that theory—there is still the need to explain and defend that general characteristic in each case. The shared practice—even if it were universally shared—would still need some defence.

The issue to address is not so much whether there *must* be *for strictly formal reasons* (such as the discipline of 'the language of morals'), equal consideration for all, at some level, in all ethical theories of social arrangement.[10] That is an interesting and hard question, but one I need not address in the present context; the answer to it is, in my judgement, by no means clear. I am more concerned with the question whether ethical theories must have this basic feature of equality to have substantive plausibility in the world in which we live.

It may be useful to ask *why* it is that so many altogether different substantive theories of the ethics of social arrangements have the common feature of demanding equality of *something*—something important. It is, I believe, arguable that to have any kind of plausibility, ethical reasoning on social matters must involve elementary equal consideration for all at *some* level that is seen as critical. The absence of such equality would make a theory arbitrarily discriminating and hard to defend. A theory may accept—indeed demand—inequality in terms of many variables, but in defending those inequalities it would be hard to duck the need to relate them, ultimately, to equal consideration for all in some adequately substantial way.

Perhaps this feature relates to the requirement that ethical reasoning, especially about social arrangements, has to be, in some sense, credible from the viewpoint of others—potentially *all* others. The question 'why this system?' has to be answered, as it were, for all the participants in that system. There are some Kantian elements in this line of reasoning, even though the equality demanded need not have a strictly Kantian structure.[11]

Recently Thomas Scanlon (1982) has analysed the relevance and power of the requirement that one should 'be able to justify one's actions to others on grounds that they could not reasonably

---

[10] For a classic exposition and defence of such an analytically ambitious claim, see Hare (1952, 1963).

[11] For reasons for taking note of differences (e.g. of personal commitments or obligations) that tend to be ignored at least in some versions of the Kantian uniformist format, see Williams (1981), Hampshire (1982), Taylor (1982). On some related issues, see Williams (1973*a*), where it is also discussed why 'the various elements of the idea of equality' pull us in 'different directions' (p. 248). But the acknowledgement of the importance of different obligations and commitments does not, of course, do away with the general need to make our ethics credible to others.

reject'.[12] The requirement of 'fairness' on which Rawls (1971) builds his theory of justice can be seen as providing a specific structure for determining what one can or cannot reasonably reject.[13] Similarly, the demands of 'impartiality'—and some substantively exacting forms of 'universalizability'—invoked as general requirements have that feature of equal concern in some major way.[14] Reasoning of this general type certainly has much to do with the foundations of ethics, and has cropped up in different forms in the methodological under-pinning of substantive ethical proposals.[15]

The need to defend one's theories, judgements, and claims to others who may be—directly or indirectly—involved, makes equality of consideration at some level a hard requirement to avoid. There are interesting methodological questions regarding the status of this condition, in particular: whether it is a logical requirement or a substantive demand,[16] and whether it is connected with the need for 'objectivity' in ethics.[17] I shall not pursue these questions further here, since the main concerns of this monograph do not turn on our answers to these questions.[18]

What is of direct interest is the plausibility of claiming that equal consideration at some level—a level that is seen as important—is a demand that cannot be easily escaped in presenting a political or ethical theory of social arrangements. It is also of considerable pragmatic interest to note that impartiality and equal concern, in

[12] See also Scanlon (1988a). On related matters, see Rawls (1971, 1988c), B. Williams (1972, 1985), Mackie (1978a), Ackerman (1980, 1988), Parfit (1984), O'Neill (1989).

[13] See also Rawls's later—more explicit—analysis of this connection, in Rawls (1985, 1988a, 1990).

[14] See Mackie (1978a). Impartiality-based reasoning is used by Harsanyi (1955) and Hare (1963) to defend the choice of utilitarian ethics. The idea of equal concern, in the form of the requirement of impartiality, is invoked even in setting up theories that explicitly take an 'anti-egalitarian' form. For example, in presenting his case for 'morals by agreement', Gauthier (1986) asserts—correctly in terms of his particular definition of equality—that 'equality is not a fundamental concern in our theory', but goes on immediately to explain: 'we have appealed to the equal rationality of the bargainers to show that their agreement satisfies the moral standard of *impartiality*' (p. 270, emphasis added).

[15] On this see Sen (1970a: ch. 9).

[16] This issue can be compared with John Mackie's (1978a) examination of whether the need for universalization is 'a logical thesis' or 'a substantive practical thesis' (p. 96).

[17] On the scope of objectivity, see Nagel (1980, 1986), McDowell (1981, 1985), Wiggins (1985, 1987), H. Putnam (1987, 1991), and Hurley (1989). On the other hand, see also Harman (1977), Mackie (1978a, 1978b) and B. Williams (1981, 1985).

[18] Some particular aspects of this question are discussed in Sen (1983b, 1985a).

some form or other, provide a shared background to all the major ethical and political proposals in this field that continue to receive argued support and reasoned defence.[19] One consequence of all this is the acceptance—often implicit—of the need to justify disparate advantages of different individuals in things that matter. That justification frequently takes the form of showing the integral connection of that inequality with equality in some *other* important—allegedly *more* important—space.[20]

Indeed, it is equality in that more important space that may then be seen as contributing to the contingent demands for *inequality* in the other spaces. The justification of inequality in some features is made to rest on the equality of some other feature, taken to be more basic in that ethical system. Equality in what is seen as the 'base' is invoked for a reasoned defence of the resulting inequalities in the far-flung 'peripheries'.

1.3. HUMAN DIVERSITY AND BASAL EQUALITY

Human beings differ from each other in many different ways. We have different external characteristics and circumstances. We begin life with different endowments of inherited wealth and liabilities.

---

[19] The remark here applies specifically to *social arrangements*—and thus to theories in political philosophy rather than personal ethics. In the ethics of *personal* behaviour, powerful arguments have been presented in favour of permitting or requiring explicit *asymmetries* in the treatment of different people. Such arguments may relate, for example, to the permissibility—perhaps even the necessity—of paying special attention to one's own interests, objectives and principles, *vis-à-vis* those of others. Or they may relate to the requirement of assuming greater responsibility towards one's own family members and others to whom one is 'tied'. Different types of asymmetries involved in personal ethics are discussed in B. Williams (1973*a*, 1973*b*, 1981), Mackie (1978*a*), Nagel (1980, 1986), Scheffler (1982), Sen (1982*b*, 1983*b*), Regan (1983), and Parfit (1984). While these requirements can also be seen in terms of demands for equality of rather special types, they would tend to go against the usual political conceptions of 'anonymous' equality (on this see Sen 1970*a*).

[20] This greater importance need not be seen as *intrinsic* to the space itself. For example, equality of primary goods in Rawls's (1971, 1982, 1985, 1988*a*) analysis, or of resources in Ronald Dworkin's (1981, 1987) theory is not justified on grounds of the intrinsic importance of primary goods or of resources. Equality in these spaces is seen as important because they are *instrumental* in giving people equitable opportunity, in some sense, to pursue their respective goals and objectives. This distance does, in fact, introduce—I would claim— some internal tension in these theories, since the derivative importance of primary goods or resources depends on the respective opportunities to convert primary goods or resources into the fulfilment of the respective goals, or into freedoms to pursue them. The conversion possibilities can, in fact, be

We live in different natural environments—some more hostile than others. The societies and the communities to which we belong offer very different opportunities as to what we can or cannot do. The epidemiological factors in the region in which we live can profoundly affect our health and well-being.

But in addition to these differences in natural and social environments and external characteristics, we also differ in our personal characteristics (e.g. age, sex, physical and mental abilities). And these are important for assessing inequality. For example, equal incomes can still leave much inequality in our ability to do what we would value doing. A disabled person cannot function in the way an able-bodied person can, even if both have exactly the same income. Thus, inequality in terms of one variable (e.g. income) may take us in a very different direction from inequality in the space of another variable (e.g. functioning ability or well-being).

The relative advantages and disadvantages that people have, compared with each other, can be judged in terms of many different variables, e.g. their respective incomes, wealths, utilities, resources, liberties, rights, quality of life, and so on. The plurality of variables on which we can possibly focus (the *focal variables*) to evaluate interpersonal inequality makes it necessary to face, at a very elementary level, a hard decision regarding the perspective to be adopted. This problem of the choice of the 'evaluative space' (that is, the selection of the relevant focal variables) is crucial to analysing inequality.

The differences in focus are particularly important because of extensive human diversity. Had all people been exactly similar, equality in one space (e.g. incomes) would tend to be congruent with equalities in others (e.g. health, well-being, happiness). One of the consequences of 'human diversity' is that equality in one space tends to go, in fact, with inequality in another.

For example, we may not be able to demand equality of welfare levels and other such 'patterning'—to use Nozick's helpful description—once we demand the equality of libertarian rights as specified by Nozick (1974). If equal rights, in this form, are accepted, then so must be all their consequences, and this would

very *diverse* for different people, and this does, I would argue, weaken the rationale of the derivative importance of equality of holdings of primary goods or resources. On this, see Chs. 3 and 5 (also Sen 1980*a*, 1990*b*).

include all the generated inequalities of incomes, utilities, well-being, and positive freedoms to do this or be that.

I am not examining, here, how convincing this defence is.[21] The important issue in the present discussion is the nature of the strategy of justifying inequality through equality. Nozick's approach is a lucid and elegant example of this general strategy. If a claim that inequality in some significant space is right (or good, or acceptable, or tolerable) is to be defended by reason (not by, say, shooting the dissenters), the argument takes the form of showing this inequality to be a consequence of *equality* in some other—more centrally important—space. Given the broad agreement on the need to have equality in the 'base', and also the connection of that broad agreement with this deep need for impartiality between individuals (discussed earlier), the crucial arguments have to be about the reasonableness of the 'bases' chosen. Thus, the question: 'equality of what?' is, in this context, not materially different from the enquiry: 'what is the right space for basal equality?' The answer we give to 'equality of what?' will not only endorse equality in that chosen space (the focal variable being related to the demands of basal equality), but will have far-reaching consequences on the distributional patterns (including necessary *inequalities*) in the other spaces. 'Equality of what?' is indeed a momentous—and central—question.

1.4. EQUALITY VERSUS LIBERTY?

The importance of equality is often contrasted with that of liberty. Indeed, someone's position in the alleged conflict between equality and liberty has often been seen as a good indicator of his or her general outlook on political philosophy and political economy. For example, not only are libertarian thinkers (such as Nozick 1974) seen as anti-egalitarian, but they are diagnosed as anti-egalitarian *precisely because* of their overriding concern with liberty.[22] Similarly, those diagnosed as egalitarian thinkers (e.g. Dalton 1920, Tawney 1931, or Meade 1976) may appear to be less concerned with liberty precisely because they are seen as being wedded to the demands of equality.

In the light of the discussion in the previous sections, we must

---

[21] Some criticisms of that approach can be found in Sen (1982*b*, 1984).

[22] I refer here specifically to Nozick (1973, 1974). For a reassessment and refinement of his position, see Nozick (1989).

argue that this way of seeing the relationship between equality and liberty is altogether faulty. Libertarians must think it important that people should have liberty. Given this, questions would immediately arise regarding: *who, how much, how distributed, how equal?* Thus the issue of equality immediately arises as a *supplement* to the assertion of the importance of liberty.[23] The libertarian proposal has to be completed by going on to characterize the distribution of rights among the people involved.[24] In fact, the libertarian demands for liberty typically include important features of 'equal liberty', e.g. the insistence on equal immunity from interference by others. The belief that liberty is important cannot, thus, be in conflict with the view that it is important that the social arrangements be devised to promote equality of liberties that people have.

There can, of course, be a conflict between a person who argues for the equality of some variable *other than* liberty (such as income or wealth or well-being) and someone who wants only equal liberty. But that is a dispute over the question 'equality of *what?*' Similarly, a distribution-independent general promotion of liberty (i.e. promoting it wherever possible without paying attention to the distributive pattern) could, of course, conflict with equality of some other variable, say, income, but that would be (1) partly a conflict between concentrating respectively on liberty and on incomes, and (2) partly one between a concern for distributive patterns (of incomes in this case) and non-distributive aggregative considerations (applied to liberty). It is neither accurate nor helpful to think of the difference in either case in terms of 'liberty *versus* equality'.

Indeed, strictly speaking, posing the problem in terms of this latter contrast reflects a 'category mistake'. They are not alternatives. Liberty is among the possible *fields of application* of equality,

[23] There can be quite different ways of defending the importance of liberty. One distinction relates to the different concepts of goodness and rightness. First, liberty can be seen as a *good* thing that people should have, and the violation of liberty may be seen as making the state of affairs less good. Second, liberty may be taken to be not a part of the idea of goodness, but a feature of *right* social arrangements. There are distinctions—not unrelated to the above contrast—also between what duties *others* have if someone's liberties are violated. I have tried to discuss these questions elsewhere (see Sen 1970a, 1982b, 1983a, 1992a), and will not pursue them further here.

[24] See, in this context, Rawls's (1971) discussion of the priority of 'equal liberty' (ch. 4). See also Berlin (1955–6, 1969), Wollheim (1955–6), Hayek (1960, 1967), Buchanan (1975, 1986), Haksar (1979), Gutmann (1980), Goodin (1988), Suppes (1988), and Lukes (1990).

and equality is among the possible *patterns* of distribution of liberty.[25]

As was discussed earlier, the need to face explicitly the choice of space is an inescapable part of the specification and reasoned evaluation of the demands of equality. There are, at one end, demands of equal libertarian rights only, and at the other end, various exacting demands of equality regarding an extensive list of *achievements* and also a corresponding list of *freedoms* to achieve. This study is much concerned with this plurality and its manifold consequences.

1.5. PLURALITY AND ALLEGED EMPTINESS

The recognition of plurality of spaces in which equality may be assessed can raise some doubts about the content of the idea of equality. Does it not make equality less powerful and imperative as a political idea? If equality can possibly speak with so many voices, can we take any of its demands seriously?[26]

Indeed, the apparent pliability of the contents of equality has appeared to some analysts as a source of serious embarrassment for the idea of equality. As Douglas Rae (1981) has put it (in his meticulous and helpful exploration of the various contemporary notions of equality), 'one idea that is more powerful than order or efficiency or freedom in resisting equality' is 'equality itself' (p. 151).

While Rae argues that the idea of equality is, as it were, 'overfull', others have argued, on similar grounds, that equality is 'an empty idea'—it is 'an empty form having no substantive content of its own'.[27] Since equality can be interpreted in so many different

[25] There can, of course, be some ambiguity regarding what is called a 'pattern'. Sometimes the term 'pattern' may be used to impose particular specifications of constituent characteristics, e.g. the Union Jack demands some blue and some red. The appropriate analogy for equality and liberty is with the distinction between, say, the pattern of intensities of colours (e.g. the same intensity for each unit, or maximal intensity altogether), and the use of particular colours (e.g. blue) the intensities of which are examined.

[26] There is also a related but distinct issue as to whether equality can provide a deep enough justification for any social structure. Robert Goodin (1988) asks an interesting question as to whether the 'apparent egalitarianism' underlying 'welfare state practices' are ultimately just 'epiphenomenal' (pp. 51–69). The argument depends, as Goodin notes, on how equality is defined, and his affirmative answer to the question draws on the conflict between different views of equality (including that implicit in what he calls 'impartiality').

[27] Westen (1982: 596).

ways, the requirement of equality cannot, in this view, be taken to be a truly substantive demand.

It is certainly true that merely demanding equality without saying equality of what, cannot be seen as demanding anything specific. This gives some plausibility to the thesis of emptiness. But the thesis is, I believe, erroneous nevertheless. First, even before a specific space is chosen, the general requirement of the need to value equality in *some space that is seen to be particularly important* is not an empty demand. This relates to the discipline imposed by the need for some impartiality, some form of equal concern. At the very least, it is a requirement of scrutiny of the basis of the proposed evaluative system. It can also have considerable cutting power, in questioning theories without a basal structure and in rejecting those that end up without a basal equality altogether. Even at this general level, equality is a substantive and substantial requirement.

Second, once the context is fixed, equality can be a particularly powerful and exacting demand. For example, when the space is fixed, demands for equality impose some ranking of patterns, even before any specific index of equality is endorsed. For example, in dealing with the inequality of incomes, the so-called 'Dalton principle of transfer' demands that a small transfer of income from a richer person to a poorer one—keeping the total unchanged—must be seen to be a distributive improvement.[28] In its context, this is a fairly persuasive rule in ranking distributions of the same total income by the general requirement of equality without invoking any specific index or measure.

In addition to such ordering of patterns in a *given* space, even the broader exercise of the choice of space itself may have clear links with the motivation underlying the demand for equality. For example, in evaluating justice, or social welfare, or living standards, or quality of life, the exercise of choice of space is no longer just *formal*, but one of substantive discrimination. As I shall try to show in the chapters that follow, the claims of many of these spaces can be forcefully disputed once the context is fixed. Though this need not lead us to *one* precise characterization of the demands of equality that is important in every context, this is far from a real

[28] On this see Dalton (1920), Kolm (1969), Atkinson (1970*b*, 1983). On some further normative implications of this property, see Dasgupta, Sen, and Starrett (1973) and Rothschild and Stiglitz (1973), and also *OEI*, ch. 3.

embarrassment. In each context, the demands of equality may be both distinct and strong.

Third, the diversity of spaces in which equality may be demanded really reflects a deeper diversity, to wit, different diagnoses of objects of value—different views of the appropriate notions of individual advantage in the contexts in question. The problem of diversity is, thus, not unique to equality evaluation. The different demands of equality reflect divergent views as to what things are to be directly valued in that context. They indicate different ideas as to how the advantages of different people are to be assessed *vis-à-vis* each other in the exercise in question. Liberties, rights, utilities, incomes, resources, primary goods, need-fulfilments, etc., provide different ways of seeing the respective lives of different people, and each of the perspectives leads to a corresponding view of equality.

This plurality—that of assessing the advantages of different persons—reflects itself in different views not merely of equality, but also of any other social notion for which individual advantage substantially enters the informational base. For example, the notion of 'efficiency' would have exactly the same plurality related to the choice of space.[29] Efficiency is unambiguously increased if there is an enhancement of the advantage of each person (or, an advancement for at least one person, with no decline for any), but the content of that characterization depends on the way advantage is defined. When the *focal variable* is fixed, we get a specific definition of efficiency in this general structure.

Efficiency comparisons can be made in terms of different variables. If, for example, advantage is seen in terms of individual utility, then the notion of efficiency immediately becomes the concept of 'Pareto optimality', much used in welfare economics. This demands that the situation is such that no one's utility can be increased without cutting down the utility of someone else. But efficiency can also be similarly defined in the spaces of liberties, rights, incomes, and so on. For example, corresponding to Pareto optimality in the space of utilities, efficiency in terms of liberty would demand that the situation is such that no one's liberty can be increased without cutting down the liberty of someone else. There is, formally, an exactly similar multiplicity of efficiency

---

[29] While the plurality is exactly similar in principle, it is possible that empirically there may be more space-related divergence between inequality comparisons than between efficiency comparisons; on this see Sen (1992*b*).

notions as we have already seen for equality, related to the plurality of spaces.

This fact is not surprising, since the plurality of spaces in which equality may be considered reflects a deeper issue, viz. plurality regarding the appropriate notion of individual advantage in social comparisons. The choice between these spaces is undoubtedly an integral part of the literature of inequality evaluation. But the plurality of spaces really reflects diversities in substantive approaches to individual advantage, and in the informational base of interpersonal comparisons. Space plurality is not a unique problem—nor of course a source of special embarrassment—for the idea of equality as such.

1.6. MEANS AND FREEDOMS

It was suggested earlier that the class of normative theories of social arrangements with which we are concerned demand—for reasons that we discussed—equality in some space or other. This equality serves as the 'basal equality' of the system and has implications on the distributive patterns in the other spaces. Indeed, basal equality may be directly responsible for inequalities in the other spaces.

It may be useful to discuss an example or two of the choice of space and its importance. In modern political philosophy and ethics, the most powerful voice in recent years has been that of John Rawls (1971). His theory of 'justice as fairness' provides an interesting and important example of the choice of space and its consequences. In his 'Difference Principle', the analysis of efficiency and equality are both related to the individual holdings of primary goods.[30]

With that system, the diversity of inherited wealth and of talents

[30] It is the Difference Principle which is concerned with the distribution of primary goods in the Rawlsian two principles of justice as fairness. It is worth noting—so as not to oversimplify matters—that (1) Rawls's first principle, which has priority, deals only with personal liberties (and demands *equal* liberty); (2) the Difference Principle is concerned not only with distributive considerations but also with efficiency (in the form that any change that improves the position of all—including the worst off group—is regarded as an improvement), and (3) the principles stated are not meant as mechanical formulae, and a good deal of explanation and analysis of their use is presented by Rawls as part and parcel of his theory of justice as fairness (for recent clarifications on the exact claims in this theory, see Rawls 1985, 1988*a*, 1988*b*, 1988*c*, 1990; see also Laden 1991*a*). Notwithstanding these qualifications, it is obvious that equality of the holdings of primary goods has an important place in Rawls's structure of political ethics.

would not generate income inequality in the same way as in Nozick's system, since the primary goods—on the distribution of which Rawls's Difference Principle imposes an egalitarian requirement—include incomes among their constitutive elements. Incomes are, thus, directly covered in the Rawlsian demands of basal equality. But the relationship between *primary goods* (including incomes), on the one hand, and *well-being*, on the other, may vary because of personal diversities in the possibility of converting primary goods (including incomes) into achievements of well-being. For example, a pregnant woman may have to overcome disadvantages in living comfortably and well that a man at the same age need not have, even when both have exactly the same income and other primary goods.

Similarly, the relationship between *primary goods* and the *freedom* to pursue one's objectives—well-being as well as other objectives—may also vary.[31] We differ not only in our inherited wealths, but also in our personal characteristics. Aside from purely individual variations (e.g. abilities, predispositions, physical differences), there are also systematic contrasts between groups (for example between women and men in specific respects such as the possibility of pregnancy and neonatal care of infants). With the same bundle of primary goods, a pregnant woman or one with infants to look after has much less freedom to pursue her goals than a man not thus encumbered would be able to do. The relationship between *primary goods*, on the one hand, and *freedom* as well as *well-being*, on the other, can vary with interpersonal and intergroup variations of specific characteristics.[32]

Inequalities in different 'spaces' (e.g. incomes, primary goods, liberties, utilities, other achievements, other freedoms) can be very different from each other depending on interpersonal variations in the *relations* between these distinct—but interconnected—variables. One consequence of the basic fact of human diversity is to make it particularly important to be sure of the space in which inequality is to be evaluated. Person 1 can have more utility than 2 and 3, while 2

[31] On this question, see Sen (1990*b*).

[32] Rawls (1985, 1987, 1988*a*) himself has emphasized *another* type of diversity among the individuals, to wit, differences between their respective conceptions of the good. This leads to differences in the objectives which they respectively have reasons to pursue. That heterogeneity has to be distinguished from the diversity in the ability to convert resources and primary goods into the fulfilment of objectives (or into the *ability* to fulfil objectives). Neither diversity entails the other, and it is important to consider both types of interpersonal variations. These issues are discussed in Ch. 5.

has more income than 1 and 3, and 3 is free to do many things that 1 and 2 cannot. And so on. Even when the rankings are the same, the relative distances (i.e. the extent of the superiority of one position over another) could be very diverse in the different spaces.

Some of the most central issues of egalitarianism arise precisely because of the contrast between equality in the different spaces. The ethics of equality has to take adequate note of our pervasive diversities that affect the relations between the different spaces. The *plurality* of focal variables can make a great difference precisely because of the *diversity* of human beings.

1.7. INCOME DISTRIBUTION, WELL-BEING AND FREEDOM

Our physical and social characteristics make us immensely diverse creatures. We differ in age, sex, physical and mental health, bodily prowess, intellectual abilities, climatic circumstances, epidemiological vulnerability, social surroundings, and in many other respects. Such diversities, however, can be hard to accommodate adequately in the usual evaluative framework of inequality assessment. As a consequence, this basic issue is often left substantially unaddressed in the evaluative literature.

An important and frequently encountered problem arises from concentrating on inequality of *incomes* as the primary focus of attention in the analysis of inequality. The extent of real inequality of opportunities that people face cannot be readily deduced from the magnitude of inequality of *incomes*, since what we can or cannot do, can or cannot achieve, do not depend just on our incomes but also on the variety of physical and social characteristics that affect our lives and make us what we are.

To take a simple illustration, the extent of comparative deprivation of a physically handicapped person *vis-à-vis* others cannot be adequately judged by looking at his or her income, since the person may be greatly disadvantaged in converting income into the achievements he or she would value.[33] The problem does not arise only

---

[33] The importance of coming to grips with cases of this kind was discussed fairly extensively in *OEI*, ch. 1. It was treated there mainly as the basis of a critique of utilitarianism and its exclusive concern with *summing* utilities. I have nothing to withdraw from that critique, but the problem is, in fact, much more pervasive than I had argued there. It will become clear, as we review other standard approaches, that nearly all of them tend to fail to do justice to the problem that is illustrated by this case.

from the fact that income is just a means to our real ends, but (1) from the existence of *other* important means, and (2) from interpersonal variations in the *relation* between the means and our various ends.

These issues have on the whole tended to be neglected in the literature on the measurement of inequality in economics. For example, consider the approach to constructing 'inequality indices' based on social loss of equivalent income pioneered by Atkinson (1970*b*).[34] This approach has been, in many ways, remarkably influential and productive in *integrating* considerations of income-inequality with the overall evaluation of social welfare.[35] The extent of inequality is assessed in this approach by using the same response function $u(y)$ for *all* individuals, defined over personal incomes.[36] This strategy of inequality measurement, thus, incorporates the restrictive feature of treating everyone's incomes symmetrically no matter what difficulties some people have compared with others in converting income into well-being and freedom.[37]

[34] This welfare-economic approach to inequality evaluation is further discussed in Ch. 6 below.

[35] The approach is extensively discussed in *OEI*, ch. 3. For illuminating accounts and assessments of the recent literature on inequality evaluation—including the influence of Atkinson's approach on that literature—see Blackorby and Donaldson (1978, 1984) and Foster (1985). Atkinson (1983) himself has provided a critical evaluation of that literature and commented on some of the questions that have been raised. See also Kolm (1969, 1976) on related matters.

[36] This u function has usually been interpreted as a 'utility function'. But u need not necessarily be seen as 'utility'; on this see Atkinson (1983: 5–6). Social welfare is taken to be an additively separable function of individual incomes. The bits of social welfare dependent on the respective persons' incomes are derived from the same function for everyone and then added up together to yield aggregate social welfare. If u *is* taken as utility (a permissible view, providing perhaps the simplest—certainly the most common—interpretation), then the assumption of the same u function for all amounts to that of the same utility function for everyone. But more generally, no matter what interpretation of $u(y)$ is chosen, *that* function must have this characteristic of being the same for all. Similarly, in the extension of the Atkinson measure to a not-necessarily additively separable format proposed in my *OEI* (pp. 38–42), the assumption of a *symmetric* aggregate W function entails that everyone's income would have the same overall impact. While formally all this is consistent with many different underlying stories, the central case is based on the presumption of the *same* conversion relation (between income and achievement) for different people. On the general issue of conversion, see Fisher and Shell (1972), Sen (1979*c*), and Fisher (1987).

[37] Taking the same utility function for all, relating utility to income (or to income and work) is also quite standard in many other branches of resource allocation, e.g. in the literature on 'optimum taxation' pioneered by James Mirrlees (1971); Tuomala (1971) provides a helpful account of that literature. This applies also to the literature on cost-benefit analysis (see the critical survey by Drèze and Stern, 1987).

It is, of course, true that the object of this approach is to assess inequality specifically in the distribution of *incomes*, not in levels of well-being. But that assessment is done in the light of what is *achieved* from the respective person's income, and these achievements make up the aggregate 'social welfare'. Income inequality is assessed by Atkinson in terms of the loss of social welfare (in units of equivalent aggregate income) as a result of inequality in the distribution of aggregate income.[38] Given this motivation, it will in general be necessary to bring in the effects of other influences on people's lives and well-being to assess *income* inequality itself.[39] In general the measurement of inequality has to bring in information regarding other spaces—both (1) for the purpose of evaluating inequality in these spaces *themselves*, and (2) for that of assessing *income inequality* in a broader framework, taking note of the presence of other influences on the objective (in Atkinson's case, social welfare) in terms of which income inequality is to be ultimately assessed. These issues will be further examined in Chapter 6.

The tendency to assume away interpersonal diversities can originate not only from the pragmatic temptation to make the analytics simple and easy (as in the literature of inequality measurement), but also, as was discussed earlier, from the rhetoric of equality itself (e.g. 'all men are created equal'). The warm glow of such rhetoric can push us in the direction of ignoring these differences, by taking 'no note of them', or by 'assuming them to be absent'. This suggests an apparently easy transition between one space and another, e.g. from incomes to utilities, from primary goods to freedoms, from resources to well-being. They reduce—again only *apparently*—the tension between different approaches to equality.

But that comfort is purchased at a heavy price. As a result of that assumption, we are made to overlook the substantive inequalities in, say, well-being and freedom that may directly *result* from an equal distribution of incomes (given our variable needs and disparate personal and social circumstances). Both pragmatic shortcuts and grand rhetoric can be helpful for some purposes and altogether unhelpful and misleading for others.

---

[38] The approach (see Atkinson 1970*b*, 1975, 1983) develops a line of analysis originally explored by Dalton (1920), and revived also by Kolm (1969). The main lines of the approach and the underlying analytics are also discussed in *OEI*.

[39] For insightful remarks on this and related issues, see Atkinson (1983: Part I).

2

FREEDOM, ACHIEVEMENT AND RESOURCES

2.1. FREEDOM AND CHOICE

A person's position in a social arrangement can be judged in two different perspectives, viz. (1) the actual achievement, and (2) the freedom to achieve. Achievement is concerned with what we *manage* to accomplish, and freedom with the *real opportunity* that we have to accomplish what we value. The two need not be congruent. Inequality can be viewed in terms of achievements and freedoms, and they need not coincide. That distinction is relevant for judging efficiency as well, which can be seen in terms of individual achievements *or* freedoms to achieve. Thus, the distinction between achievement and freedom is quite central to social evaluation.[1]

There are, of course, different ways of judging achievement, e.g. by utility (such as pleasures achieved or desires fulfilled), or by opulence (such as incomes earned or consumptions enjoyed), or by the quality of life (such as some measures of living standards).[2] As was discussed in the previous chapter, the choice between these different spaces is a question of profound significance in evaluating our lives and attainments, and it is also of central importance in inequality evaluation (specifically in answering the question 'equality of what?'). But even with any given way of characterizing achievement, there is a further issue, viz. the distinction between (1) the extent of *achievement*, and (2) the *freedom* to achieve.

Some well-known approaches to the evaluation of individual advantage and to the assessment of good social orders have been concerned directly with achievement only, treating the importance

---

[1] The relevance of the perspective of freedom in the context of evaluation of different types of economies has been examined by Kornai (1988), Lindbeck (1988), and Sen (1988a), in a symposium arranged by the European Economic Association.

[2] I have addressed some of these issues in my Tanner Lectures on 'the standard of living'. See Sen *et al.* (1987), which also includes comments and further analyses presented by the discussants, viz. John Muellbauer, Ravi Kanbur, Keith Hart, Bernard Williams, and Geoffrey Hawthorn, who also edited this volume.

of the freedom to achieve as being entirely instrumental—as means to actual achievements. Utilitarianism is an obvious example. The utilitarian approach is characterized by (1) confining interpersonal comparisons for social assessment to achievements only, and (2) identifying achievements with the utilities achieved. The two together yield the utilitarian informational focus on interpersonally compared individual utilities for personal and social assessment.

Similarly, the Bergson–Samuelson social-welfare functions, as presented and explored in their classic formulations (see Bergson 1938; Samuelson 1947), tend to confine direct attention only to achievements (e.g. preference-fulfilment, consumer satisfaction), valuing individual freedom only indirectly as means to achievement. To some extent this applies also to the corresponding Arrovian social-choice frameworks,[3] which too have been mainly geared towards individual preferences over states of affairs, rather than taking note of the freedom to choose *among* states of affairs. But much depends on how states are characterized—in particular whether the choices available to *move* to other states are taken to be *part* of each particular state.[4] Recent developments in social-choice theory have attempted to bring in considerations of freedom into the framework of evaluation, in the specific context of valuing liberty.[5]

[3] See Arrow (1951, 1963).

[4] Since completing this manuscript, I have tried to examine the possibility of integrating the perspective of freedom in the structure of social choice theory in my Kenneth Arrow Lectures at Stanford University in May 1991 ('Freedom and Social Choice').

[5] An attempt in that direction was made in Sen (1970a, 1970c). The large literature on the treatment of liberty in social choice theory has been well discussed and scrutinized by Suzumura (1983), Wriglesworth (1985), and Riley (1987), among others. In dealing with the importance of liberty, the social-choice format has both advantages and limitations compared with (1) traditional deontological statements, (2) standard welfare-economic formulations, and (3) game-theoretic interpretations. These and related issues have been discussed, along with examining ways of integrating considerations of liberty in social choice frameworks, in an extensive literature, including *inter alia*, Sen (1970a, 1976c, 1982b, 1982c, 1983a, 1992a), Ng (1971, 1979), Batra and Pattanaik (1972), Peacock and Rowley (1972), Nozick (1973, 1974), Bernholz (1974, 1980), Gibbard (1974), Blau (1975), Fine (1975b), Seidl (1975, 1986b, 1990), Campbell (1976, 1989), Farrell (1976), Kelly (1976a, 1976b, 1978), Aldrich (1977), Breyer (1977), Perelli-Minetti (1977), Ferejohn (1978), Karni (1978), Stevens and Foster (1978), Suzumura (1978, 1980, 1983, 1991), Austen-Smith (1979, 1982), Mueller (1979), Barnes (1980), Breyer and Gardner (1980), Breyer and Gigliotti (1980), Fountain (1980), Gardner (1980), McLean (1980), Weale (1980), Gaertner and Krüger (1981, 1983), Gärdenfors (1981), P. J. Hammond (1981, 1982), Schwartz (1981, 1986), Sugden (1981, 1985), Levi (1982, 1986), Wriglesworth (1982, 1985), Chapman (1983), K. Basu (1984), Gaertner (1985, 1986), Kelsey (1985, 1988), Schotter (1985), Coughlin (1986), Barry (1986), Elster and Hylland (1986), Hylland (1986), Webster

The exclusive focus on achievements has recently been seriously challenged by arguments for basing political evaluation on the *means* to achievement, such as the Rawlsian concern with the distribution of 'primary goods', the Dworkinian concentration on the distribution of 'resources', and so on. Since the means in the form of resources, primary goods, etc., undoubtedly enhance the freedom to achieve (other things remaining the same), it is not unreasonable to think of these moves as taking us *towards* freedom—away from attention being confined exclusively to evaluating achievement. If we aim at equality in the space of resources or of primary goods, this can be seen as moving the evaluative exercise towards the assessment of freedom away from that of achievement as such.

But it must be recognized at the same time that equalizing ownership of resources or holdings of primary goods need not equalize the substantive freedoms enjoyed by different persons, since there can be significant variations in the *conversion* of resources and primary goods into freedoms. The conversion problems can involve some extremely complex social issues, especially when the achievements in question are influenced by intricate intragroup relations and interactions.[6] But, as was discussed earlier, variations in conversion can also arise from simple physical differences. For example (to illustrate with a simple case referred to earlier), a poor person's freedom from undernourishment would depend not only on her resources and primary goods (e.g. through the influence of income on the ability to buy food), but also on her metabolic rates, gender, pregnancy, climatic environment, exposure to parasitic diseases, and so on. Of two persons with identical incomes and other primary goods and resources (as characterized in the Rawlsian or Dworkinian frameworks), one may be entirely free to avoid undernourishment and the other not at all free to achieve this.[7]

The move away from achievement to the *means* of achievement (in

(1986), Harel and Nitzan (1987), MacIntyre (1987, 1988), Mezzetti (1987), Nurmi (1987), Riley (1987, 1989*a*, 1989*b*), Sonstegaard (1987), Subramanian (1987), Allen (1988), Gigliotti (1988), Pattanaik (1988), S. O. Hansson (1988), Deb (1989), Gärdenfors and Pettit (1989), A. Hamlin (1989), Hurley (1989), Vallentyne (1989), Xu (1990), Gaertner, Pattanaik, and Suzumura (1992), among other contributions.

[6] This is a particularly important question in the assessment of poverty involving the failure to achieve some minimal social functionings such as taking part in the life of the community. On this see Sen (1983*d*), and also Ch. 7 below.

[7] On the practical importance of this type of issue, with empirical illustrations, see Sen (1985*b*), particularly Appendices A and B. See also Arneson (1989*a*, 1990*a*, 1990*b*, 1991), and G. A. Cohen (1989, 1990, 1992).

the form of Rawls's focusing on primary goods or Dworkin's concentration on resources[8]) may well have helped to shift the attention of the literature in the *direction* of seeing the importance of freedom, but the shift is not adequate to capture the *extent* of freedom. If our concern is with freedom as such, then there is no escape from looking for a characterization of freedom in the form of alternative sets of accomplishments that we have the power to achieve. Before that more exacting question is addressed (in Section 2.3 and in Chapters 3–5), another aspect of the achievement–freedom distinction related to standard economic theory may be worth examining.

2.2. REAL INCOME, OPPORTUNITIES AND SELECTION[9]

The distinction between achievement and freedom can be illustrated by two different interpretations of real-income analysis that can be found in the literature and which are often not clearly distinguished. The evaluation of real income can be seen as the assessment of the benefit that a person receives from a *particular bundle* of commodities that he or she acquires: 'Is x a better bundle for this person than y?' The comparison is directly of the nature of the bundles selected, and we may call it the 'selection view'. Alternatively, the focus can be not just on the particular bundles purchased, but on *the set* of all bundles that the person *could have* bought with that income: 'Does the budget set A give this person a better set of options than does the budget set B?' This may be called the 'options view'.

The rationale of the axiomatic structure of real-income comparisons depends on the interpretation of the comparisons, and both the selection view and the options view have been extensively used— explicitly or by implication.[10] The use of the options view has taken the form of asserting the superiority of choosing x from set A over choosing y from set B if set A offers, *inter alia*, the possibility of choosing y as well.[11] This is the 'revealed preference' approach to

---

[8] In Dworkin's proposal much would, in fact, depend on the scope and reach of his insurance mechanisms against personal handicaps.

[9] This section invokes some standard procedures in economic theory. This makes it a little bit more 'technical' than the rest of the monograph, but no great specialized knowledge has been presupposed. Also, the text is so organized that a non-economist reader should be able to follow subsequent sections even if this section is skipped.

[10] These uses have been examined and scrutinized in Sen (1979c).

[11] Note that this is not a *full* comparison of the two sets A and B, but takes the form of looking at A in the light of the chosen element y from B.

real-income comparison.[12] Its rationale is based on utilizing the price-and-purchase data to make a particular comparison of the freedom to choose, to wit, whether in *A* one could choose what was chosen from *B*.

The selection view, on the other hand, is focused on comparing just the bundles *x* and *y*, and this is done by assuming a particular structure of preferences (specifically *convexity*—essentially, non-increasing marginal rates of substitution). The data on prices and purchases are used to ascertain the relative weights attached to the different commodities *locally* (i.e. for the respective amounts actually purchased), and the assumption of non-increasing marginal rates of substitution is used to determine whether the bundle *x* chosen from *A* can be declared to be superior to *y* chosen from *B*.[13] The opportunities of choice, as such, are not compared in this exercise.

The two approaches give similar results in real-income comparison under standard assumptions, but (1) they involve very different strategies, and (2) they lead to different results once the standard assumptions (e.g. competitive markets) are dropped.[14] Here we are concerned with the differences between the two strategies, in particular with the contrast between comparing *options* and that of comparing the goodness of the *selected* bundles directly.

I should, however, add that even in the use of the options view in the revealed-preference approach—as the analysis has actually been carried out—no *intrinsic* importance has, in fact, been attached to the extent of freedom of choice as such. Instead, the opportunities of choice have been seen only as *means* to acquiring preferred bundles of commodities. But it is possible to extend the analytics of the logic of options-comparisons used by the revealed-preference

[12] See Samuelson (1938, 1947); also Houthakker (1950) and Little (1950). Comparison of options of choice is used in the 'revealed preference' approach to infer the person's utility function on the basis of his choices from different sets of bundles. That programme of getting to utility from choices has a number of problematic features, including the use of some demanding presumptions about the nature of the goals pursued by the person, and the interpretation of the goal function as the individual's personal utility function (on this, see Sen 1973*b*, 1977*c*). Here we are not directly concerned with the strategy of 'recovering' personal utility functions from the observed choices, but with the illumination provided by the procedure of comparing a person's *options* of choice rather than just the *chosen* bundles. Thus we are making use of a part of the chain of 'revealed preference' reasoning, but not all of it.

[13] See Hicks (1939, 1940), Samuelson (1947), and Graaff (1957).

[14] On this see Majumdar (1969) and Sen (1979*c*).

approach in the direction of attaching intrinsic importance to the freedom of choice itself.[15] While the selection view goes straight at the goodness of commodity bundles (nothing else is involved), the options view can also be used to compare the extents of the freedom of choice. In the revealed-preference literature, no intrinsic value is attached to freedom as such and it is assessed in purely instrumental terms (in terms of the value of the chosen bundle), but the same technique of analysis can be adapted to take note of the intrinsic value of freedom (if freedom is seen as important in itself).

2.3. FREEDOM DISTINGUISHED FROM RESOURCES

We come back now to the distinction between *freedom* and the *means to freedom* (such as primary goods or resources, which help one to achieve more freedom). We may begin with seeing the distinction in the context of commodity consumption, though that is not our ultimate focus of attention. The 'budget set' represents the extent of the person's freedom in this space, i.e. the freedom to achieve the consumption of various alternative commodity bundles. This budget set is derived on the basis of the person's resources (in this case, the level of income and the opportunity to buy commodities at given prices). The distinction between (1) the resources on which the budget set depends, and (2) the budget set itself, is a simple illustration of the general distinction between the *means* to freedom and the *extent* of freedom (in this case all seen in terms of consumption bundles that can be achieved).

A shift in the attention from achievement to resources (e.g. from the *chosen* commodity bundle to the income with which such bundles could be bought) can indeed be seen (as was stated earlier) as a move in the *direction* of paying greater attention to freedom, since resources tell us about the *set* of commodity bundles from which we can choose.[16] The strategy of judging individual advantage by the person's command over resources, as opposed to what the

---

[15] On the importance of the distinction between *instrumental* and *intrinsic* valuation of freedom, and on its implications for economic theory, see Sen (1988a).

[16] Note, however, that the resources owned or freedoms enjoyed by a person at a particular point of time may have been the result of achievements in the past. In considering the contrast between achievements and means of freedom, there is no intention to deny that connection. Indeed, a fuller formulation of the relationship would require a proper intertemporal accounting of the interconnections involved.

individual actually achieves, is to refocus our vision from achievement to the means of freedom, and that is, in an obvious sense, a homage to freedom.

Various important moves in contemporary political and moral philosophy (e.g. Rawls's focus on primary goods in his theory of justice, Dworkin's arguments for 'equality of resources'), which have been partly motivated by a concern for the importance of freedom, have tended to concentrate on the individual's command over *resources*—in one form or another—as the basis of interpersonal comparisons of individual advantage.

While this has been a move in the right direction (as far as freedom is concerned), the gap between *resources that help* us to achieve freedom and the extent of *freedom itself* is important in principle and can be crucial in practice. Freedom has to be distinguished not merely from achievement, but also from resources and means to freedom.[17]

This problem of interpersonal variation may look rather unlikely in the case of converting resources into commodity bundles, since the assumptions of uniform prices, competitive markets, etc., are standardly made in the economic literature on these matters. But that is partly a quirk of theory, and in actuality non-uniform prices and other interpersonal variations in conversion are quite common. But more importantly, once we shift attention from the commodity space to the space of what a person can, in fact, do or be (or what kind of a life a person can lead), the sources of interpersonal variations in conversion can be numerous and powerful.[18]

The resources a person has, or the primary goods that someone holds, may be very imperfect indicators of the freedom that the

---

[17] Even in the commodity space, the *set* of commodity bundles over which the person has command is a better representation of freedom (in that commodity space) than the resources that can be used to establish command over a set of commodity bundles. The latter will take us to the former, but the conversion will depend on certain contingent circumstances, e.g. markets and prices. If these conversions vary from person to person, then one person can be ahead in the resource space but behind in terms of the freedom in the commodity space (e.g. with differential rents as a part of public-housing policy).

[18] One of the more discussed examples of interpersonal variations relates to nutritional 'requirements' of different people. For different ways of dealing with these variations, see Sukhatme (1977, 1982), Srinivasan (1981, 1992), Gopalan (1983), Lipton (1983), Blaxter and Waterlow (1985), Payne (1985), Vaidyanathan (1985),

person really enjoys to do this or be that.[19] As was discussed in the previous chapter, the personal and social characteristics of different persons, which can differ greatly, can lead to substantial interpersonal variations in the conversion of resources and primary goods into *achievements*. For exactly the same reason, interpersonal differences in these personal and social characteristics can make the conversion of resources and primary goods into the *freedom* to achieve similarly variable.

If we are interested in the freedom of choice, then we have to look at the *choices* that the person does in fact have, and we must not assume that the same results would be obtained by looking at the *resources* that he or she commands. The moves towards resource-based interpersonal comparisons in contemporary political philosophy (such as those of Rawls and Dworkin) can certainly be seen as taking us in the *direction* of paying attention to freedom, but the moves are substantially inadequate.[20] In general, comparisons of resources and primary goods cannot serve as the basis for comparing freedoms. Valuing freedom imposes exacting claims on our attention—claims that cannot be met by looking at something else.[21]

Scrimshaw (1987), Payne and Lipton (1988), Anand and Harris (1990, 1992), Dasgupta and Ray (1990), Osmani (1990a, 1992a, 1992b), Bhargava (1991), among other contributors.

[19] For further discussion of this issue, see Sen (1980a, 1991b). On related matters, see Lehning (1989) and Pogge (1989).

[20] More on this in Ch. 5 when we consider the problem of inequality evaluation in the context of theories of justice.

[21] In the next chapter we examine and scrutinize the idea of freedom to achieve well-being as a prelude to examining inequalities in freedoms.

3

FUNCTIONINGS AND CAPABILITY

3.1. CAPABILITY SETS

This chapter explores the 'capability' perspective on the assessment of (1) well-being, and (2) the freedom to pursue well-being. The approach has been discussed in some detail elsewhere.[1] Here I shall confine the presentation to only a few elementary aspects of this perspective.

The well-being of a person can be seen in terms of the quality (the 'well-ness', as it were) of the person's being. Living may be seen as consisting of a set of interrelated 'functionings', consisting of beings and doings. A person's achievement in this respect can be seen as the vector of his or her functionings. The relevant functionings can vary from such elementary things as being adequately nourished, being in good health, avoiding escapable morbidity and premature mortality, etc., to more complex achievements such as being happy, having self-respect, taking part in the life of the community, and so on.[2] The claim is that functionings are *constitutive* of a person's being, and an evaluation of well-being has to take the form of an assessment of these constituent elements.[3]

Closely related to the notion of functionings is that of the

[1] Various aspects of the conceptual foundation and practical problems of measurement and evaluation have been discussed in Sen (1980a, 1985a, 1985b). This chapter draws on Sen (1991b).

[2] For helpful discussion of various constitutive elements of quality of life, see Allardt (1981, 1992), Erikson and Aberg (1987), Erikson (1991), Ysander (1992). Indeed, the 'Scandinavian studies' on living conditions have done much to demonstrate and clarify the empirical possibility of examining diverse functionings as the basis of quality of life. On related matters, see also Fuchs (1983), Mack and Lansley (1985), Culyer (1986), A. Williams (1991).

[3] The philosophical basis of this approach can be traced to Aristotle's writings, which include a penetrating investigation of 'the good of man' in terms of 'life in the sense of activity' (see particularly *The Nicomachean Ethics*, I. 7). Aristotle had gone on to examine—both in *Ethics* and in *Politics*—the political and social implications of concentrating on well-being in this sense, involving 'human flourishing'. On the Aristotelian approach and its connections with the recent explorations of the capability perspective, see Nussbaum (1988a, 1988b).

capability to function. It represents the various combinations of functionings (beings and doings) that the person can achieve. Capability is, thus, a set of vectors of functionings, reflecting the person's freedom to lead one type of life or another.[4] Just as the so-called 'budget set' in the commodity space represents a person's freedom to buy commodity bundles,[5] the 'capability set' in the functioning space reflects the person's freedom to choose from possible livings.

It is easy to see that the well-being of a person must be thoroughly dependent on the nature of his or her being, i.e. on the functionings achieved. Whether a person is well-nourished, in good health, etc., must be intrinsically important for the wellness of that person's being. But, it may be asked, how do *capabilities*—as opposed to *achieved functionings*—relate to well-being?

The relevance of a person's capability to his or her well-being arises from two distinct but interrelated considerations. First, if the achieved functionings constitute a person's well-being, then the capability to achieve functionings (i.e. all the alternative combinations of functionings a person can choose to have) will constitute the person's freedom—the real opportunities—to have well-being. This 'well-being freedom' may have direct relevance in ethical and political analysis.[6] For example, in forming a view of the goodness of the social state, importance may be attached to the freedoms that different people respectively enjoy to achieve well-being. Alternatively, without taking the route of incorporating well-being freedom in the 'goodness' of the social state, it may be simply taken to be 'right' that individuals should have substantial well-being freedom.[7]

---

[4] There are several technical problems in the representation and valuation of functioning vectors (more generally, functioning *n*-tuples) and the capability sets of such vectors (or *n*-tuples); see Sen (1985*b*, 1991*b*).

[5] On this see Ch. 2, Sect. 2.2.

[6] The particular relevance of 'well-being freedom' as opposed to achieved well-being in social and political ethics is discussed in my Dewey Lectures (Sen 1985*a*), particularly in lectures 2 and 3. Those lectures also deal with the distinction between 'well-being freedom' and 'agency freedom'. The latter stands for freedom of a more general kind—the freedom to achieve whatever one's objectives are (possibly going well beyond the pursuit of one's own well-being). See Ch. 4 below.

[7] See Rawls (1988*a*) on the importance of the distinction between 'the right' and 'the good'. See also Sugden (1989) for a forceful presentation of the case for seeing the duties of the state in terms of ideas of the right rather than being based on maximizing the good. In Sen (1987) it is argued *inter alia* that the distinction may be less clear-cut and perhaps even less fundamental than is frequently assumed.

This freedom, reflecting a person's opportunities of well-being, must be valued at least for *instrumental* reasons, e.g. in judging how good a 'deal' a person has in the society. But in addition, as we have been discussing, freedom may be seen as being intrinsically important for a good social structure. A good society, in this view, is also a society of freedom.[8] It is also possible to use the notion of 'rightness' as opposed to 'goodness' of the society to argue for the same substantive arrangements. Those who see that distinction as being very fundamental, and argue for 'the priority of right over ideas of the good' (as Rawls 1988*a* puts it), would have to approach this question from that end.

The second connection between well-being and capability takes the direct form of making *achieved* well-being itself depend on the *capability* to function. Choosing may itself be a valuable part of living, and a life of genuine choice with serious options may be seen to be—for that reason—richer.[9] In this view, at least some types of capabilities contribute *directly* to well-being, making one's life richer with the opportunity of reflective choice. But even when freedom in the form of capability is valued only instrumentally (and the level of well-being is not seen as dependent on the extent of freedom of choice as such), capability to function can nevertheless be an important part of social evaluation. The capability set gives us information on the various functioning vectors that are

---

[8] The perspective of freedom is much associated with the important works of libertarian writers (e.g. Hayek 1960, 1967; Nozick 1974; J. M. Buchanan 1975, 1986; among recent contributors). But an early argument for concentration on the basic value of freedom can be found in Marx's political philosophy, with his emphasis on bringing 'the conditions for the free development and activity of individuals under their own control'. In Marx's vision, the liberated future society would 'make it possible for me to do one thing to-day and another tomorrow, to hunt in the morning, fish in the afternoon, rear cattle in the evening, criticize after dinner, just as I have in mind, without ever becoming hunter, fisherman, shepherd or critic' (Marx 1845–6: 22). This is, of course, an *overall* view of freedom (what one can, everything considered, do) in contrast with *negative* rights (what one is not prevented from doing) emphasized in much of the libertarian literature; on this distinction, see Berlin (1969). On alternative approaches to the intrinsic value of freedom, see my 'Freedom of Choice: Concept and Content' (Sen 1988*a*). On the Marxian approach to freedom, see Kolakowski (1978), C. Taylor (1979), Brenkert (1980, 1983), A. E. Buchanan (1982), Elster (1986), Lukes (1985), G. A. Cohen (1986, 1988, 1989), Ramachandran (1990), among other contributors.

[9] This is not to say that every additional choice makes a person's well-being go up, nor that the *obligation* to choose necessarily adds to one's freedom. These issues will be taken up in the next chapter.

within reach of a person, and this information is important—no matter how exactly well-being is characterized.

In either form, the capability approach clearly differs crucially from the more traditional approaches to individual and social evaluation, based on such variables as *primary goods* (as in Rawlsian evaluative systems), *resources* (as in Dworkin's social analysis), or *real income* (as in the analyses focusing on the GNP, GDP, named-goods vectors[10]). These variables are all concerned with the *instruments* of achieving well-being and other objectives, and can be seen also as the *means* to freedom. In contrast, functionings belong to the constitutive elements of well-being. Capability reflects freedom to pursue these constitutive elements, and may even have—as discussed earlier in this section—a direct role in well-being itself, in so far as deciding and choosing are also parts of living.[11]

3.2. VALUE OBJECTS AND EVALUATIVE SPACES

In an evaluative exercise, two distinct questions have to be clearly distinguished: (1) What are the objects of value? (2) How valuable are the respective objects? Even though *formally* the former question is an elementary aspect of the latter (in the sense that the objects of value are those that have *positive* weights), nevertheless the identification of the objects of value is *substantively* the primary exercise which makes it possible to pursue the second question.

Furthermore, the exercise of identification of the set of value-objects, with positive weights, itself precipitates a 'dominance

---

[10] For a critical survey of the analytical literature on this, see Sen (1979c).

[11] A fuller discussion of the motivational and strategic issues underlying the capability approach can be found in Sen (1980a, 1985a, 1985b, 1991b). For critiques and extensions of that approach, and also contributions in related but different traditions, see Roemer (1982, 1986a), Streeten (1984), Beitz (1986), Culyer (1986), P. Dasgupta (1986, 1988, 1990), de Beus (1986), De Leonardo, Maurie, and Rotelli (1986), Delbono (1986), Hamlin (1986), Helm (1986), Kakwani (1986), Luker (1986), O'Neill (1986, 1992), Riley (1986, 1987), Zamagni (1986), Asahi (1987), K. Basu (1987a), Brannen and Wilson (1987), Erikson and Aberg (1987), Hawthorn (1987), K. Hart (1987), Kanbur (1987), Kumar (1987), Muellbauer (1987), Ringen (1987), B. Williams (1987), Wilson (1987), Gaertner (1988, 1991), Goodin (1988), Arneson (1989a, 1990b), G. A. Cohen (1989, 1990), Drèze and Sen (1989), K. Griffin and Knight (1989), Nussbaum (1988a, 1988b), Suzumura (1988), Stewart (1988), Pogge (1989), Seabright (1989, 1991), Desai (1990), Hossain (1990), Steiner (1990), Van Parijs (1990a, 1990b), Ahtisaari (1991), D. A. Crocker (1991a, 1991b), A. Williams (1991), Bliss (1992), Brock (1992), A K. S. Kumar (1992) among others.

ranking' (*x* higher than *y* if it yields more of at least one of the valued objects and at least as much of each). This dominance ranking, which can be shown to have standard regularity properties such as transitivity, can indeed take us some distance—often quite a distance—in the evaluative exercise.[12]

The identification of the objects of value specifies what may be called an *evaluative space* (briefly discussed in Chapter 1). For example, in standard utilitarian analysis, the evaluative space consists of the individual utilities (defined in the usual terms of pleasures, happiness, or desire-fulfilment). Indeed, a complete evaluative approach entails a class of 'informational constraints' in the form of ruling out direct, evaluative use of various types of information (those that do not belong to the evaluative space).[13]

The capability approach is concerned *primarily* with the identification of value-objects, and sees the evaluative space in terms of functionings and capabilities to function. This is, of course, itself a deeply evaluative exercise, but answering question (1), on the identification of the objects of value does not, on its own, yield a particular answer to question (2), regarding their relative values. But the selection of space can also have a good deal of discriminating power, both because of what it *includes* as potentially valuable and because of what it *excludes* from the list of objects to be weighted as intrinsically important.

For example, the capability approach differs from utilitarian evaluation (more generally 'welfarist' evaluation[14]) in making room for a variety of doings and beings as important in themselves (not just *because* they may yield utility, nor just to the *extent* that they yield utility).[15] In this sense, the perspective of capabilities

[12] On this see Sen (1970*a*, 1970*b*).

[13] An evaluative system can, in fact, be helpfully analysed in terms of the informational constraints that it entails—the types of information that it 'rules out' from being used. On this strategy of 'informational analysis of evaluative principles', see Sen (1977*b*, 1979*d*).

[14] Utilitarianism may be factorized into three distinct components, viz. (1) *consequentialism* (decision variables such as acts, rules, etc., must be judged by the goodness of the consequent states of affairs); (2) *welfarism* (states of affairs must be judged by the individual utilities in that state); and (3) *sum-ranking* (individual utilities must be judged by simply summing them). On the nature of the factorization, and the variants of utilitarianism within this general structure, see Sen (1979*a*, 1979*b*) and Sen and Williams (1982), 'Introduction'.

[15] There are various ways of defining utility (such as happiness, pleasure, or desire-fulfilment) in distinct versions of utilitarianism (see e.g. Gosling 1969). But the remark here applies to all of them. On the other hand, if 'utility' is defined, as

provides a fuller recognition of the variety of ways in which lives can be enriched or impoverished. It also differs from those approaches that base the evaluation on objects that are not, in any sense, personal functionings or capabilities, e.g. judging well-being by real income, wealth, opulence, resources, liberties, or primary goods.

3.3. SELECTION AND WEIGHTING

There are always elements of real choice regarding the functionings to be included in the list of relevant functionings and important capabilities. The general format of 'doings' and 'beings' permits additional 'achievements' to be defined and included. Some functionings may be easy to describe, but of no great interest in most contexts (e.g. using a *particular* washing powder—much like other washing powders[16]). There is no escape from the problem of evaluation in selecting a class of functionings—and in the corresponding description of capabilities. The focus has to be related to the underlying concerns and values, in terms of which some definable functionings may be important and others quite trivial and negligible.[17] The need for selection and discrimination is neither an embarrassment, nor a unique difficulty, for the conceptualization of functionings and capabilities.[18]

In the context of some types of welfare analysis, e.g. in dealing with extreme poverty in developing economies, we may be able to go a fairly long distance in terms of a relatively small number of centrally important functionings (and the corresponding basic

James Griffin (1986) puts it, 'not as a substantive value at all, but instead as a formal analysis of what it is for something to be prudentially valuable to some person' (pp. 31–2), then the whole issue will turn on precisely how that 'formal analysis' is conducted. Whether the particular reinterpretation of utilitarianism proposed by Griffin leaves the approach still within the utilitarian fold, in any clearly distinctive sense, is an issue that I do not address here. Nor do I examine here the question of the correspondence between Griffin's general strategy as outlined in the quoted statement above and his particular use of the strength of prudential desire in substantive ethical analyses.

[16] Bernard Williams (1987) raises this issue in his comments on my Tanner Lectures on the standard of living; on this, see his discussion (pp. 98–101), and my response (pp. 108–9), in Sen *et al.* (1987).

[17] On the need to relate the evaluational concerns to the underlying motivation, see Brock (1991), who discusses this general question helpfully in terms of concrete issues in health care. See also Béteille (1983*a*), Verba *et al.* (1987), D. A. Crocker (1991*b*).

[18] I have tried to discuss some of the general methodological issues involved in 'description as choice' in Sen (1980*b*).

capabilities, e.g. the ability to be well-nourished and well-sheltered, the capability of escaping avoidable morbidity and premature mortality, and so forth).[19] In other contexts, including more general problems of economic development, the list may have to be much longer and much more diverse.[20]

In his review article of an earlier work of mine, Charles Beitz (1986) has illuminatingly discussed various features of the capability approach and has also forcefully raised an important critical issue (one that has been aired in different forms by several other critics as well):

The chief theoretical difficulty in the capabilities approach to interpersonal comparisons arises from the obvious fact that not all capabilities stand on the same footing. The capacity to move about, for example, has a different significance than the capability to play basketball.[21]

This is a natural worry to face, and it is important that the question be posed and addressed. It is certainly clear that some types of capabilities, broadly conceived, are of little interest or importance, and even the ones that count have to be weighted *vis-à-vis* each other. But these discriminations constitute an integral part of the capability approach, and the need for selection and weighting cannot really be, in any sense, an embarrassment (as 'a theoretical difficulty').[22]

The varying importance of different capabilities is as much a part of the capability framework as the varying value of different com-

[19] See Sen (1984, 1988b). The term 'basic capabilities', which I had used in 'Equality of What?' (Sen 1980a), was intended to separate out the ability to satisfy certain elementary and crucially important functionings up to certain levels. The term can, of course, be plausibly used in other ways as well, given the ambiguity of the concept of basicness, e.g. in the sense of referring to a person's *potential* capabilities that could be developed, whether or not they are actually realized (this is the sense in which the term is used by Nussbaum 1988a, 1988b).

[20] The range of functionings and capabilities that may be of interest for the assessment of a person's well-being or agency achievements can be very wide indeed; on this see my Dewey Lectures (Sen 1985a).

[21] Beitz (1986: 287). See also Arneson (1989a, 1990b) and G. A. Cohen (1989, 1990).

[22] The Aristotelian approach, referred to earlier, suggests a more assertive resolution of the weighting problem in the form of an ordered list of distinct functionings and capabilities, even though the ways of achieving specific capabilities may vary; on this see Nussbaum (1988a, 1988b). On the merits of the general approach of what is sometimes called 'perfectionism', see Haksar (1979). In general, the weighting problem may not be as totally and fully resolved as the Aristotelian approach suggests, but it is possible to make fruitful use of the capability approach even without such a linear ordering.

modities is a part of the real-income framework. Equal valuation of all constitutive elements is needed for neither. We cannot criticize the commodity-centred evaluation on the ground that different commodities are weighted differently. Exactly the same applies to functionings and capabilities. The capability approach begins with identifying a relevant space for evaluation, rather than arguing that everything that can be put into the format of that space must, for that reason, be important—not to mention, equally significant.

The primary claim is that in evaluating well-being, the value-objects are the functionings and capabilities. That claim neither entails that all types of capabilities are equally valuable, nor indicates that any capability whatsoever—even if totally remote from the person's life—must have some value in assessing that person's well-being. It is in asserting the need to examine the value of functionings and capabilities as opposed to confining attention to the *means* to these achievements and freedoms (such as resources or primary goods or incomes) that the capability approach has something to offer. The relative valuation of different functionings and capabilities has to be an integral part of the exercise.

3.4. INCOMPLETENESS: FUNDAMENTAL AND PRAGMATIC

I move now to a different, but related, issue. The capability approach can often yield definite answers even when there is no complete agreement on the relative weights to be attached to different functionings. First, a particular selection of value-objects (in this case, the functionings and capabilities that are accepted as valuable) would yield a 'dominance partial order' even without specification of relative weights. Having more of *each* relevant functioning or capability is a clear improvement, and this is decidable without waiting to get agreement on the *relative* weights to be attached to the different functionings and capabilities.

More importantly, that dominance-partial ordering can be extended even without a full agreement on relative values. For example, if there are four conflicting views claiming respectively that the relative weight to be attached to x vis-à-vis y should be ½, ⅓, ¼, and ⅕, there is, then, an implicit agreement that the relative weight on x should not exceed ½, nor fall below ⅕. But even this agreement will, in general, permit us to order pairs—possibly many pairs—not covered by the dominance ranking. For example, with the weights

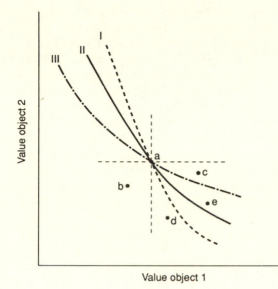

FIG. 3.1. *Dominance and Intersection*

specified, having one unit of x and two of y would be clearly better than having two units of x and one of y (even though neither pair dominates the other in the sense of having more of each x and y).

The 'intersection approach', which articulates only those judgements that are *shared* implications of *all* of the possible alternative weights, can indeed take us quite a distance.[23] It makes no further

[23] On the mathematical and interpretational issues underlying the intersection approach, see Sen (1970*a*, 1970*b*, 1973*a*, 1985*b*, 1986*a*), Blackorby (1975), Fine (1975*a*), K. Basu (1979), Bezembinder and van Acker (1979, 1986). See also the different but motivationally related literature on 'fuzzy' sets and measures (e.g. Zadeh 1965; Gouguen 1967; Bellman and Zadeh 1970), with possible application to measuring inequality and related social variables (e.g. S. R. Chakravarty and Roy 1985; K. Basu 1987*b*).

demands on agreement than what already exists. In Figure 3.1, the axes represent the value-objects (e.g. relevant functionings). That agreement (viz. on the identification of value-objects) already pre-cipitates a dominance ranking, e.g. *a* is superior to *b*. But the dom-inance ranking is incomplete and cannot rank *a* *vis-à-vis* *c*, *d*, or *e*.

Now consider the different 'indifference curves' (more generally, surfaces, when there are more than two value-objects) that are regarded as possible, without it being clear which one gives the correct valuation (or even that there *is* only one correct valuation). Let the permissible indifference curves through *a* be I, II, and III. Since *a* lies below *c* according to all of them, the intersection approach declares *a* to be inferior to *c*. Similarly, since *a* lies above *d* according to all of them, *a* can be declared to be better than *d*. Thus the dominance-partial ordering is extended by the intersection method. Even after this extension, the result may be still a partial order, illustrated by the fact that *a* is above *e* according to some indifference curve and below it according to another, so that *a* and *e* cannot be ranked in this case. The intersection approach increases decisiveness and articulation, but does not eliminate undecidability. That residual undecidability—when present—would not be a reason for embarrassment, since all it does is reflect the fact that with partially dissonant valuations, agreed completeness cannot be achieved.

It is important not to see the use of the capability approach as an 'all or nothing' exercise. Indeed, the nature of interpersonal com-parisons of well-being as well as the task of inequality evaluation as a discipline may admit incompleteness as a regular part of the respective exercises. An approach that can rank the well-being of every person against that of every other in a straightforward way, or one that can compare inequalities without any room for ambiguity or incompleteness, may well be at odds with the nature of these ideas. Both well-being and inequality are broad and partly opaque concepts. Trying to reflect them in the form of totally complete and clear-cut orderings can do less than justice to the nature of these concepts. There is a real danger of overprecision here.

In so far as there is genuine incompleteness, disparity, or ambi-valence in relative weights, they should be reflected in correspond-ing ambiguities in the characterization of the weighted value of well-being. This relates to a methodological point, which I have tried to defend elsewhere, that if an underlying idea has an essential ambiguity, a *precise* formulation of that idea must try to *capture* that ambiguity rather than lose it.[24]

The use of partial ordering has two different types of justification in interpersonal comparison or in inequality evaluation. First, as has been just discussed, the ideas of well-being and inequality may have enough ambiguity and fuzziness to make it a mistake to look for a complete ordering of either. This may be called the 'fundamental reason for incompleteness'. Second, even if it is not a mistake to look for one complete ordering, we may not be able in practice to identify it. While there may be disagreements about parts of that ordering and disputes as to how we should deal with those parts, there could still be agreement on other parts. The 'pragmatic reason for incompleteness' is to use whatever parts of the ranking we manage to sort out unambiguously, rather than maintaining complete silence until everything has been sorted out and the world shines in dazzling clarity.

The pragmatic course can, of course, work sequentially, and it is possible to extend partial orderings as and when we sort out the unresolved parts. But despite acknowledging the possibility of extension, it may be a mistake to say nothing and make no judgements whatever even about those parts that *are* clear, until everything is resolved. 'Waiting for toto' may not be a cunning strategy in a practical exercise.

3.5. CAPABILITY OR FUNCTIONINGS?

Capability is primarily a reflection of the freedom to achieve valuable functionings. It concentrates directly on freedom as such rather than on the means to achieve freedom, and it identifies the real alternatives we have. In this sense it can be read as a reflection of substantive freedom. In so far as functionings are constitutive of well-being, capability represents a person's freedom to achieve well-being.

That connection may seem simple enough, but—as was discussed in the first section of this chapter—capability may be relevant even for the *level of well-being achieved*, and not only for the *freedom to achieve well-being*. The achievement of well-being is not indepen-

---

[24] On this see Sen (1970a, 1989b). This is, of course, not a special problem exclusively for the capability approach. The same issues arise generally in many of the conceptual frameworks in social, economic, and political theory.

dent of the process through which we achieve various functionings and the part that our own decisions play in those choices. If this line of reasoning is seen to be important over a wide domain, there will be a case for relating capability to achieved well-being—and not only to the freedom to achieve well-being.

However, this move might seem rather complicated and perhaps even confusing. For one thing, it would seem to disrupt the neat structure of (1) *functionings achieved* being related to the achievement of *well-being*, and (2) the *capability* to function being related to the *freedom* to achieve well-being. While—it could be argued—freedom of choice (and therefore capability) might indeed have some direct influence on the level of well-being achieved, nevertheless it would surely be an 'overkill' to see achieved well-being 'just as' a function of the capability set, rather than of the *actual functionings* achieved. In trying to make room for one little influence, aren't we likely to miss out the simple and important relationship between achieved functionings and achieved well-being?

In sorting out this tangled issue, the first thing to note is that capability is defined in terms of the *same* focal variables as functionings. In the space of functionings, any *point* represents an n tuple of functionings. Capability is a *set* of such functioning n tuples, representing the various alternative combinations of functionings from which the person can choose one combination.[25] Since an important part of the force of the capability approach lies in moving us away from the space of commodities, incomes, utilities, etc., on to the space of the constitutive elements of living, it is particularly important to note that there is no difference *as far as the space is concerned* between focusing on functionings *or* on capabilities. A functioning combination is a *point* in such a space, whereas capability is a *set* of such points.

Next, we must note that the capability set contains *inter alia* information about the actual functioning combination chosen, since it too is obviously among the feasible combinations. In fact, there is nothing to prevent us from basing the evaluation of a capability set exactly on the assessment of the *chosen combination* of functionings from that set. Indeed, if freedom had only *instrumental* importance for a person's well-being and no intrinsic relevance, then it would be appropriate—in the evaluation of well-being—to identify the value of the capability set simply with the value of the *chosen* functioning

[25] For formal characterizations, see Sen (1985*b*: chs. 2 and 7).

combination. This will coincide with valuing a capability set by the value of the best element (or, more generally, *a* best element, since it need not be unique) of this set, if the person does in fact choose in a way that maximizes his or her well-being. These different procedures, which may or may not yield the same result, can be seen as examples of what may be called 'elementary evaluation,' i.e. valuing a set by the value of one distinguished element of it (e.g. the chosen one, the best one, or some such).[26]

The possibility of elementary evaluation of the capability set makes it clear that *even if* we are ultimately concerned only with achievements, not with freedoms (except instrumentally as means to the achievements), the capability set can, in fact, still be used for the evaluation. The capability set gives us more information than we need, but the chosen combination is a *part* of the capability set.[27] In this sense, there is a case for seeing the theory of evaluation of well-being in terms of capability in general, whether or not the elements other than the chosen one are actually invoked (depending on the importance that is attached to the process of choice).[28]

Furthermore, freedom of choice can indeed be of direct importance for the person's quality of life and well-being. The nature of this connection may be worth discussing a bit more. Acting freely and being able to choose are, in this view, directly conducive to well-being, not just because more freedom makes more alternatives available. This view is, of course, contrary to the one typically assumed in standard consumer theory, in which the contribution of a set of feasible choices is judged exclusively by the value of the best element available.[29] Even the removal of all elements of a feasible set (e.g. a 'budget set') *other than* the chosen best element would be seen as 'no real disadvantage', since the freedom to choose does not,

[26] See Sen (1985*b*: 60–1).

[27] To use this procedure, we do, of course, need to know what is chosen from each set, and not just what the set is from which the choice is being made. This can be done through actual observation, or through some behavioural assumption (such as the maximization of the relevant objective function).

[28] In fact, in my first presentation of the capability view in 'Equality of What?' (Sen 1980*a*), no real distinction was made between the capability view and the functioning view of well-being. On this issue, see also Cohen (1990), Desai (1990), Ahtisaari (1991).

[29] Thus in standard consumer theory set evaluation will take the form of elementary evaluation. For particular departures from that tradition, see Koopmans (1964) and Kreps (1979). However, even there the motivation is not so much to value the freedom one has as a good thing in itself, but to take note of uncertainty regarding one's *own future preferences* by instrumentally valuing the advantage of having more options in the future. On the motivational distinctions, see Sen (1985*b*).

in this view, in itself matter. In contrast, if choosing is seen as a part of living, and 'doing *x*' is distinguished from 'choosing to do *x* and doing it', then even the achievement of well-being must be seen as being influenced by the freedom reflected in the capability set.

It is, in fact, possible to represent functionings in such a way that they already reflect the alternatives available and thus the choices enjoyed. For example, 'fasting' as a functioning is *not* just starving; it is *choosing to starve when one does have other options*. In examining a starving person's achieved well-being, it is of direct interest to know whether he is fasting or simply does not have the means to get enough food. Similarly, choosing a life-style is not exactly the same as having that life-style no matter how chosen, and one's well-being does depend on how that life-style happened to emerge.[30]

There is, in principle, some real advantage in being able to relate the analysis of *achieved* well-being on the wider informational base of the person's *capability set*, rather than just on the selected element of it. This is, however, not to deny that quite often this potential advantage would have to be forgone given the difficulty of getting information regarding the capability set as opposed to the observed functionings. In fact, the capability set is not directly observable, and has to be constructed on the basis of presumptions (just as the 'budget set' in consumer analysis is also so constructed on the basis of data regarding income, prices and the presumed possibilities of exchange). Thus, in practice, one might have to settle often enough for relating well-being to the achieved—and observed—functionings, rather than trying to bring in the capability set (when the presumptive basis of such a construction would be empirically dubious).[31]

But we must distinguish between what becomes acceptable on grounds of practical difficulties of data availability, and what would be the right procedure had one not been so limited in terms of information. In arguing for the importance of the capability set in

[30] The importance of choice in the value of living has been emphasized by several authors, including Aristotle (*Nicomachean Ethics*, books II and V; in Ross 1980) and Marx (1844, 1845–6). There are many formal as well as conceptual problems involved in valuing both achievements and freedoms, and in making room for each in the evaluative structure. I have tried to discuss these problems elsewhere, and will not pursue them further here; in Sen (1985*a*, 1991*b*).

[31] Indeed, as will be argued in Ch. 4, sometimes even the analysis of *freedom*, and not just of achieved well-being, may have to be partly based on the *observed states of being* (bringing in the perspective of freedom in terms of the power to get what one *would* choose, rather than focusing just on the *act* of choice).

the analysis of achieved well-being, we are not closing our eyes to the practical problems of informational availability, nor to the value of the second-best analysis that we can do even with limited data. But it is also important to be quite clear as to what data, in principle, can be relevant and useful, even though *in many cases* we might not be able to get them. Practical compromises have to be based with an eye both to (1) the range of our ultimate interests, and (2) the contingent circumstances of informational availability.

Even when the pragmatic acceptance of limitations of data availability force us to set our sights lower than the full representation of capability sets, it is important to keep the underlying motivations clearly in view and to see practical compromises as the best we can do under the circumstances. As a matter of fact, the informational base of functionings is still a much finer basis of evaluation of the quality of life and economic progress than various alternatives more commonly recommended, such as individual utilities or commodity holdings.

The capability approach can, thus, be used at various levels of sophistication. How far we can go would depend much on the practical considerations regarding what data we can get and what we cannot. Ideally, the capability approach should take note of the full extent of freedom to choose between different functioning bundles, but limits of practicality may often force the analysis to be confined to examining the *achieved* functioning bundle only. This is obviously more of a problem when we use the capability approach to assess *freedom* rather than the actual *well-being* attained, but even for the latter, data limitation can be—for reasons already mentioned—a substantial drawback.

3.6. UTILITY *VIS-À-VIS* CAPABILITY

We end this chapter with a brief contrast of the capability approach with the alternative of relying on utility as a guide to personal well-being and as the basis of social ethics and the assessment of equality. The utilitarian notion of value, which is invoked explicitly or by implication in much of welfare economics, sees value, ultimately, only in individual utility, which is defined in terms of some mental condition, such as pleasure, happiness, desires.

The 'desire-fulfilment' interpretation of utility is sometimes seen as quite distinct from a 'mental state' view, on the ground that here utility is achieved through the objective realization of a desired state rather than through achieving some mental state like that of being pleased (see J. Griffin, 1982, 1986). The distinction is indeed important. It is also certainly true that no mental metric is, in fact, involved in determining the *existence* of some utility in the sense of desire-fulfilment—all we need to check is whether the desired object has or has not been achieved. However, for a fuller welfarist evaluation, more is needed than just ascertaining the existence of utility, and specifically it requires measurement and comparison of utilities, in some form or other. For this purpose, *intensities of desire* would have to be compared, if the approach has to be based on relating the importance of desire-fulfilment to the strength of the desire. Indeed, the mental metric of *desire* as such would have to be extensively invoked to make use of the *desire-fulfilment* view of utility in utilitarian and other utility-based evaluations.

It might appear that there is no particular reason why the valuation of functionings or capabilities themselves should not be done by the use of mental metrics, e.g. the strength of desires, and if so done, why such a utility-based accounting could not be seen as a possible *part* of the capability approach. There is indeed no reason why such desire-based accounting of capabilities and functionings could not count as a specific version of the capability approach broadly defined. But there are problems related to motivational contrasts.

There are different problems with different interpretations of utility, but they share the programme of getting the evaluation done *indirectly* through using some psychological metric like happiness or desire. This is precisely where the main difficulty lies. While being happy may count as an important functioning, it cannot really be taken to be all there is to leading a life (i.e. it can scarcely be the only valuable functioning). If the utility-based valuation is done in terms of pleasure or happiness, then in effect the other functionings would get disenfranchised, and would be valued only indirectly and only to the extent that they contribute to pleasure or happiness.

If, on the other hand, desire-fulfilment is taken as the criterion, then a very particular method of evaluating capabilities and functionings would have been chosen. The adequacy of this particular perspective for the evaluation of capabilities and functionings is deeply disputable, since any mechanical use of a metric of desires rather than facing the problem of reasoned assessment does injustice to the exercise of normative evaluation.[32]

The problem is particularly acute in the context of entrenched inequalities and deprivations. A thoroughly deprived person, leading a very reduced life, might not appear to be badly off in terms of the mental metric of desire and its fulfilment, if the hardship is accepted with non-grumbling resignation. In situations of long-standing deprivation, the victims do not go on grieving and lamenting all the time, and very often make great efforts to take pleasure in small mercies and to cut down personal desires to modest—'realistic'—proportions. Indeed, in situations of adversity which the victims cannot individually change, *prudential reasoning* would suggest that the victims should concentrate their desires on those limited things that they *can* possibly achieve, rather than fruitlessly pining for what is unattainable. The extent of a person's deprivation, then, may not at all show up in the metric of desire-fulfilment, even though he or she may be quite unable to be adequately nourished, decently clothed, minimally educated, and properly sheltered.

The problem of entrenched deprivation is particularly serious in many cases of inequality. It applies particularly to the differentiation of class, community, caste, and gender. While the nature of these deprivations can be brought out more clearly by concentrating on socially generated differences in important capabilities, some of that gain would be wasted if the capabilities themselves were to be assessed, after all, in the metric of utilities. A return to the old conformism as a supplement to the capability perspective would tend to wipe out—at least partially—the gains from the change, especially by undervaluing those capabilities which the chronically deprived dare not covet. The exercise of evaluation of capabilities cannot be left to the mere totalling of utilities generated by these capabilities. The difference can be quite far-reaching in the case of deep-rooted and resilient inequalities.

---

[32] This is a difficult issue, and the summary of a complex argument presented here is not satisfactory. For a fuller treatment of this question, see my second Dewey Lecture (Sen 1985*a*: 185–203). On related matters, see also Davidson (1986), Gibbard (1986), and Scanlon (1975, 1990, 1992).

4

FREEDOM, AGENCY AND WELL-BEING

4.1. WELL-BEING *VIS-À-VIS* AGENCY

In the discussion of freedom in the last chapter, our attention was confined to the freedom to achieve functionings relevant for one's own well-being. But a person can—and typically does—also have goals and values other than the pursuit of one's own well-being. In the Dewey Lectures (Sen 1985*a*), I have tried to discuss the distinction between 'the agency aspect' and 'the well-being aspect' of a person, and have argued that a person cannot be reduced to just one dimension to force these two aspects to coincide.

A person's agency achievement refers to the realization of goals and values she has reasons to pursue, whether or not they are connected with her own well-being. A person as an agent need not be guided only by her own well-being, and agency achievement refers to the person's success in the pursuit of the totality of her considered goals and objectives.[1] If a person aims at, say, the independence of her country, or the prosperity of her community, or some such general goal, her agency achievement would involve evaluation of states of affairs in the light of those objects, and not merely in the light of the extent to which those achievements would contribute to her own well-being.

Corresponding to the distinction between agency achievement and well-being achievement, there is a differentiation also between a

---

[1] The need for reflection, or for having reasons for one's goals and objectives, is a qualification that can be quite exacting. Any whim or caprice that a person happens to have at a certain time need not provide the basis of an 'agency objective' in the sense used here. On the relevance of this constraint, see Sen (1985*a*). On some general issues regarding reasoned defence of one's objectives, see Rawls (1971), Glover (1977), Hare (1981), B. Williams (1981, 1985), Hirschman (1982), Schelling (1984), Parfit (1984), Nagel (1986), Wiggins (1987), Hurley (1989), among others. In the context of economic analysis, the often neglected need for 'rational assessment' has been well posed by Broome (1978). In this monograph I shall not specifically concentrate on this aspect of the problem, and will simply assume that a person's 'objectives' and 'goals' refer to those objectives and goals for which he has reasons (rather than referring to any impulse or whim that he happens to have).

person's 'agency freedom' and 'well-being freedom'. The former is one's freedom to bring about the achievements one values and which one attempts to produce, while the latter is one's freedom to achieve those things that are constitutive of one's well-being. It is the latter that is best reflected by a person's *capability set*, for reasons already discussed, while the former—agency freedom—would have to be seen in broader terms, including aspects of states of affairs that relate to one's agency objectives (whether or not they directly contribute to one's well-being). I have discussed the distinction more extensively elsewhere,[2] and will not pursue it further here.

It should be emphasized that there is no claim here that the two aspects—agency and well-being—would be independent of each other. They are distinguishable and separate, but thoroughly interdependent. The pursuit of well-being can be one of the important goals of the agent. Also, the failure to achieve *non*-well-being goals can lead to frustration and thus to a loss of well-being. There are other connections. The point is the recognition of a significant distinction, *not* the assertion of any possibility of analysing one *independently* of the other.

4.2. AGENCY, INSTRUMENTALITY AND REALIZATION

In analysing the agency objectives, it is possible to make a further distinction between (1) the occurrence of those things that one values and one aims at achieving, and (2) the occurrence of such things brought about by one's *own* efforts (or, in the bringing about of which one has *oneself* played an active part).[3] The former refers to the realization of one's objectives, regardless of one's own role in bringing about that realization. The latter, in contrast, is a more specific notion of agency success, concentrating on one's success specifically *as* an agent.[4]

If my agency objectives include the independence of my country, or the elimination of famines, the first view of agency achievement

[2] In my third Dewey Lecture (Sen 1985*a*).

[3] In my Dewey Lectures (Sen 1985*a*), my primary focus was on the distinction between the 'well-being aspect' and the 'agency aspect', and as a consequence, I did not distinguish between the two different features of the agency aspect sharply. The motivational discussion included both types of agency considerations. I am most grateful to Susan Brison for an entirely persuasive discussion on the importance of disentangling the two elements.

[4] The value that people attach (and have reason to attach) to 'involvement' is one of the important features of this distinction. On this see Hirschman (1982).

would be well met if the country *does* become independent, or if famines *are* in fact eliminated, irrespective of the part I personally manage to play in bringing about that achievement. This idea of agency success is based on a straightforward comparison between the objectives I wish to promote—or what I would in fact promote if I were the effective agent—and the actual realization of those objectives (no matter who does the actual promoting).

The second view is a more *participatory* one. I have to look specifically at my own role in the promotion of those objectives. In this view, my agency success, in this narrower sense, would depend precisely on the role I myself play in bringing about the achievement of those objectives. We can perhaps usefully distinguish between '*realized* agency success' and '*instrumental* agency success' to refer respectively to the two cases.

In some contexts this distinction between the two elements in a person's agency aspect can be important. To some extent the question is closely related to the nature of our values, i.e. whether what we value is the achievement irrespective of the instrumental process, or whether the valuation relates directly to the part we ourselves play in bringing about the results. Indeed, by specifying the objectives more fully, e.g. by distinguishing between 'the occurrence of *A*' and 'the occurrence of *A* through our own efforts', it is formally possible to embed the particular feature of 'instrumental agency success' within the general format of 'realized agency success'. But this is a formal route, which I shall not explore further here.[5]

The question of instrumentality relates closely also to the notion of the 'control' that one exercises over the realization of outcomes. In some views of freedom, definitive and great importance is attached to a person having the control himself in bringing about what he wants to achieve. Later on in this chapter, I shall have the occasion to scrutinize the idea of 'freedom as control' and will discuss some problems in seeing freedom exclusively in that perspective. But before that I would like to investigate further some of the implications of the general distinction between the agency aspect and the well-being aspect of a person.

---

[5] The question relates to the way states of affairs are to be seen—an issue of some importance in analysing the limits of consequentialism; on this see Sen (1982*b*, 1983*b*).

4.3. CAN FREEDOM CONFLICT WITH WELL-BEING?

In arguing for a freedom-based evaluative system, a general presumption is sometimes made that more freedom is always advantageous—at least not detrimental. Is that supposition correct?[6] It seems clear enough that it cannot be, in general, correct. Indeed, sometimes more freedom of choice can bemuse and befuddle, and make one's life more wretched.[7] There are costs of decision-taking, and it may be comfortable to lie back and relax while others make the detailed choices. It is possible to construct different types of scenarios in which more freedom makes one certainly less happy, and possibly even less fulfilled.[8]

This interesting matter raises two different types of issues. One is the question as to whether freedom—both agency freedom and well-being freedom—can conflict with well-being, and if so, in what sense, and for what reasons? This issue (i.e. possible conflicts between freedom and well-being) I shall investigate first. But there is a second—no less important—issue that is also raised by the possibly contrary effects of the expansion of some types of choices. Is that contrariness best seen simply as a conflict between freedom, on the one hand, and advantage, on the other, with some increase in freedom being *disadvantageous*? Or is that problem largely a reflection of an ambiguity regarding the nature of freedom itself which needs to be sorted out? I shall take up this second issue (related to the nature of freedom) in the next section, after discussing the possible conflicts between freedom and well-being.

Given what has already been discussed in this monograph, it should come as no surprise that freedom and well-being need not always move in the same way, or even in the same direction. In pursuing this question, the distinction between *well-being freedom* and *agency freedom* is particularly important. There would be nothing contrary in the fact that an enhancement of *agency freedom*

[6] For arguments and illustrations showing that more freedom can be disadvantageous, see Elster (1979), G. Dworkin (1982), Schelling (1984), and Frankfurt (1987).

[7] Dithering can also kill, as illustrated by the sad case of Buridan's ass, which died of starvation unable to choose between two haystacks in front of it. A commanding authority could have saved its life. On the importance of self-command, see Schelling (1984).

[8] There is also an interesting issue regarding the intercultural variation of the importance we attach to taking decisions ourselves and having a range of choice. It has been argued that in some cultures, more freedom of choice is not viewed with favour. On related issues, dealing *inter alia* with cultural variations, see Apffel Marglin and Marglin (1990).

(i.e. an increase in one's ability to promote goals that one has reasons to promote) can lead to a reduction of *well-being freedom* (and correspondingly to a decline in *achieved well-being*). Indeed, it is precisely because of such conflicts that the distinction between agency and well-being is important.[9]

For example, if instead of being far away from a scene of crime—a crime that I would like to prevent—I happen to be bang on the spot, my agency freedom is certainly enhanced (I can now do something to stop that terrible event which I would much like to prevent), but as a result my well-being may go down (e.g. I may get wounded in the process of prevention even if my efforts are successful). The fact that, everything considered, I do regard the fight to be worth it (i.e. my other agency objectives dominate over any diminution of well-being that I may suffer) does not, of course, entail that my well-being *as such* cannot go down as a result of my chosen efforts.[10] If freedom is taken to be *agency* freedom, then it is quite possible to see contrary movements in which freedom (i.e. agency freedom) does go up, while achieved well-being goes down.

In fact, not only *well-being achievement* but also *well-being freedom* can often move in the opposite direction to *agency freedom*. Indeed, even in the 'crime-prevention case' discussed above, not only is my well-being reduced as a result of my being at the scene of the crime rather than far away, there is a possible reduction also in my *freedom* to achieve well-being (despite the increase in my agency freedom). For example, I might not be able to escape getting involved in the event if I am too close (there may be 'no exit'), so that my increased ability to stop the crime may go hand in hand with a diminished ability to pursue my own well-being. But perhaps more importantly, even if I *can* leave without interference (if I can choose to 'chicken out'), being at that hot spot I may no longer be able to be at peace with myself and have the comfort of *both* being safe and feeling non-guilty, which I could have enjoyed had I been far away (not having the need to consciously opt out of help-

---

[9] On this, see my third Dewey Lecture (Sen 1985a: esp. 203–8).

[10] A false identification of well-being success and agency success can, of course, occur in the model of the 'rational fool', a common behavioural assumption in economic theory whereby each person is seen as promoting his own well-being in every choice that he makes. On the limitations of that behavioural framework, see Sen (1973b, 1977c, 1987). See also Hirschman (1982), McPherson (1982, 1984), Akerlof (1984), Walsh (1987, 1991), Hausman and McPherson (1991), Meeks (1991).

ing the person in peril).[11] So this is a case in which my well-being freedom may also go down, and there need not be any conflict between the directional movements of well-being achievement and well-being freedom (both down, as opposed to agency freedom and achievement, which are both up).

Thus, well-being and freedom can move in opposite directions no matter which interpretation of freedom is chosen. If by freedom we mean *agency freedom*, then it is quite possible that an expansion of (agency) freedom may go hand in hand with a reduction in well-being freedom as well as well-being achievement. If, on the other hand, we take freedom to mean *well-being freedom*, then any conflict between freedom and achieved well-being cannot, of course, arise from the shrinkage of opportunities of well-being achievement with increased (well-being) freedom. But there can still be a conflict between the two (i.e. between well-being freedom and well-being achievement), since a person's choice is not necessarily guided only by the pursuit of his or her well-being. If the increase in well-being freedom is accompanied by other changes that shift one's choices towards pursuing other—non-well-being—objectives, then well-being *achievement* might quite possibly go down while well-being *freedom* goes up. This last case may at first sight appear to be a bit odd (how can an *increased* freedom to pursue well-being *reduce* the achievement of well-being?), but there is no real puzzle here. The change that brings about the expansion of well-being freedom may also allow a person to pursue other (non-well-being) goals more forcefully and this can quite possibly lead to a deterioration of the extent of well-being the person chooses to achieve.

An illustration may be useful. Consider a doctor who is ready to sacrifice her own well-being to go and work in some terribly poor and miserable country, but is prevented from doing that because of a lack of means and opportunity to go to that far-away land. Consider next a rise in her income—it need not matter how this came about— and in this new economic situation she has both more well-being

---

[11] This kind of problem comes close to the issue of 'moral luck', on which see B. Williams (1973a, 1981, 1985), Nagel (1979), and Nussbaum (1985). Note, however, that in terms of the duality between well-being and agency explored in this monograph (and in Sen 1985a), a person can be both *luckier* in the sense of being better able to promote her *agency* objectives and *less lucky* in the sense of being more constrained in pursuing her own *well-being*. In this monograph I do not further explore the distinctions involved in the general context of 'moral luck'.

freedom (e.g. she can buy lots of nice things for herself) and more agency freedom (she can also go to the far-away land and sacrifice her own well-being for tireless work in pursuit of the greater good of suffering humanity). If she chooses the latter, it is quite possible that she would have less well-being achievement (though greater agency success). Her well-being achievement may, thus, go down just as her well-being freedom as well as agency freedom *both* go up.

Freedom and well-being achievement can, thus, move in opposite directions, no matter whether we interpret freedom as agency freedom or as well-being freedom. How common such a conflict will be is, of course, a different question. Greater opportunities of pursuing well-being—an enhancement of well-being freedom—may well be frequently seized. Also, as discussed in the earlier sections of this chapter, increased freedom may *itself* contribute to the achievement of well-being, since choosing and deciding may be valuable parts of living well. But notwithstanding all this, there *can* be a conflict between the achievement of well-being, on the one hand, and freedom in either form (viz. well-being freedom as well as agency freedom). The reasons for possible conflicts can vary, but they relate ultimately to the substantive content of the distinction between the two aspects—well-being and agency—of a person. That distinction not only indicates two different perspectives in which inequality may be assessed, but also provides reason, as we have just argued, for expecting that well-being may not move in the same direction as freedom judged in *either* perspective.

4.4. FREEDOM AND DISADVANTAGEOUS CHOICES

Even when freedom and well-being do not move together, it does not, of course, follow that an increase in a person's freedom would be to his or her disadvantage. There are different ways of judging advantage, related partly to the distinction between well-being and agency objectives, and partly to the contrast between available opportunities and resulting states. The realized level of well-being need not be the only guide to the opportunities that a person values most. But there is also the second question that was posed earlier (at the beginning of Section 4.3) concerning the possibility that increased freedom might be *disadvantageous* to the person by forcing on the person the necessity to spend time and effort in making lots of choices that he or she would rather not have to make. There can be inconvenience and hassle from having to make more choices, and this may well be far from advantageous, no matter how exactly we define advantage.

This question does, in fact, take us in the direction of an important issue regarding the nature of freedom, to wit, whether any increase in choices that one can—and has to—make must be seen as an expansion of freedom. This issue is, as will be presently argued, quite central to the assessment of social structures and public policies related to enhancing freedom.

Freedom is a complex notion. Facing more alternatives need not invariably be seen as an expansion of a person's freedom to do the things she would like to do.[12] If a life without hassle is valued (and the frantic routine of constant decision-taking is not treasured), the freedom to achieve the preferred form of life is not necessarily enhanced by a multiplication of trivial choices. What may apparently look like a conflict between freedom and advantage may not, thus, be anything of the sort, and may be the result of misspecifying freedom by overlooking the *loss of option* of leading a peaceful and unbothered life (entailed by a proliferation of minor choices that *have to be*—willy-nilly—made).

There is an inescapable need for evaluation in judging whether the forgone opportunity of a hassle-free life may not be more important than the greater chance of being able to take all these minor decisions. The question really turns on the need to judge what options are important and what are not. The expansion of choices to be made is both an *opportunity* (the choices *can* be made by oneself) and a *burden* (the choices *have to be* made by oneself). It is easy to think of circumstances when given *the choice of having to make these particular choices*, one would have good reason to say no. This indicates that the expansion of those *particular choices* and obligations need not be seen as a valued expansion of freedom.

The significant recognition that choosing is a part of living, which we discussed earlier, cuts both ways. Some types of choosing can be *valuable* parts of living, giving us reason to treasure them. But there are other choices that we may have no great reason to value, and the *obligatory* requirement to face and deal with them may impose on us losses of time and energy which we may have good reasons to resent.

[12] For different axiomatic approaches to assessing the extents of freedom, see Koopmans (1964), Kreps (1979), Sen (1985b, 1991a), Suppes (1987), Pattanaik and Xu (1990).

Thus the expansion of some types of choices can reduce our ability to choose life-styles that we might treasure.

So the conflict here is not really between our freedom *tout court*, on the one hand, and our advantages, on the other, but primarily between different *types* of freedoms—the freedom to exercise active choice over a range of (possibly trivial) options and the freedom to lead a leisured life without the nuisance of constantly having to make trivial choices. Some of the perceived conflict between freedom and advantage arises from an underspecification of freedom—ignoring the fact that we may have good reasons to choose *not* to have the necessity of making all these unwanted choices. The problem relates to the inescapable requirement of valuation involved in the assessment of freedom, as has already been discussed.

4.5. CONTROL AND EFFECTIVE FREEDOM

A related issue concerns the distinction between freedom and *direct control*. I have tried to argue elsewhere (Sen 1982c), that the perspective of 'freedom as control' is seriously limited. Many freedoms take the form of our ability to get what we value and want, without the levers of control being *directly* operated by us. The controls are exercised in line with what we value and want (i.e. in line with our 'counterfactual decisions'—what we *would* choose), and in this sense they give us more power and more freedom to lead the lives that we would choose to lead. To confuse freedom with control can drastically reduce the scope and force of that great idea.

To illustrate, consider first a fairly minor example. When a proof-reader checks the proofs of this book to weed out the printing errors and to get the spelling right, he will not be taking away my freedom to have my book printed the way I would like it to be. The *control* will be in other hands, but the proof-reader will be doing what I would, counterfactually, have done, if I were to correct all the proofs myself with eyes as efficient as that of the proof-reader. Whether he is following my direct instructions, or *knows* what my instructions *would have been if sought*, is not a matter of great importance here, in judging what freedoms I really do have. As long as the levers of control are systematically exercised in line with *what I would choose* and *for that exact reason*, my 'effective freedom' is uncompromised, though my 'freedom as control' may be limited or absent.[13]

In modern society, given the complex nature of social organization, it is often very hard, if not impossible, to have a system that gives each person all the levers of control over her own life. But the fact that others might exercise control does not imply that there is no further issue regarding the freedom of the person; it does make a difference how the controls are, in fact, exercised.

The distinction between 'instrumental agency success' and 'realized agency success' (discussed earlier on in this chapter) is relevant here. The 'freedom as control' view *is* concerned only with the 'instrumental' aspect of the problem. The focus, in this case, is entirely on the person herself being the active agency in bringing about the achievement. The broader issue of 'realized' success is left open in this perspective. The idea of 'effective freedom' is related to that broader view of success.

To take a rather more momentous example than getting the spelling right in correcting proofs, the freedom to live in an epidemic-free atmosphere may be important for us, and given the choice, we would choose to achieve that. But the controls of general epidemic prevention may not be in our hands—it may require national and possibly even international policies. If we do not have control over the process of elimination of epidemics, there is no more to be said, as far as our 'freedom as control' is concerned, in this field. But in a broader sense, the issue of freedom is still there. A public policy that eliminates epidemics is enhancing our freedom to lead the life— unbattered by epidemics—that we *would choose* to lead.[14]

Of course, the elimination of epidemics also increases our well-being achievement.[15] That is another issue (not unrelated, but not

[13] What is being called 'effective freedom' here was called 'freedom as power' in Sen (1982c). G. A. Cohen and Jean Drèze have given me good reasons to think that the word 'power' is not very helpful in making this distinction, and that it is hard to differentiate 'power' from 'control' in ordinary usage. Hence the attempt here to use a different term to refer to a person's ability to get systematically what he *would choose* no matter who actually controls the levers of operation.

[14] If someone does have the odd preference for having one of the epidemic diseases, then his preference-fulfilment would not be well served by this epidemiological policy. The negative implication may extend, in this case, to freedom as well, if the preference in question turns out to be reasonably defendable.

[15] There is, of course, an important question here about the connections between the choices of *different* individuals. In this case, it is reasonable to expect a congruence of our general preferences on the matter of epidemic prevention. It is because of this congruence that our respective powers to lead lives we would like to lead do not get

the same either), and the one with which we are directly concerned here is our freedom to lead a life we *would choose* to live. The fact that it would probably also increase our well-being, in this case, is a different matter. If the levers of control were used by those in charge of them to, say, *promote* epidemics, rather than to eliminate them, our 'freedom as control' would not be changed (i.e. would continue to be absent), but our 'effective freedom' (in particular, the freedom to lead the types of lives we would choose to lead) would be severely compromised.

In assessing the freedoms that we enjoy and in examining how unequal we are in that respect, the informational basis of the evaluation has to take into account our counterfactual choices (what we *would* choose) and their relation to what is made to happen. An exclusive concentration on the levers of control would be inadequate for analysing our freedoms. While this may look like adding to the already heavy informational demand for analysing freedoms, it need not, in fact, make the practical problems of such analyses more intractable. Sometimes the nature of counterfactual choices are very easy to guess, e.g. that people would choose to avoid epidemics, pestilence, famines, chronic hunger. The elimination of these unloved things, through public policy aimed at giving people what they would want, can be seen as an enhancement of people's real freedom. In this sense, even simple observations of realized states may have direct relevance to the analysis of freedoms enjoyed, once we reject relying exclusively on the limited view of 'freedom as control'.

This recognition has some fairly far-reaching relevance to the nature of empirical analysis of freedoms enjoyed by different people and of the inequalities in the freedoms that we have. In the next section, this question is further explored.

4.6. FREEDOM FROM HUNGER, MALARIA AND OTHER MALADIES

The term 'freedom' is often used to refer to such matters as 'freedom from hunger' or 'freedom from malaria'. It has sometimes been suggested that this is a misuse of the concept of freedom, and the

into conflict with each other. The relationship between power and control would vary systematically with the nature of the objectives in question, and that is indeed a central issue in the investigation both of the norms of public policy and of the nature of 'social rationality'. The former issue has been discussed in the literature on public goods and the allocation of resources in that context.

ideas captured by the expressions have nothing much to do with freedom in the real sense.[16] Not having malaria, or not being hungry, does add to one's well-being, but—so the argument runs—it is not a matter of having *more freedom* in any sense.[17]

This diagnosis can be disputed on the basis of the analysis presented in the earlier sections of this chapter. In terms of that analysis, the idea of *counterfactual choice*—what one would have chosen if one had the choice—is relevant to one's freedom.[18] Indeed, one's control over the actual process of choice can scarcely be the only reference in the ideas of liberty and freedom. When Isaiah Berlin (1969) talks of 'a man's, or a people's, liberty to choose to live as they desire' (p. 179), the point of direct reference is the ability to choose to live as one desires, rather than the mechanism of control. If people do desire a life without hunger or malaria, the elimination of these maladies through public policy does enhance their 'liberty to choose to live as they desire'. The fact that the levers of control are not in the hands of most people who are made more free in this respect does not compromise the importance of the enhancement of their effective freedom to live as they would choose.

However, the rationale of the *contrary* view (viz. that 'freedom from malaria' is a misnomer—it is not a *freedom* as such) need not of course be based only on concentrating on levers of control. It could certainly be argued that the elimination of malaria through public policy does not *increase* the range of options that one has, as far as having or not having malaria is concerned. (e.g. 'We first had to have malaria; could not escape it. Now, we don't have to have malaria, but we *cannot*, on the other hand, *have* it, even if we so choose. So

[16] The point was forcefully made by several participants in a conference on 'quality of life' arranged at the World Institute of Development Economics Research in Helsinki in July 1988.

[17] One must, of course, distinguish between freedom *from malaria* as such and the other freedoms that *result from not having malaria* (e.g. being able to move about freely, take on work, etc.). The latter is not in dispute. The question in assessing the idea of 'freedom from malaria' is whether there is an issue of freedom regarding malaria itself (i.e. other than the freedom to do various things that are made possible as a result of the eradication of malaria).

[18] The relevance of counterfactual choice in the analysis of personal liberty and negative freedoms has been extensively discussed in the literature on social-choice theory. On this and related matters, see Sen (1970*a*, 1983*a*), Campbell (1976), Farrell (1976), Kelly (1976*a*, 1976*b*, 1978), Suzumura (1980, 1983, 1991), Green (1980), Gaertner and Krüger (1981, 1983), Hammond (1981, 1982, 1985), Basu (1984), Nurmi (1984, 1987), Wriglesworth (1985), Elster and Hylland (1986), and Riley (1987, 1989*a*, 1989*b*), among other contributions (see footnote 5 in Ch. 2, pp. 32–3).

there has been no increase in the freedom to *choose!*') Indeed, if in assessing freedom we look only at *how many* alternatives we have, then there is no increase in freedom in this respect.[19]

This is precisely where the role of counterfactual choice becomes relevant—indeed central.[20] One values living without malaria, desires such a life, and would have chosen it, *given the choice*. Being able to live as one would value, desire and choose *is* a contribution to one's freedom (not just to one's well-being or agency achievement, though it is *also* that). The fact that the term 'freedom' is used in the expression 'freedom from malaria' is not in itself decisive in any way, but the relation of the results to what one would have chosen (and would have had reasons to choose) is a matter of direct relevance to freedom—the freedom to choose to live as one would desire.

Indeed, it would be absurd to say we have now achieved freedom from '*non*-malaria'. That is clear enough, but *why* is it absurd? This is because non-malaria is not a burden, and we would have no particular reason to reject it (i.e. to choose malaria instead), if counterfactually we were given that choice. So the language happens to be, in fact, in line with the analysis of freedom involving counterfactual choice. Of course, linguistic occurrence is not to be taken as a proof that the counterfactual-choice view of freedom is correct. Rather, it is the aptness of the counterfactual-choice view, for reasons already discussed, that shows that the language is not aberrant here. It fits into a broad general concept of freedom, rather than having to be seen as invoking some peculiarly remote idea of freedom.

It is not so much that statements such as those of Franklin Roosevelt on 'the four essential human freedoms' (e.g. 'the third is freedom from want', 'the fourth is freedom from fear') 'prove' the relevance of counterfactual choice. Rather the converse. Seeing

---

[19] On the axiomatic derivations of that procedure and possible critiques of the chosen axioms, see Pattanaik and Xu (1990) and Sen (1990*a*, 1991*a*).

[20] Sometimes a bit of fog is added to the idea of freedom by insisting that a person cannot be said to have the freedom to achieve *x* if he is not, at the same time, free to ensure the achievement of *not x*. This is, however, an odd restriction. Ann is free not to marry Bill irrespective of what Bill wants, but that freedom is not conditional on Ann being able to ensure that she marries Bill (i.e. *not* 'not marry' Bill) irrespective of what Bill wants. Similarly, Bill may be free to make sure that he dies before becoming 90 years old (assuming that the anti-suicide laws have limited power), but that freedom is not conditional on Bill being able to make sure that he does *not* die before becoming 90.

freedom, *inter alia*, in terms of counterfactual choice helps us to understand and interpret these statements and makes them cogent (rather than our having to view them as examples of misused—if moving—rhetoric). Roosevelt *was* talking about freedom.

Freedom as a value demands that certain things be considered seriously *for that reason* (whether or not it is valued for any other reason as well). The notion of freedom as effective power to achieve what one *would* choose is an important part of the general idea of freedom.

I end this section with one final observation. I have discussed the scope of the idea of freedom at some length here partly because freedom is one of the most powerful social ideas, and its relevance to the analysis of equality and justice is far-reaching and strong. When we assess inequalities across the world in being able to avoid preventable morbidity, or escapable hunger, or premature mortality, we are not merely examining differences in well-being, but also in the basic freedoms that we value and cherish. That viewpoint is important. And as it happens, the available data regarding the *realization* of disease, hunger, and early mortality tell us a great deal about the presence or absence of certain central basic *freedoms*. Given the motivation underlying the analysis of inequality, it is important not to miss this momentous perspective.

4.7. THE RELEVANCE OF WELL-BEING

It is possible to argue that in an important sense the agency aspect of a person is more comprehensive than the well-being aspect. A person's goals will, in the case of most 'normal' people, include *inter alia* the pursuit of their own well-being. Indeed, the overall balance of agency objectives might be seen, with some plausibility, as reflecting the weights that the person herself would attach to her own well-being *among* the things that she wishes to promote. On this ground, it could be tempting to argue that in judging the relative advantages of different people, the proper basis of comparison should be just their respective agency freedoms. The information on agency aspect would *inter alia* include the value of each person's own well-being, in the light of whatever importance she herself gives to it in her agency objectives. Treating the person herself as the best judge of how she may be viewed by others, it might look as if the agency aspect would tell all that is relevant for others to know.

This argument overlooks many things. One issue relates to the lasting importance of the plurality of our concerns even when for the purpose of action we choose one compromise or another. The fact that we may have to arbitrate between conflicting demands in the interest of deciding what we should do need not indicate, especially when we face deep dilemmas, that this is the end of the story as far as evaluation is concerned. William Butler Yeats spoke of one such dilemma:

> The intellect of man is forced to choose
> Perfection of the life, or of the work.[21]

What the person chooses is obviously important, but no matter which of the two gets chosen by 'the intellect of man', the fact of that choice does not make the remaining one—life *or* work—devoid of importance for that reason.[22] The fact that you may have chosen the 'perfection of the work' over that of your 'life', or have chosen to give priority to other goals in your agency objectives over your own well-being is not a reason to think that your life or your well-being is henceforth of no importance—to you or to others.[23]

Another important issue concerns the very different roles that the well-being and the agency aspects can have in the use of interpersonal comparisons for *diverse* exercises. Society might accept some responsibility for a person's well-being, especially when that is in some danger of being particularly low. But this does not imply that society must take an equal interest in the promotion of that person's other agency objectives as well. For example, society may be seen as having a special responsibility to make sure that no one has to

---

[21] W. B. Yeats, *Variorum Edition of the Poems of W. B. Yeats*, ed. P. Allt and R. K. Alspach (New York: Macmillan, 1957), 495. Vivian Walsh, who drew my attention to these lines, has provided an illuminating and elegant analysis of the scope and limits of rationality underlying human behaviour and economic choices (see Walsh 1991).

[22] On this issue see B. Williams (1973*a*, 1981), Marcus (1980), and Nussbaum (1985).

[23] This is so even when the person's choice is based on a complete ordering in terms of agency objectives. That ordering and the identified 'best' choice reflect your view of the relevant 'trade-offs' for that decision, rather than reflecting the *unimportance* of the outweighed considerations in general, or even in the *specific context* of that choice. But in addition to that, it must also be recognized that sometimes our agency decisions may not be based on a complete ordering (or on the existence of a 'best' alternative), and the 'losing side' may not in fact have been 'outweighed' by your own reason even in the specific context of that choice. On these issues, see Sen (1970*a*, 1982*a*) and Levi (1986).

starve, or fail to obtain medical attention for a serious but eminently treatable ailment. On the other hand, this carries no implication that the society must take an equally protective attitude about the person's agency goal of, say, erecting a statue in honour of some hero he particularly admires (even when the person himself attaches more importance to erecting the statue than to being well-nourished and having medical coverage).

There are, however, other contexts in which the relevant interpersonal comparisons may be precisely those of agency aspect—either of agency achievement or of agency freedom. We might wish to know who has how much power to pursue their own respective goals.[24] We might also have interest in checking how successful they respectively are in bringing about what they are trying to achieve. We may have political and ethical views regarding societies in which some people can promote all their ends while others have to face great barriers which they cannot overcome.

Depending on the context, the agency aspect or the well-being aspect might achieve prominence. It would be a mistake to expect that *one* of these aspects would be uniformly more relevant than the other as a basis of interpersonal comparison for *every* interesting exercise. Along with the plurality of spaces (discussed already), we have to take adequate note of the plurality of *purposes*. The evaluation of inequality cannot but be purpose-dependent, and the important need is to provide an appropriate match between (1) the purposes of inequality evaluation, and (2) the choice of informational focus. This question will be pursued at a more general level in the next chapter.

The well-being aspect is especially important in such matters as social security, poverty alleviation, removal of gross economic inequality, and in general in the pursuit of social justice. That case, as we have discussed, is not conditional on the person himself attaching overwhelming priority to his own well-being in his agency objective. A self-sacrificing idealist who is ready to sacrifice fully his own well-being for some 'cause' does not thereby make it okay for others to ignore his well-being so long as his 'cause' is not harmed. One's claim to help from others in the society for one's survival and well-

---

[24] The inequality of social power relates to the institutional structure of its organization and control. For insightful analyses of various aspects of the inequality of social power and its economic and political implications in the context of an advanced capitalist economy, see Galbraith (1952, 1958, 1967). See also Dahrendorf (1988).

being need not be conditional on one's self-centredness in giving precedence to one's interests *vis-à-vis* other goals and values in one's overall agency objectives.

The well-being aspect of a person has great importance of its own for the analysis of social inequality and the assessment of public policy. Problems of social injustice and inequity between different classes and groups relate strongly to extensive disparities in well-being—including the freedom that we respectively enjoy to achieve well-being.[25] In some of the analyses that will follow in the rest of the book, particular attention will be paid to inequalities in well-being freedom and correspondingly to disparities in well-being achievement. However, even for that analysis, the relevance of the agency aspect has to be kept in view, since the person's actual *use* of her well-being freedom will depend *inter alia* on her agency objectives (since these will influence her actual choices).[26]

Thus, the broader agency concerns remain relevant to the social or economic analysis of inequality even if the primary focus of the analysis of inequality is on well-being, or on the freedom to achieve well-being. The distinction between agency and well-being— discussed in this chapter—remains, therefore, important even when our evaluative focus is on inequality of well-being (freedom or achievement), as will be the case in some of the problems discussed in the chapters that follow. The specification of our evaluative focus (to individual well-being) must not be confused with any assumed narrowing of human beings in terms of motivation.

[25] In any evaluative structure in which the focus is on the *freedoms* that people have (i.e. in which the *focal variables* are freedoms rather than outcomes), no patterning of *outcomes* as such would directly emerge from the equality of the focal variables. The outcome pattern will depend on the decisions of the persons themselves. This applies, obviously, to 'well-being freedom' as well. Even when complete equality of well-being freedom is clearly definable and is entirely realized, this need not lead to an equality of well-being *achieved*, since different individuals may give different priority to the pursuit of their own well-being (in making use of their respective well-being freedoms).

[26] Also, other people's help to the deprived and the miserable may well relate to the helpers' agency objectives. This applies not just to charity and other transfers, but also to political action. For example, it has been observed that a democracy with a free press tends to eliminate the occurrence of famines through general public pressure on the government to take timely avertive action (threatening its electoral prospects if it fails to do this); on this see Sen (1984, 1988*c*), Reddy (1988), Drèze and Sen (1989), Article 19 (1990), D'Souza (1990), Ram (1991), among others. The well-being of the vulnerable famine victims (typically a small minority) may greatly depend on the agency actions of others, in democratic politics.

5

JUSTICE AND CAPABILITY

5.1. THE INFORMATIONAL BASES OF JUSTICE

Any evaluative judgement depends on the truth of some information and is independent of the truth or falsity of others. The 'informational basis of a judgement' identifies the information on which the judgement is directly dependent and—no less importantly—asserts that the truth and falsehood of any other type of information cannot *directly* influence the correctness of the judgement.

The informational basis of judgements of *justice*, thus, specifies the variables that are directly involved in assessing the justice of alternative systems or arrangements (the role, if any, of the other variables being only derivative). For example, in the utilitarian view of justice, the informational basis consists only of the utilities of the respective individuals in the states of affairs under evaluation. I have tried to argue elsewhere that the examination of the informational basis of each evaluative approach provides a useful way of investigating and scrutinizing that approach.[1]

Most theories of justice can also be usefully analysed in terms of the information used in two different—though interrelated—parts of the exercise, viz. (1) the selection of *relevant personal features*, and (2) the choice of *combining characteristics*. To illustrate, for the standard utilitarian theory, the only intrinsically important 'relevant personal features' are *individual utilities*, and the only usable 'combining characteristic' is *summation*, yielding the *total* of those utilities. The set of 'welfarist' theories, of which utilitarianism is a particular example, retains the former part (viz. takes utilities as the only relevant personal features), but can use other combining characteristics, e.g. utility-based maximin (or lexicographic

---

[1] The diverse roles of the informational bases of normative choice and judgements have been discussed in Sen (1974, 1977*b*, 1979*d*, 1985*a*). The part played, in particular, by 'informational constraints', which are typically implicitly imposed, can be both complex and far-reaching.

maximin), summation of concave transforms of utilities (such as summing the logarithms of utilities).[2]

Examples of selection of 'relevant personal features' other than utilities include *liberties* and *primary goods* (Rawls 1971), *rights* (Nozick 1974), *resources* (R. Dworkin 1981), *commodity bundles* (Foley 1967; Pazner and Schmeidler 1974, Varian 1974, 1975; Baumol 1986), and various *mixed* spaces (Suzumura 1983; Wriglesworth 1985; Riley 1987). Note that in some cases the personal features are broadly of the *outcome* type (e.g. commodity bundles enjoyed), as they are with welfarist theories (illustrated by utilitarianism), whereas in other cases they relate to *opportunities*, defined in some way or other (e.g. primary goods, rights, resources).

The selection of personal features has to be supplemented by the choice of a combining formula, e.g. *sum-maximization*,[3] *lexicographic priorities and maximin*,[4] *equality*,[5] or one of various *other* combining rules.[6]

The substantive contents of theories of justice have, thus, included widely different informational bases and also quite divergent uses of the respective information. That informational variation corresponds closely to the question of plurality of focal variables with which we are concerned in this monograph. As was argued earlier, each theory of justice includes choosing—explicitly or by implication—a particular demand for 'basal equality', which in its turn influences the choice of the focal variable for assessing inequality. The respective claims of the different conceptions of

---

[2] Arguments for quite different combining characteristics in even the *same* utility space can be found, among others, in Suppes (1966, 1977), Kolm (1969, 1976), Sen (1970a, 1977b), Mirrlees (1971), Rawls (1971), Phelps (1973), P. J. Hammond (1976a), Strasnick (1976), Arrow (1977), Blackorby and Donaldson (1977), d'Aspremont and Gevers (1977), Maskin (1978), Gevers (1979), Roberts (1980a), Blackorby, Donaldson, and Weymark (1984), d'Aspremont (1985), Thomson and Varian (1985). While the axiomatics of the combining structures explored in these and related contributions are mostly defined in the utility space, they can, in most cases, also be readily presented in other spaces, involving other personal features (such as indices of primary goods, or of resources, or of capabilities). Thus, the axiomatic structures, in fact, have a wider interest than the nature of the space might suggest.

[3] See Harsanyi (1955), d'Aspremont and Gevers (1977), Maskin (1978).

[4] See Rawls (1971), Hammond (1976a), Strasnick (1976), d'Aspremont and Gevers (1977), Sen (1977b).

[5] See Foley (1967), Nozick (1974), R. Dworkin (1981), Van Parijs (1990a).

[6] See Varian (1975), Gevers (1979), Roberts (1980a), Suzumura (1983), Blackorby, Donaldson, and Weymark (1984), d'Aspremont (1985), Wriglesworth (1985), Baumol (1986), Riley (1987), Moulin (1989, 1990), among many other contributions.

justice have a close connection with the relevance of the corresponding views of equality.

5.2. RAWLSIAN JUSTICE AND THE POLITICAL CONCEPTION

By far the most influential—and I believe the most important—
theory of justice to be presented in this century has been John
Rawls's 'justice as fairness'. The main aspects of that theory are well
known and have been extensively discussed.[7] Some features have
received particular attention. This includes Rawls's use of the
device of 'the original position'—a hypothetical state of primordial
equality in which people (without knowing exactly who they are
going to be) are seen as choosing between alternative principles that
would govern the basic structure of the society. That procedure is
seen as fair, and the principles regarding the basic social structure
that would be picked by that fair procedure are seen as just.

The rules of justice include a pair of principles. The formulation
of these principles has undergone some change since their presentation in *The Theory of Justice* (Rawls 1971: 60, 83, 90–5), partly to
clarify what was ambiguous, but also to respond to some early
critiques (e.g. by H. L. A. Hart 1973). In his 1982 Tanner Lectures,
Rawls stated these principles thus:

1. Each person has an equal right to a fully adequate scheme of equal basic
liberties which is compatible with a similar scheme of liberties for all.
2. Social and economic inequalities are to satisfy two conditions. First, they
must be attached to offices and positions open to all under conditions of fair
equality of opportunity; and second, they must be to the great benefit of the
least advantaged members of society.[8]

The first principle involves a weakening of the condition of liberty
('a fully adequate scheme' demands rather less than the original
requirement of 'the most extensive total system' specified in the 1971
version). The second principle continues to include the so-called
'Difference Principle' in which the focus is on producing 'the greatest
benefit of the least advantaged', with advantage being judged by the
holding of 'primary goods' (Rawls 1971: 90–5). But 'fair equality of
opportunity' receives renewed emphasis here.

While these features of Rawls's theory have received wide atten-

---

[7] An early set of responses can be found in Norman Daniels's collection *Reading
Rawls* (Daniels 1975). See also Phelps's (1973) collection on 'economic justice'.
[8] Reprinted in Rawls *et al.* (1987: 5).

tion even among economists, it is important to interpret these features in the light of some of the political aspects of his approach. In particular Rawls himself has insisted on the need to see his theory as 'a political conception of justice' (see Rawls 1985, 1987, 1988*a*, 1988*b*, 1988*c*, 1990). I begin with an examination of that feature and the bearing it might have on the importance of questions of equality in particular social circumstances.

Two distinct features of Rawls's characterization of his political conception of justice can be fruitfully separated out. One feature relates to the *subject-matter* of the political conception: 'a political conception of justice ... is a moral conception worked out for a specific kind of subject, namely, for political, social, and economic institutions.'[9] This does not specify any particular principle that would have to be used for a moral conception to be political. The matter turns on whether the *subject* is 'political', in the sense of dealing with 'political, social, and economic institutions'.

The other feature, in contrast, relates precisely to a particular principle to be used, associated with a specific form of social judgement and choice, viz. that of 'a constitutional democracy', in which 'the public conception of justice should be, so far as possible, independent of controversial philosophical and religious doctrines'. 'To formulate such a conception, we apply the principle of toleration to philosophy itself: the public conception of justice is to be political, not metaphysical.'[10] In this characterization, the subject-matter is not in itself critical, and the crucial 'political' feature is the 'toleration' of possibly divergent comprehensive doctrines (subject to these ideas of the good themselves satisfying certain features of toleration, i.e. 'the ideas included must be political ideas').

In Rawls's analysis these two distinct features are closely related, so much so that he seems to view them inseparably together. It is, however, possible for an approach to be 'political' in the sense of the subject-matter (as specified by Rawls) without its endorsing the feature of 'toleration' as a qualifying condition for a theory having some claims to justice. I make this point here not because I regard the issue of toleration to be unimportant—quite the contrary, I regard it to be *one of the central* issues in thinking politically about justice.[11] But there can be important issues of justice and injustice in the choice of 'political, social, and economic institutions' *even when*

---

[9] Rawls (1985: 224).   [10] Rawls (1985: 223).
[11] On this, see Sen (1970*a*, 1985*a*).

pluralist tolerance of the kind outlined by Rawls simply does not obtain. While 'toleration', in the sense discussed by Rawls, of different comprehensive views of the good is undoubtedly one of the most important political aspects of living together in a society, it is nevertheless not the only thing that is 'political' in social living.[12] The definitional exclusion contained in Rawls's 'political conception' limits the scope of the concept of justice drastically and abruptly, and it would often make it hard to identify political rights and wrongs that a theory of justice *should* address.

Specifically, on grounds of the absence of toleration a whole lot of comprehensive doctrines may be ruled out of court (indeed, in some social situations none of the ones actually championed by different political groups may remain), and yet there may be very perspicuous problems of inequality, deprivation, and injustice in the disputes between the different sides. To be without a theory that can deal with such problems (when the different sides are intolerant), and to see the disputes as lying *outside* the purview of the so-called political conception of justice, would appear to be oddly limiting for the domain of a political conception of justice.

Consider, for example, the well-known dictum of social choice apparently enunciated by Emperor Haile Selassie during the Ethiopian famines of 1973, explaining the absence of famine relief measures undertaken by his government: 'We have said wealth has to be gained through hard work. We have said those who don't work starve.'[13] This is, of course, an old no-nonsense principle, which has often been articulated, and which might even be seen—by stretching a point—as having some biblical support.[14] That 'principle' was, in fact, very efficiently practised in Selassie's Ethiopia, and at the height of the 1973 famine, there was little state-arranged relief.[15]

It is not hard to argue that the Emperor's political ethics regard-

[12] There is a related—but larger—issue regarding the exact role of 'neutrality' in political liberalism and the feasibility and desirability of imposing neutrality on theories of justice and fairness. For divergent assessments of that question, see e.g. Dworkin (1978, 1985), Fishkin (1983), Raz (1986), Larmore (1987), Ackerman (1988), Rawls (1988a), Pogge (1989), Van Parijs (1991). The discussion here bears on that issue, but I shall not, here, go on to a fuller treatment of that larger problem.

[13] Quoted in L. Wiseberg, 'An International Perspective on the African Famines,' in Glantz (1976: 108).

[14] 'If any would not work, neither should he eat' (2 *Thess.* 3: 10).

[15] The Emperor's principles were not, in fact, the only reason for the disastrous delay in arranging public relief, and there were other factors involved, including a misdiagnosis of the nature of the famine and of its causation (on which see Sen 1981a, ch. 7, and also Glantz 1976). But I am not concerned with those issues here.

ing the choice of social and political institutions, as expressed in the dictum, violates requirements of justice quite robustly. Indeed, at the substantive level, one can easily point to the drastic inequalities in capabilities between famine victims and the rest of the society, and also—in this case—to great inequalities in the holdings of primary goods. The argument can proceed by pointing to the wrongness of denying to out-of-work famine victims—unable to find remunerative work for survival—reasonable claims on support from the rest of the society.[16] There are different ways of working out this argument in political ethics, and invoking Rawls's device of the 'original position' would be one of the most effective ways.

But neither the Emperor, nor the opponents of his regime, who eventually overthrew him in a bloody uprising while the famine raged on, gave any indication of accepting any principle of toleration of the other's view of the good. Indeed, each side pursued their own objectives with no quarter given to the objectives of the others, and as far as one can judge, had no interest in looking for a political solution based on toleration with the desire of living together. In terms of a political conception of justice that requires such toleration, it would be hard to pass any judgement about justice in this case. And yet it would be peculiar to claim that no decidable issue of justice in a political conception was involved in the dispute about institutional famine relief, and that the principles of social choice embodied in Haile Selassie's statement (to wit, no state relief for the out-of-work famine victims) simply lay *outside* the domain of the political conception of justice. Justice, in this restrictive political conception, would seem to have a high admission price.[17]

All this need not be seen as being at all embarrassing for a theory of justice that self-consciously 'starts from within a certain political tradition', and that is presented with the 'hope that this political conception of justice may at least be supported by what we may call an "overlapping consensus", that is, by a consensus that includes all the opposing philosophical and religious doctrines likely to persist and to gain adherents in a more or less just constitutional

[16] This case, incidentally, also illustrates well the force of Judith Shklar's (1990) general argument that the sense of *injustice* is a specially cogent starting point for social analysis and assessment.

[17] It is, of course, easy to indict Selassie of being intolerant. But the injustice in question relates not just to that, but to the principles of famine relief—more correctly *non*-relief—followed by his government. The insistence on toleration as a common agreed basis would prevent that question from even being raised.

democratic society' (Rawls 1985: 225–6). So there is no real problem here for Rawls's analysis in terms of his own programme.

It is, however, important to ask whether this particular political conception gives the idea of justice—even justice in a *political* sense—its due. Many blatant injustices in the world take place in social circumstances in which the invoking of 'political liberalism' and the 'principle of tolerance' may be neither easy nor particularly helpful. And yet to leave these matters out of the scope of a 'political conception of justice' would be to reduce its domain severely. There are many conspicuous issues of justice and injustice involved in the political choice of social institutions all over the world, and it is not easy to accept the definition of a political conception of justice that rules most of them out of court on grounds of ideological remoteness from constitutional democracies. The limits of 'the political' need not be seen to be so close.[18] The pervasive problems of inequality and injustice in the world call for a less restrictive approach.

While the preceding discussion points to the limited domain of the Rawlsian conception of justice, especially in the light of the emphasis he has recently placed on the aspect of 'toleration', it is important to recognize that the Rawlsian perspective—particularly the Difference Principle—has been widely used in the literature on economic and social development. The insights that people have obtained from Rawls's analysis of 'justice as fairness' seem to have gone greatly beyond the limits he has himself imposed, and it is not clear to me that these insights have been all misderived and misdirected. When it comes to evaluating Rawls's theory of justice as a whole, it is of course necessary to see it within the specific constraints imposed by the author himself, but the 'Rawlsian outlook' in a less constrained form has had a profound impact on a much wider range of contemporary political, social, and economic thinking. In particular, the literature on the evaluation of inequality has not been quite the same again since Rawls's classic book made its first appearance.

5.3. PRIMARY GOODS AND CAPABILITIES

There have been various approaches focusing on equality of *opportunities*—characterized in different ways—in the recent literature of

[18] The point is not about the use of the word 'political', but rather about the motivation underlying the idea of a political conception. It is, however, possible also to argue that Rawls uses a particularly narrow definition of the term political.

justice. Rawls's concentration on the distribution of 'primary goods'—including 'rights, liberties and opportunities, income and wealth, and the social bases of self-respect'[19]—in his Difference Principle can be seen as a move in that direction. This approach can also be interpreted, as I argued earlier on in this monograph, as taking us in the direction of the overall freedom actually enjoyed by people, and this has the effect of reorienting the direction of the analysis of equality and justice towards freedoms enjoyed rather than being confined to the outcomes achieved. An important problem arises from the fact that primary goods are not constitutive of freedom as such, but are best seen as *means* to freedom (an issue that we discussed in Section 3.3 earlier). Ronald Dworkin's (1981, 1987) case for 'equality of resources' can also be seen as belonging broadly in the same general area of substantive accounting, since resources are also means to freedom, and Dworkin has, in fact, presented a specific way of accounting resources and adjudicating 'the equality of resources'.

One problem is that of valuation. Since means are ultimately valued for something else, it is not easy to set up a scheme of valuation of means that would be really independent of the ends. It is by skilful use of this connection that John Roemer (1986*b*) has established a mathematical result which he has interpreted as 'equality of resources implies equality of welfare' (the title of his article). The result has been based on an elaborate set of axioms, but the basic insight behind the result can be seen as seeking the value of *resources* in terms of what the resources *yield*. Since resources are not valued for their own sake, such a connection has some obvious plausibility. By taking a model in which the only ultimate end is welfare, the result that equality of resources must yield equality of welfare has emerged in Roemer's theorem.

The congruence of resource valuation with welfare valuation can be, in fact, replaced by a similar congruence with whatever is taken to be the end the promotion of which is the reason for valuing the resources. The real issue behind this interesting result is the dependence of the valuation of means on the valuation of ends (and not specifically the interdependence of resources and welfare).

In what follows I shall be concerned primarily with Rawls's theory of justice as fairness, but some of the comments will apply also to Dworkin's approach.

[19] See Rawls (1971: 60–5).

The main issue is the adequacy of the informational base of primary goods for the political conception of justice in Rawls's sense, and the need if any for focusing on capabilities. Primary goods are 'things that every rational man is presumed to want', and include 'income and wealth', 'the basic liberties', 'freedom of movement and choice of occupation', 'powers and prerogatives of offices and positions of responsibility', and 'the social bases of self-respect'.[20] Primary goods are, thus, general purpose means or resources useful for the pursuit of different ideas of the good that the individuals may have.

Earlier in this monograph (especially in Chapter 3), I have disputed the alleged adequacy, for a freedom-oriented assessment of justice, of this concentration on *means* to freedom, rather than on the *extent* of the freedom that a person actually has. Since the conversion of these primary goods and resources into freedom of choice over alternative combinations of functionings and other achievements may vary from person to person, equality of holdings of primary goods or of resources can go hand in hand with serious inequalities in actual freedoms enjoyed by different persons. The central question, in the present context, is whether such inequalities of freedom are compatible with fulfilling the underlying idea of the political conception of justice.

In the capability-based assessment of justice, individual claims are not to be assessed in terms of the resources or primary goods the persons respectively hold, but by the freedoms they actually enjoy to choose the lives that they have reason to value.[21] It is this actual freedom that is represented by the person's 'capability' to achieve various alternative combinations of functionings.

It is important to distinguish capability—representing freedom actually enjoyed—both (1) from primary goods (and other resources), and (2) from achievements (including combinations of functionings actually enjoyed, and other realized results). To illustrate the first distinction, a person who has a disability can have more primary goods (in the form of income, wealth, liberties, and so on) but less capability (due to the handicap). To take another example, this time from poverty studies, a person may have more income and more nutritional intake, but less freedom to live a well-nourished existence because of a higher basal metabolic rate, greater

---

[20] See Rawls (1971: 60–5); Rawls (1982: 162); Rawls (1988a: 256–7).

[21] Various aspects of this claim and their diverse implications were discussed in Chs. 3 and 4.

vulnerability to parasitic diseases, larger body size, or simply because of pregnancy. Similarly, in dealing with poverty in the richer countries, we have to take note of the fact that many of those who are poor in terms of income and other primary goods also have characteristics—age, disability, disease-proneness, etc.—that make it more difficult for them to convert primary goods into basic capabilities, e.g. being able to move about, to lead a healthy life, to take part in the life of the community. Neither primary goods, nor resources more broadly defined, can represent the capability a person actually enjoys.

To illustrate the *second* distinction, a person may have the same capability as another person, but nevertheless choose a different bundle of functionings in line with his or her particular goals. Furthermore, two persons with the same actual capabilities and even the same goals may end up with different outcomes because of differences in strategies or tactics that they respectively follow in using their freedoms.

In responding to my critique, Rawls has tended to assume that it is based on presuming that everyone has the same common ends— *shared* objectives pursued by all. This is based on the belief that if they had distinct objectives, then the differential conversion rates of primary goods into capabilities could not be ascertained. That assumption (viz. the *same* objectives for all), if made, would certainly go against Rawls's political conception of justice, which admits interpersonal variation of ends, with each person having his own 'comprehensive view of the good'. Rawls summarizes *his interpretation* of my objection thus:

... the idea of primary goods must be mistaken. For they are not what, from within anyone's comprehensive doctrine, can be taken as ultimately important: they are not, in general, anyone's idea of the basic values of human life. Therefore, to focus on primary goods, one may object, is to work for the most part in the wrong space—in the space of institutional features and material things and not in the space of basic moral values.[22]

Rawls's response to his interpretation of my objection is the following:

In reply, an index of primary goods is not intended as an approximation to what is ultimately important as specified by any particular comprehensive doctrine with its account of moral values.[23]

[22] Rawls (1988*a*: 256–9).
[23] Rawls (1988*a*: 259). Rawls also has a rather different line of answering my criticism in his 'Reply to Sen' (Rawls 1988*b*). He argues that his full theory of justice

The main problem with this reply lies in the misinterpretation of the nature of the objection. Capability reflects a person's freedom to choose between alternative lives (functioning combinations), and its valuation need not presuppose unanimity regarding some one specific set of objectives (or, as Rawls calls it, 'a particular comprehensive doctrine'). As was discussed earlier, it is important to distinguish between freedom (reflected by capability) and achievement (reflected by actual functionings), and the evaluation of capability need not be based on one particular comprehensive doctrine that orders the achievements and the lifestyles.[24]

The second problem, related to the first, concerns Rawls's claim that primary goods are 'not intended as an approximation to what is ultimately important as specified by any *particular* comprehensive doctrine' (emphasis added). This is a legitimate enough concern for Rawls's 'political conception of justice', but the lack of correspondence with primary goods does not lie only there. It lies also in the fact—more important in the present context—that a disadvantaged person may get less from primary goods than others *no matter what comprehensive doctrine* he or she has.

To illustrate the point, consider two persons 1 and 2, with 2 disadvantaged in some respect (e.g. physical disability, mental handicap, greater disease proneness). They do *not* have the same ends or objectives, or the same conception of the good. Person 1 values *A* more than *B*, while 2 has the opposite valuation. Each values 2*A* more than *A*, and 2*B* more than *B*, and the orderings of the two (representing the relevant parts of their respective 'comprehensive doctrines') are the following:

has more 'flexibility' than I recognize, and some of the interpersonal variations I am concerned with can be taken note of at later stages, such as 'legislative' and 'judicial' ones. It is not altogether easy to be sure what overall procedures and allocational principles would be in fact satisfied by such a complex stagewise structure, but if it is indeed the case that all the relevant interpersonal variations will be effectively dealt with at some stage or other, then that would certainly reduce the force of the criticism. Some of the issues raised by interpersonal variations in the conversion of primary goods into capabilities would then end up receiving attention after all.

[24] In the capability format, achievement is given by an n-tuple of relevant functionings, while capability itself is a *set* of such n-tuples from which one can be chosen. On some alternative forms of representation, and their relevance to the analysis of individual advantage and thus to the study of inequality, see also Chs. 3 and 4.

Person 1	*Person 2*
2*A*	2*B*
2*B*	2*A*
A	*B*
B	*A*

With the given set of primary goods, person 1 can achieve 2*A* or 2*B*, also—though there may be no great merit in this—*A* or *B*. On the other hand, given 2's disadvantage, with the very same primary goods, she can achieve only *A* or *B*. Person 1 proceeds to achieve 2*A* (the best feasible outcome for him), while 2 settles for *B* (the best feasible outcome for her). The problem is not just that 2 is at a disadvantage in terms of one *particular* comprehensive doctrine (her own or that of person 1), but she has a worse deal than 1 *no matter* which comprehensive doctrine we take. Equality of primary goods has given 2 less *freedom to achieve* and not just less *achievement* with respect to some *one* comprehensive doctrine.

If the comparisons were made not in terms of primary goods, but in terms of capabilities, 2's worse deal would be obvious. Person 1's capability set consists of (*A*, *B*, 2*A*, 2*B*), whereas 2's capability is just a proper subset of it, to wit (*A*, *B*), with the best elements—no matter which comprehensive doctrine is considered—lost. Capability represents *freedom*, whereas primary goods tell us only about the *means* to freedom, with an interpersonally variable relation between the means and the actual freedom to achieve. Rawls is right to think that my objection did relate to primary goods being *means* only, but that problem is not disposed of by saying that they are not meant as an approximation of 'any particular comprehensive doctrine'.[25]

[25] Dominance in the space of capabilities does not require agreement on any one comprehensive doctrine, since one capability set can be a proper subset of another (as in the example given). Furthermore, even when the capability sets are not subsets of each other, for agreement to exist on their ranking, we do not need the acceptance of any one comprehensive doctrine. Partial rankings of capabilities can be based on superiority in terms of *each* of the relevant comprehensive doctrines. However, to insist on a *complete ordering* can be problematic. (There is a similar problem of complete indexation of the holdings of primary goods for Rawls's Difference Principle, since different primary goods can be disparately effective in the pursuit of different comprehensive ends; on this and related problems, see Plott 1978, Gibbard 1979, Blair 1988, Sen 1992c.) But partial orderings can be an adequate basis for many evaluative judgements, especially in dealing with serious problems of inequality. How extensive the rankings of capability sets turn out to be will depend on (1) the divergence between the relevant comprehensive views, and (2) the differences between the sets to be ranked. The analytical problems involved are discussed in Sen (1970a, 1970b, 1985b). See also Ch. 3 above.

5.4. DIVERSITIES: ENDS AND PERSONAL CHARACTERISTICS

There are in fact two sources of variation in the relation between a person's *means* in the form of primary goods (or resources) and *achievement* of ends. One is *inter-end* variation—different conceptions of the good that different people may have. The other is *inter-individual* variation in the relationship between resources (such as primary goods) and the freedom to pursue ends. Rawls shows great sensitivity to the first variation, and is keen on preserving respect for this diversity (rightly so, in line with his pluralist political conception). To deal with this problem, Rawls assumes that the *same* primary goods serve all the different ends.[26]

As far as the second *inter-individual* variation is concerned (i.e. in the relation between resources and freedoms), the problem created by this is in no way reduced by the existence of the first variation (i.e. over ends and objectives). A person's actual freedom to pursue her ends depends both on (1) what ends she has, and (2) what power she has to convert primary goods into the fulfilment of those ends. The latter problem can be serious *even with* given ends, but it is *not* the case that it can be serious *only with* given ends. The reach and relevance of the second problem is not reduced by the existence of the first.

To conclude, human beings are diverse, but diverse in different ways. One variation relates to the differences in ends and objectives. The ethical and political implications of this diversity we now understand much better as a result of Rawlsian analysis of justice as fairness. But there is another important diversity— variations in our ability to convert resources into actual freedoms. Variations related to sex, age, genetic endowments, and many other features, give us very divergent powers to build

---

[26] Presumably for the sake of fairness it must not be the case that some people's ends are so *imperfectly* served by the primary goods (compared with the ends of others) that the first group may have a legitimate complaint about judging individual deals in terms of primary goods. Rawls's comprehensive assertion that 'approximation' of primary goods to 'no other space of values' is needed (indeed has to be shunned) would seem to overlook the nature of this particular problem. If every possible list of primary goods (and every way of doing an index) makes some people's ends very well served and others' very poorly indeed, then the important feature of 'neutrality' will be lost, and the entire line of reasoning of 'justice as fairness' may be significantly undermined. Thus, some strong requirements *are* imposed on the relation between primary goods and the spaces of other values. I shall not discuss this issue further in this essay. See also Ruth Anna Putnam (1991).

freedom in our lives even when we have the same bundle of primary goods.[27]

The Rawlsian approach to justice has transformed the way we think about that issue, and his theory has had the effect of shifting our concerns from inequalities only in outcomes and achievements to those in opportunities and freedoms. But by concentrating on the *means* to freedom rather than on the *extent* of freedom, his theory of a just basic structure of the society has stopped short of paying adequate attention to freedom as such. While the motivation for focusing on the *means* of freedom might have, it would appear, rested on Rawls's belief that the only alternative would be to choose one *particular* comprehensive view of outcomes and achievements, that presumption is, as shown above, not quite correct. Freedom can be distinguished *both* from the *means* that sustain it and from the *achievements* that it sustains.

Rawls's theory of justice has many distinct features, and the questions raised here must not be seen as an attempt to undermine the entire approach. Indeed, it would be difficult to try to construct a theory of justice today that would not have been powerfully influenced by the illumination provided by Rawls's deep and penetrating analysis.[28] The point of criticism relates specifically to the tension between Rawls's concentration on primary goods and his concern for the freedoms we enjoy to pursue our ends. In so far as freedoms are what we are concerned with, I have tried to argue that there is a different—more accurate—way of examining the distributive issue. Rawls is, in fact, concerned with many other things as well, including the importance of certain liberal institutions and processes, and the need to restrain public policy when personal liberty is threatened. The discussion on equality of effective freedoms presented here does not dispute these aspects of Rawls's concerns.

[27] Some of the empirical issues involved are discussed in Sen (1984, 1985*b*, 1988*c*) and Kynch and Sen (1983).

[28] In proposing his alternative political theory, Robert Nozick says: 'Political philosophers now must either work within Rawls' theory or explain why not. The considerations and distinctions we have developed are illuminated by, and help illuminate, Rawls' masterful presentation of an alternative conception. Even those who remain unconvinced after wrestling with Rawls' systematic vision will learn much from closely studying it' (Nozick 1974: 183). Needless to say, the last remark will apply even more to those who remain unconvinced *only of particular parts* of Rawls's overall conception. But here we are concerned specifically with such a part, and hence the concentration on the *differences* with Rawls, rather than on the many points of agreement and on the great debt owed to Rawls for teaching us what it is like to examine justice.

The point may be illustrated by taking up the role that liberty is given in Rawlsian theory of justice. Rawls gives complete priority to the principle of liberty over other principles of justice, and this rather extreme formulation has been cogently disputed by Herbert Hart (1973).[29] On the other hand, it can be argued (on this, see Sen 1970a, 1983a) that some additional recognition is indeed needed for liberty over and above the attention it may receive as one primary good, or as one influence on well-being, or even as one of the causal determinants of a person's capability. Indeed, a person's capability may be reduced in exactly the same way in two cases: (1) through a violation of his liberty (by someone violating her freedom over a personal domain), and (2) through some internal debilitation that she suffers). Even though the two cases are not distinguishable in the capability space, an adequate theory of justice cannot really ignore the differences between the two cases. In this sense, the capability perspective, central as it is for a theory of justice, cannot be entirely adequate for it. There is a real need to bring in the demands of liberty as an additional principle (even if that principle is not given the total priority that Rawls recommends). The importance of the *over-all* freedom to achieve cannot eliminate the special significance of *negative* freedom.[30]

Our focus in the present discussion has been only on a specific part of Rawls's theory of justice and the relation between one of his concerns and his proposed way of dealing with it. But in that specific—and I believe crucial—part of Rawlsian theory of justice, the point to emerge from our analysis is—I would argue—of some conceptual and practical importance. Equality of freedom to pursue our ends cannot be generated by equality in the distribution of primary goods. We have to examine interpersonal variations in the transformation of primary goods (and resources, more generally) into respective capabilities to pursue our ends and objectives.

If our concern is with equality of freedom, it is no more adequate to ask for equality of its *means* than it is to seek equality of its *results*. Freedom relates to both, but does not coincide with either.

---

[29] Note, however, that the principle of liberty that receives this priority is itself made less demanding in the later formulation chosen by Rawls, quoted earlier in this chapter, compared with the 1971 version. The change is largely in response to Hart's (1973) forceful critique.

[30] On this see Sen (1970a, 1976c, 1985a: Lecture 3).

6

WELFARE ECONOMICS AND INEQUALITY

6.1. SPACE CHOICE AND EVALUATIVE PURPOSE

As was discussed in the earlier chapters, the evaluation of inequality has to take note of both the plurality of spaces in which inequality can be assessed, and the diversity of individuals. The relative advantages and disadvantages that people have, compared with each other, can be seen in many different perspectives, involving different concentrations, e.g. liberties, rights, incomes, wealths, resources, primary goods, utilities, capabilities, and so on, and the question of inequality assessment turns on the selection of the space in which equality is to be assessed. While the pictures of inequality in the different spaces are not unrelated to each other, the pervasive diversities of human beings make them non-congruent—indeed, frequently far apart.

That much has already been discussed in some detail. It is, however, also worth emphasizing that the relative appropriateness of the different spaces depends ultimately on the motivation underlying the exercise of inequality evaluation. Inequality is measured for some *purpose*, and the choice of space as well as the selection of particular inequality measures in that space would have to be made in the light of that purpose. There is, of course, nothing at all surprising in the recognition that the nature of interpersonal comparisons and the assessment of inequality should depend on what we are after.[1]

Sometimes we may be interested in knowing how disparate the levels of well-being of different people happen to be, e.g. between different classes or distinct communities, or between women and men in a particular group. In the light of the discussion in the last chapter, one could argue that comparisons in the *functioning space* may be more relevant for the analysis of well-being than in the spaces of incomes, primary goods, or resources. And yet in some

[1] On this see Broome (1987).

other context we may be interested precisely in the relative positions of different individuals (or groups) in terms of incomes, or primary goods, or resources. Even if the distribution of incomes gives us little idea of the inequalities in well-being as such, it does not follow that income distribution is of no direct interest, since there are possible motivations other than well-being comparison.

For example, we may be interested in knowing what effect *income inequality* has, say, on crime, or on social discontent, or for that matter—*inter alia*—on the distribution of well-being. Similarly, we may wish to check what kind of a distribution of *primary goods* (or of *resources*) a state or a political system is working towards, and this may be an interesting issue to investigate in understanding the role of public policy—not in promoting well-being or freedom as such, but in making the means of freedom available to all.[2] The argument for paying greater attention to functionings (or capabilities) in assessing inequalities of well-being (or of freedom) must not be seen as an *all-purpose* preference for those variables.

6.2. SHORTFALLS, ATTAINMENTS AND POTENTIALS

Before I go into some specific questions that have been much discussed in the recent welfare-economic literature on inequality, I would like to address a distinction that has some general relevance in judging individual advantage. Should a person's position be judged, positively, in terms of the level of achievement, or negatively, in terms of the *shortfall vis-à-vis* what she could have maximally achieved? The two general approaches in assessing achievement are closely linked but nevertheless distinct.[3]

---

[2] This is, in fact, a part of Rawls's (1971) and Ronald Dworkin's (1981) motivation in placing the emphases they do on distributions in these spaces. See also Dahrendorf (1988).

[3] Shortfalls have been used as the basis of evaluation in welfare-economic literature in various forms. For example, Frank Ramsey's (1928) formulation of the problem of optimum saving was in terms of the minimization of the shortfall from the maximum level of aggregate utility (the so-called 'bliss'). In fact, Ramsey's shortfall minimization problem is well defined over infinite time in a way that the direct formulation of the problem (as the maximization of the utility-sum over an infinite horizon) would not have been (on which, see Sukhamoy Chakravarty 1969). To take another type of case, Dalton's (1920) measure of inequality looks for the shortfall *vis-à-vis* the maximal value of social welfare that could be achieved through equal distribution. Similarly, Atkinson's (1970*b*) measure of inequality looks for the income equivalent of the social-welfare shortfall. Dalton's and Atkinson's measures of in equality are discussed later on in this chapter. See also Musgrave (1959) on different concepts of 'sacrifice'.

The two approaches can yield different results for two distinct reasons. First, if the maximal value from which shortfall is calculated is varied between the persons (e.g. on the ground that what is maximally achievable by that *specific* person may not be the same as the achievement that another person could have maximally attained), then the ordering of absolute attainments can differ from that of the respective shortfalls. Second, even when the same maximal value is taken for all, a difference may arise from the fact that the comparisons may be done not in absolute terms, but in the scale of 'proportionate' attainments and shortfalls. There may be a case for that shift in perspective when the extent of 'difficulty' in achievement is seen as becoming relatively more acute with the rise in absolute attainment.[4]

The second issue may or may not be an immediate one in the particular context of assessing the level of interpersonal inequality; the formulation of achievements in proportionate terms would often be rather remote. But the first issue—that of interpersonal variations in maximal potentials—is peculiarly relevant when inequality assessment is addressed after a clear recognition of human diversity.

Equality between persons can be defined either in terms of *attainments*, or in terms of the *shortfalls* from the maximal values that each can respectively attain. For 'attainment equality' of achievements, we compare the actual levels of achievement.[5] For 'shortfall equality', what are compared are the shortfalls of actual achievements from the respective maximal achievements.[6] Each of the two

---

[4] For example, in assessing the performance of countries in terms of average life expectancy at birth, increasing the life expectancy figure from, say, 40 years to 50 years is a 25% increase, whereas raising it from 60 years to 70 years is only a 17% increase. It is, nevertheless, arguable that the latter is a much harder task, since further improvements get increasingly more difficult as we get closer to the maximal possible value. To alter the perspective, if we take, as our working assumption, 80 years (say) as the maximal value of average life expectancy at birth, then a move from 40 to 50 years is a reduction of the shortfall by 25%, whereas raising life expectancy from 60 to 70 years would involve a reduction of the shortfall by 50%. It can be argued that the latter ranking is relatively more in line with the recognition of the difficulty in raising life expectancy further, as the absolute achievements become higher. The underlying issues are discussed in Sen (1981*b*). Empirical examples of the use of proportionate shortfall comparisons for intercountry contrasts can be found there, and also in UNDP (1990). See also Desai, Boltvinnik, and Sen (1991).

[5] In the case of freedoms, attainment equality compares the levels of alternative actual achievements from which the person can choose.

[6] Correspondingly, in the case of freedoms, we have to look at the differences in shortfalls from the respective maximal freedoms to achieve.

views has some considerable interest of its own. Shortfall equality takes us in the direction of equal use of the *respective potentials*, whereas attainment equality is concerned with equal absolute levels of achievement (no matter what the maximal potentials are).

If human diversity is so powerful that it makes it impossible to equalize what is *potentially* achievable, then there is a basic ambiguity in assessing achievement, and in judging equality of achievement or of the freedom to achieve. If the maximal achievement that person 1 can have—under the most favourable circumstances—is, say, x, while person 2 can maximally manage $2x$, then equality of *attainment* would leave person 2 invariably below his or her potential achievement. It is partly to address such issues that Aristotle had incorporated a parametric consideration of what a person's 'circumstances admit', and had seen his 'distributive conception' in that light. 'For it is appropriate, if people are governed best that they should do best, *in so far as their circumstances admit*—unless something catastrophic happens.'[7]

In the case of serious disabilities, attainment equality may be hard to achieve, and it may be particularly tempting to opt for shortfall equality. There might well be a good argument in that direction, but I would like to argue that it is not the case that the choice is made clear-cut simply by the non-feasibility of attainment equality. It can be argued that even when a disabled person cannot, in any way, be given the freedom to enjoy the *same* level of the functioning in question (e.g. the same ability to move about freely as others), there is nevertheless a good case—based on fairness—for trying to *maximize* his below-par functioning ability, rather than settling for the same shortfall (absolute or proportionate) as others have from their—much higher—maximal functioning (as would be demanded by shortfall equality).

Indeed, that is the direction in which the Rawlsian logic of 'maximin' or 'lexicographic maximin' should take us—'to make the worst off as well off as possible'.[8] This is, in fact, an illustration of

---

[7] Aristotle, *Politics*, VII. 1 (1323ª17–19), emphasis added. The translation is taken from Nussbaum (1988a), who also discusses the precise role that this qualification plays in Aristotle's 'distributive conception' (pp. 146–50).

[8] There is a more complex problem of fairness when the different maximal achievements are not particular to the individual, but apply to a whole 'natural type', e.g. children *vis-à-vis* adults. Indeed, Aristotle's reasoning, presented earlier, seems to relate to inter-type comparisons, rather than to inter-individual variations (on this see Nussbaum 1988a). The lower ability of children to acquire some capabilities (e.g. in activities for which fuller bodily development or greater maturity is important)

the point made earlier in this monograph that a good deal of Rawlsian reasoning can be applied even *beyond* his own constrained framework. Rawls's own principles of justice will not directly admit the claim of the disabled in the domain of 'maximin' reasoning, since his Difference Principle restricts the use of 'maximin' to holdings of *primary goods*, whereas the deprivation of the disabled occurs in the field of *capability* (because of his unfavourable transformation possibility of primary goods into capability). But Rawls's general argument for focusing on the least advantaged does apply here (for reasons of 'fairness' that he has analysed so powerfully). That certainly provides reason enough to take seriously the claims of attainment equality even when the maximal achievements are quite diverse.

It could, of course, be objected that a policy of attainment equality would lead to a very 'low level equality' for all. In trying to achieve equality when person 1 can only achieve x, person 2 will have to be dragged down from his maximal achievement of $2x$, and *each* will have, at most, x. There is some force in that objection, but it would have been a more telling counterargument had equality been the *only* principle to be used. However, as was argued earlier (and will be discussed further in the last chapter), equality would typically be one consideration among many, and this could be combined with *aggregative* considerations including *efficiency*. These latter influences would work against choosing 'low-level equality', and against pulling person 2 down to the low level of person 1 just for the sake of achieving equality of attainments.

The real question is not about the kind of equality to ask for *if* that were the *only* principle to be used, but whether in a mixed framework in which aggregative considerations as well as equality are taken into account, the demands of equality as such are best represented by 'shortfall equality' rather than by 'attainment equality'. I have not argued for unqualified pursuit of attainment equality, but have argued against opting for shortfall equality on the simple ground

might not be seen as a definitive argument for giving priority to expanding these capabilities for the children at the cost of the larger capabilities of the adults. This problem would not arise in that form if the advantages of individuals are seen in terms of lifetime opportunities (as Rawls 1971 himself suggests), but the question is not entirely dismissible, since there is a further issue of inter-age distribution that the lifetime focus tends to avoid. There are also complex problems of fairness related to the biological advantages that women seem to have *vis-à-vis* men in longevity, even though women often live *less* long in many countries because of unequal treatment (on this see Sect. 8.2).

that attainment equality may be unfeasible or inefficient (involving the 'levelling down' of all to the condition of the lowest achiever). The case for retaining an interest in moving towards attainment equality can survive the difficulties in achieving it *fully*.

The issues involved in the distinction between attainment and shortfall will reappear in specific contexts in some of the arguments in the rest of the monograph (particularly in Chapters 8 and 9). But since they do not come in much in the standard welfare-economic discussion of inequalities, with which the rest of this chapter is concerned, the distinction will not figure further in this chapter. The literature on welfare-economic theory dealing with inequality has typically overlooked human diversities and has tended to take everyone as being exactly similar (including *inter alia* having the same maximal potentials).

6.3. INEQUALITY, WELFARE AND JUSTICE

The literature on the measurement and evaluation of inequality has expanded very rapidly over the last decade or two, and remarkable progress has been made in the understanding of many analytical aspects of the evaluative problems.[9] While the analytical contri-

[9] Recently, Blackorby and Donaldson (1978) and Foster (1985) have provided critical surveys of the developments in the contemporary literature. See also Cowell (1977), Nygrad and Sandstrom (1981), Eichhorn and Gehrig (1982), Chipman (1985), and Lambert (1989). The literature has, by now, what seems like uncountably many contributions, but here is a list to get one started: Aigner and Heins (1967), Theil (1967), Kolm (1969, 1976), Atkinson (1970b, 1975, 1983), Bentzel (1970), Newbery (1970), Tinbergen (1970), Pen (1971), Sheshinski (1972), Dasgupta, Sen, and Starrett (1973), Rothschild and Stiglitz (1973), Pazner and Schmeidler (1974), Blackorby and Donaldson (1977, 1978), Muellbauer (1974b, 1978), Wolfson (1974), Gastwirth (1975), Hammond (1976b, 1977, 1978), Mehran (1976), Pyatt (1976, 1987), Bhattacharya and Chatterjee (1988), Cowell (1977, 1980, 1985, 1988), Graaff (1977), B. Hansson (1977), Fields and Fei (1978), Kern (1978), Osmani (1978, 1982), Archibald and Donaldson (1979), Bourguignon (1979), Donaldson and Weymark (1980), Deaton and Muellbauer (1980), Dutta (1980), Fields (1980a), Kakwani (1980b, 1981, 1986), Roberts (1980b), Shorrocks (1980, 1982, 1983, 1984, 1988), Blackorby, Donaldson, and Auersperg (1981), S. R. Chakravarty (1981, 1988, 1990), Cowell and Kuga (1981), Jasso (1981), Nygrad and Sandstrom (1981), Weymark (1981), Atkinson and Bourguignon (1982), Kanbur (1982b), Mookherjee and Shorrocks (1982), Thon (1982), Anand (1983), Broder and Morris (1983), Blackorby, Donaldson, and Weymark (1984), Foster, Greer, and Thorbecke (1984), Jorgenson and Slesnick (1984a, 1984b), Le Grand (1984), Slottje (1984), Chakravarty, Dutta, and Weymark (1985), Chakravarty and Roy (1985), Fine (1985), Lambert (1985, 1989), Le Breton, Trannoy, and Uriarte (1985), Baumol (1986), Hutchens (1986), Kanbur and Stromberg (1986), Maasoumi (1986), Temkin (1986, 1989), K. Basu (1987b), Chakravarty and Dutta (1987), Ebert (1987, 1988), Le Breton and Trannoy (1987), Meyer (1987), Shorrocks

butions are not always explicit about the purpose of the exercise, it is clear that many different purposes have motivated the analytical literature.

The connection between inequality and social welfare has, however, been invoked more often than any other. That connection can be pursued in different ways, depending on what we take to be the 'argument' of the social-welfare function. For example, social welfare may be seen as a function of individual utilities, as in the welfarist framework, of which utilitarianism is a distinguished case, involving 'sum-ranking' (i.e. simply adding up the utilities).[10] Or alternatively, social welfare may be seen as a function *directly* of the vector of incomes (without being intermediated by the utilities related to those incomes), or of the combination of multiple-attribute characteristics of individual economic status or opulence.[11]

A particular approach to this class of problems is to see social welfare as a function of the person-specific distribution of each commodity (i.e. of the 'named-goods vector', as it is sometimes called[12]). Social welfare can, of course, also be seen as a function of the combination of everyone's functioning vectors (or of everyone's capability sets). The nature of the presumed social-welfare function, thus, influences the type of interpersonal comparability that may be correspondingly sought.

Therefore, even for the purpose of social-welfare assessment, there are several possible leads to the problem of choice of space in inequality evaluation. And as other purposes (i.e. purposes other than the assessment of aggregate social welfare) are taken up, the space-choice problem will also alter in conformity with the respec-

and Foster (1987), Bhattacharya, Chatterjee, and Pal (1988), Eichhorn (1988a, 1988b), Foster, Majumdar, and Mitra (1988), Foster and Shorrocks (1988a, 1988b), Dutta and Ray (1989). There are, of course, many other contributions.

[10] On the distinction between welfarism in general and utilitarianism in particular, see Sen (1979a, 1979b) and Sen and Williams (1982), 'Introduction'.

[11] On this see Kolm (1977), Atkinson and Bourguignon (1982), Maasoumi (1986, 1989), Foster, Majumdar, and Mitra (1988).

[12] The concept of a 'named good'—good *i* going to person *j* being a named good *ij*—was introduced by Hahn (1971). The named-goods vector contains the same information as the 'commodity matrix' as defined by Fisher (1956). The informational enormity of a named-goods vector can be systematically handled to get practically usable results, given some regularizing axioms, on which see Sen (1976b, 1979c), Hammond (1978), Roberts (1980b). On related matters, see Graaff (1977), Dasgupta and Heal (1979), Atkinson and Bourguignon (1982), Broder and Morris (1983), Osmani (1982), Atkinson (1983), Atkinson and Bourguignon (1987), Bhattacharya, Chatterjee, and Pal (1988).

tive objectives. In this sense, the question 'equality of what?' cannot lead to anything like a clear answer until the purpose and the motivation behind the question have been specified.

There are, in fact, two implicit programmes that have been frequently invoked as background to the exercise of inequality evaluation.[13] The first is that of using inequality evaluation for analysing social justice, and specifically for the choice of the 'basic structure' of the society in a general framework of political and social ethics, such as that of Rawls's (1971) 'justice as fairness'. This programme was already examined in Chapter 5, and it has obvious implications for normative analysis of public policy.

In contrast with this 'justice-based inequality evaluation' (much discussed in modern ethics and political philosophy), the second frequently invoked programme—more commonly used in welfare economics—is that of assessing inequality in the context of social-welfare analysis, assuming that the vector of incomes determines the level of social welfare. This is the exercise that was specifically investigated in the pioneering contributions of Dalton (1920), Kolm (1969), and Atkinson (1970*b*), and the literature that it led to (including substantial parts of my *OEI*). I shall call this the problem of 'welfare-based inequality evaluation', and I shall have a few methodological comments to make on the nature of that exercise in the next section of this chapter.

6.4. WELFARE-BASED INEQUALITY EVALUATION

In his pioneering contribution to measuring inequality in terms of social-welfare loss, Hugh Dalton (1920) used a simple utilitarian social-welfare function. Social welfare was taken to be the sum-total of individual utilities, and each individual utility was taken to be a function of the income of that individual. The same utility function was taken to apply to all individuals, and this fact, along with diminishing marginal utility from income, ensured that for any given total income to be distributed among the people, an equal distribution would maximize social welfare (i.e. would

---

[13] Another approach that has been used with illuminating results is that of surveying people's general attitude to inequality. On this, see Yaari and Bar-Hillel (1984), Amiel and Cowell (1989), Fields (1990). For a systematic use of common intuitions to judge inequality, see Temkin (1986).

generate the highest utility sum-total for that total income).[14]
Dalton identified the level of inequality for a given total income
with the percentage shortfall of the *actual* sum-total of utilities
from the *maximal* value, i.e. the sum-total that would be generated
through equally distributing the given total income over all the individuals.

Since Dalton's measure of inequality operates on utilities as
such, it is very exacting on the measurability and interpersonal
comparability of individual utilities. It is, in fact, not easy to talk
about percentage shortfalls of utility sum-totals from the maximal
sum-total (e.g. 'the sum of *utilities* is reduced by 17 per cent').[15]
Atkinson's (1970*b*) index of inequality, in contrast, operates on
incomes, and measures the social loss involved in unequal income
distribution in terms of shortfalls of equivalent incomes. Atkinson
measures the inequality of a distribution of incomes by the percentage reduction of total income that can be sustained without
reducing social welfare, by distributing the new reduced total exactly equally. It requires judgements of the kind: 'A 22 per cent
smaller total income, if *equally* distributed, would be just as good
for the society as the present [higher] income distributed as [un-
equally as] it in fact is.' The more unequal the distribution of
present incomes, the more of a reduction of total income is
sustainable, without social-welfare loss, by distributing the new
total equally. The level of the 'equally distributed equivalent
income' (in this case 22 per cent lower than the actual income) is
the crucial concept in Atkinson's approach, and the difference with
the actual income (in this case 22 per cent) gives us Atkinson's
measure of inequality.

Atkinson's and related approaches to inequality measurement
have several technical features which I have discussed elsewhere,

---

[14] This was also the basis of the famous 'Dalton's principle of transfers' (discussed
earlier), which asserts that given other things a transfer of a unit of income from a
richer to a poorer person must increase social welfare and be seen as reducing the
normative measure of inequality. The principle has been extensively used in the
literature on the normative measurement of inequality (see Atkinson 1970*b*, 1975,
1983). See also Dasgupta, Sen, and Starrett (1973) and Rothschild and Stiglitz
(1973).

[15] This requires, in fact, that the utility functions have ratio-scale measurability
and comparability, which is a very demanding assumption. On this, see Sen (1977*b*,
1986*a*), Gevers (1979), Roberts (1980*a*), Blackorby, Donaldson, and Weymark
(1984), d'Aspremont (1985), among others.

and on which I shall not comment further here.[16] Atkinson's approach has the advantage, over the Dalton formulation, of not demanding any more measurability or comparability of utilities than is already involved in the characterization of social welfare—the indexing operations being all in the space of incomes. The Atkinson approach is also more general in permitting non-utilitarian social-welfare functions, even though (as we discussed earlier) he actually chose to see social welfare as the sum-total of individual *u*-values (usually taken to be individual utilities, but open also to other interpretations). Indeed, there is no difficulty within the Atkinson approach in changing the form of the social-welfare function, as long as it is ensured that (1) social welfare is ultimately a function of the vector of incomes only, and (2) for any total income, an equal distribution must be the social-welfare maximizing distribution of that total income.[17]

The merits of this approach are clear enough, and the class of Atkinson indices (with various assumptions about the relation between individual incomes and social welfare) has been widely used not only in the literature of normative measurement, but also in public economics in general. In particular, the idea of an 'equally distributed equivalent income' links inequality measurement directly to the evaluation of public policy in a most usable way.

There are, however, several serious problems as well. First, since inequality has *descriptive* as well as *normative* content, a purely normative approach to inequality can go against certain obvious intuitions regarding inequality. For example, if individual utility is a linear function of individual income (i.e. if marginal utility is constant), then with a utilitarian social-welfare function, 'the equally distributed equivalent income' would be the *same* as the actual income (since there would be no aggregate-utility loss from inequalities in income distribution). In this case the Atkinson index of inequality, which identifies the social-welfare loss *from* inequality with inequality *itself*, would declare that every distribution of incomes—no matter how unequal—in fact has a zero level of

---

[16] They were explored particularly in ch. 3 of my *OEI*. See also Kolm (1976), Blackorby and Donaldson (1978, 1984), Atkinson (1983), Foster (1985). The problems discussed in what follows apply generally to the whole class of normative measures of inequality; I specifically concentrate on Atkinson's analysis because of its clarity and its pre-eminent position in the literature on the subject.

[17] In *OEI*, such a generalized form was presented. See also Kolm (1976) and Blackorby and Donaldson (1978, 1984).

inequality. A distribution of incomes (1, 99) would be, then, seen as *perfectly equal*, in the same way as a (50, 50) distribution would be viewed. This would run somewhat contrary to the fact that both in terms of incomes and in terms of utilities, a (1, 99) distribution is quite unequal.

More importantly, the Atkinson index of inequality can move in the opposite direction to the actual inequality of individual utilities, as we take less and less 'concave' utility functions, i.e. take marginal utility to diminish more slowly with increased income.[18] When the marginal utility goes down comparatively more slowly, the utility gap related to an income gap is *more* than it would otherwise have been, so that the directly observed level of utility inequality related to a given pattern of income inequality is *larger* than otherwise. On the other hand, with slowly diminishing marginal utility the loss of aggregate utility as a result of the income inequality is less, and thus the Atkinson measure of inequality (and the Dalton measure too) is *lower*, rather than higher. This has the somewhat perverse feature that—for any given income distribution—the *more* the inequality in the utilities that people enjoy, the *lower* is the index of inequality.[19] The Atkinson index moves (goes *down*) in a way contrary to the directly observed income inequality (which is *stationary*) and in a way contradictory to the directly observed utility inequality (which goes *up*).

The 'perversity' may or may not be in itself particularly disturbing, but it draws our attention to a feature of the normative approach to the measurement of inequality that is important to appreciate. The Atkinson index and other normative measures of inequality are, in fact, measures of the *distributional badness*—according to the chosen social-welfare function—of the particular configuration of personal incomes; they are not specifically measures of *inequality per se*—neither of incomes, nor of utilities. With a *given* configura-

---

[18] This interpretation is possible if the 'utility function' is seen as giving the values of individual utilities, rather than as a purely analytical device to express the social welfare as an additively separable function of individual incomes (y_i), with the utility $u(y_i)$ not standing for any particular feature of the person i. On these issues, see Atkinson (1983).

[19] This discussion may be a little too compressed, and it certainly could be aided by the diagrammatic version presented in Sen (1978*b*), and also in Sen (1984). The philosophical issues are best discussed in Bengt Hansson (1977); see also Atkinson (1983). Since this is not a central issue in the context of this monograph, I am resisting a fuller discussion, since it might deflect attention towards a side-issue that is related and relevant but by no means crucial to the main themes of this monograph.

tion of personal incomes (and thus, in one obvious sense, a *given* inequality of income distribution), a less concave utility function can make the Atkinson index go *down*—precisely when different persons' utilities move further apart and the inequality of *utilities* goes up.

There is nothing really perverse in all this, *if* the Atkinson index is seen as a measure of 'how bad' the income inequality is, according to the chosen social-welfare function (i.e. how much loss of aggregate welfare, or of equally distributed equivalent income, there is). In the example considered, the utility *inequality* may be larger, but the utility *sum-total* is closer to the maximal value, thanks to the slowly diminishing marginal utility. And the Atkinson index would be right to declare this to be a case of *low* index value of the loss of aggregate welfare.

The immediate context of the Atkinson approach, which has been widely used in welfare economics and in public-policy analysis, is well-defined, viz. the assessment of social-welfare implications of income inequality. The interest in income inequality in the Atkinson approach is mainly in that context. When there is slowly diminishing marginal utility, there is *less inefficiency* from unequal distribution of incomes, and it is this inefficiency in generating social welfare that the Atkinson index really measures. While it may be somewhat misleading to call this an 'inequality index' as such, the index relates very well to Atkinson's purpose of measuring the social-welfare loss from inequality.

The second issue concerns the characterization of the social-welfare function. Atkinson chose an additive form, and earlier on Dalton had chosen specifically a utilitarian social-welfare function, with no concern whatever for the distributional inequality of utilities. These features can be changed, and it is in fact even possible to drop the additive form, in addition to eschewing utilitarianism.[20] But the framework requires, as we stated earlier, that (1) social welfare must be a function, ultimately, of incomes alone, and (2) social welfare must be maximized by an equal distribution of incomes, given the total income. I have already discussed why these assumptions are disputable. Indeed, this monograph is much concerned with getting away from the limiting perspective on inequality that is provided by these—and related—assumptions, widely used in welfare economics.

[20] See Sen (1973*a*), Atkinson (1983), Blackorby and Donaldson (1984).

If social welfare is seen as a function of individual well-beings, then variations in the conversion of incomes into well-being must be taken into account, with adequate attention being paid to the variable relationship between incomes, on the one hand, and functionings and capabilities, on the other. These conversion factors influencing the relation of income to well-being must also be brought in. This can raise questions about assumption (1). Even if the parameters of the conversion rates are respectively *given*, an equal distribution of income may yield very unequal well-being levels—with differences related to group-specific parameters (such as gender, age, environments) and individual parameters (such as genetic characteristics). It is easy to envisage circumstances with wide interpersonal variations in conversion rates, in which an equal distribution of *income* would be quite bad for social welfare, so that assumption (2) may be quite unacceptable.[21]

These problems arise even with retaining the basic assumption that social welfare is a function of individual well-beings. When that assumption itself is dropped, and direct attention is paid to the freedoms enjoyed by the people (in line with the reasoning presented earlier in this monograph), both the assumptions needed for the approach would face more radical difficulties.

So the conclusion we must come to is perhaps something like this. The Atkinson approach of inequality measurement is indeed very useful within a fairly limited format in which individual diversities are left out of account. The format makes no room for substantial interpersonal variations in the conversion of individual incomes into personal well-beings, and furthermore it does not accommodate the importance of freedom as a constitutive element of a good society (and thus as a determinant of what is called social welfare). However, since that very format is standardly used in mainstream welfare economics and in standard public-policy analysis, the use of the Atkinson index does not add to the limitations already present in the tradition. In fact, it makes the accounting more systematic and efficient *within* that standard structure. So the contingent usefulness of the approach is not in doubt. The fact that it may be somewhat misleading to call the Atkinson index a measure of inequality as

---

[21] In these circumstances 'Dalton's principle of transfers' would also be, in general, unsupportable in the context of social-welfare maximization. For example, the transfer of some income from an ill person to one who is in robust health but with a little lower income may be far from a social improvement.

such (as opposed to an index of 'distributional badness' taking note also of efficiency considerations involved in generating social welfare) does not detract from the usefulness of that index. But we have to be clear as to what exactly we are doing, and why.

If the fundamental fact of human diversity and its far-reaching implications come to be recognized more widely in welfare-economic analysis and in public-policy assessment, then the approach would certainly need some radical transformation. The operations would have to move from the income space to the space of the constitutive elements of well-being and also of freedom, if the intrinsic importance of freedom, discussed earlier, is accepted. Social-welfare analysis would then take a different form, and the evaluation of inequality and of distributional badness would then have to reflect that foundational transformation.

In the next chapter, when we examine poverty measures, we shall see that something similarly critical can be said also about the currently used poverty indices.[22] These standard measures are all basically parasitic on the traditional concentration on the income space and ultimately on ignoring the fundamental fact of human diversity and the foundational importance of human freedom.

---

[22] Including, I fear, the so-called Sen index (Sen 1973c, 1976a).

7

POVERTY AND AFFLUENCE

7.1. INEQUALITY AND POVERTY

The mainstream approach to identifying poverty specifies a cut-off 'poverty line', defined as the level of income below which people are diagnosed as poor. The conventional measure of poverty, still widely used, proceeds from here to count the number of people below the poverty line—the so-called 'head count'—and defines the index of poverty as the proportion of the total population that happens to be below the poverty line (i.e. the fraction of the population identified as poor). This gives a neat and well-defined measure, and it is not hard to see why it has been so widely used in the empirical literature on poverty and deprivation.

The measurement of poverty can be seen as consisting of two distinct—though interrelated—exercises, viz. (1) *identification* of the poor, and (2) *aggregation* of the statistics regarding the identified poor to derive an overall index of poverty. In the traditional 'head count' approach, the identification exercise is done through the use of the 'poverty line' income as a cut-off. Then, the aggregation is done simply through counting the number of the poor, and calculating the proportion H—the 'head-count ratio'—of people below the poverty line. Both the exercises are, in this approach, thoroughly dependent on seeing deprivation in terms of *low income* as such.[1]

But, in addition, the *aggregation* exercise done through simple head counting pays no attention to the fact that people could be *a little* below the line, or *a lot*, and also the distribution of income among the poor *may or may not* be itself very unequal. It is this lacuna in using H as a measure of poverty that has received a tremendous amount of attention in the recent literature on formal measures of poverty. I shall first discuss that development in the 'aggregation' exercise, before turning, in the next section, to the first

---

[1] In principle, the 'head count' measure can be used with some other way of identifying the poor, rather than relying only on low income. In practice, however, it has been used almost invariably only with a low-income dividing line.

question, viz. the use of *low income* as the main characteristic of poverty, which influences both 'identification' and 'aggregation'.

There is, in fact, another aggregate statistic, like the 'head count' ratio, that has also been used—though not quite so widely—in the traditional literature.[2] This is the so-called 'income gap', which measures the additional income that would be needed to bring all the poor up to the level of the poverty line, i.e. the minimal extra income that would be sufficient to wipe out poverty—in the form of low income—altogether. This 'gap' can be expressed in per capita terms, viz. the average shortfall I of income of the identified poor from the poverty line.[3]

Note that just as the head-count ratio H is completely insensitive to the extent to which the incomes of the poor fall short of the poverty line and takes note only of the number below the line, the income-gap ratio I is completely insensitive to the number of heads involved and takes note only of the average gap of the income of the poor from the poverty line. It is natural to think that the two must complement each other, since they address different aspects of poverty. The need to put H and I (or similar indices) together is, thus, obvious enough.

It can now be asked whether the two *together* would provide an adequate informational base for poverty measurement (still sticking to the idea that poverty is best seen as *low income*)? The answer, briefly, is: no. H and I together still cannot be adequate, since neither pays any attention to the distribution of income *among* the poor. For example, a transfer of income from a poor person to one *less* poor but also below the poverty line (before and after the transfer) would leave *both* the values of H and I completely unchanged. But it can certainly be argued that aggregate poverty is *increased* by this transfer, since the *poorer* person is *even poorer* now, and this intensification of the more acute deprivation cannot be outweighed by the increase in the income of the person who was less poor even to start with. Hence we need some other statistic, presumably some measure of inequality in the distribution of income among the poor. Let us call such a measure of inequality among the poor D.

---

[2] See Beckerman (1979), Anand (1983), Beckerman and Clark (1982).

[3] There are also other ways of normalizing this, such as a proportion of national income needed to wipe out the poverty gaps of every identified poor person. See Anand (1977), Beckerman (1979).

It is easy to construct an axiomatic derivation of a poverty measure that is sensitive to all these three related but distinct considerations (still sticking to the idea that poverty is best seen as low income). This would make the axiomatically derived aggregate poverty measure P a function of H, I, and D. The axioms that I had, in fact, presented in Sen (1973c, 1976a) led to the identification of the inequality measure D of the distribution of income among the poor as the Gini coefficient G, and it thus led to a poverty measure P that depended on H, I, and G.

The axioms, postulated in a specified format of measurement, included accepting the informational sufficiency of H and I together in the special case in which all the poor had the *same* income (so that the question of inequality *among* the poor would not, then, arise).[4] In fact, in this special case the poverty measure was simply taken as the product of the two, i.e. HI. The axioms also demanded that when some of the poor are poorer than others, then the per-unit weighting of the income shortfall of each poor person must increase with his or her poverty rank, i.e. the poorest poor would have the highest weight and the richest poor the least. Taking the special case of 'rank-order weighting' giving a weight of n to the income shortfall of the n-th richest among the poor, a very specific measure of aggregate poverty emerges, which takes account of the inequality of the distribution of income among the poor through the use of the well-known Gini coefficient.[5]

Rank-order weighting has been extensively used in social-choice theory beginning with the classic use of this 'ordinal' approach to voting decisions by the French mathematician Borda (1781), and this procedure—and the general 'positional' approach underlying it—provide useful ways of 'weighting' competing claims with simple ordinal information.[6] It is interesting—and rather useful from a practical point of view—that the Borda method of weighting leads to the Gini coefficient in the special case of inequality

---

[4] This is not at all a demanding restriction; on this see Foster (1984: n. 27).

[5] The exact formula is the following: $P = H[I + (1 - I) G]$. For proper statements of the axioms and the proof of the theorem deriving this exact measure, see Sen (1976a). Note that in the special case in which all the poor have the same income, G would be zero, and thus P would equal HI.

[6] On the use of rank-order method in social choice theory, see Arrow (1951), Sen (1970a), Suzumura (1983). In the context of measurement problems in economics and development studies, the possibility of using the positional approach in general and the Borda rank-order method in particular has been explored in Sen (1974, 1976a, 1976b, 1981b).

measurement, which is one of the most common measures of income inequality.[7]

The so-called Sen measure of poverty and related distribution-sensitive indicators have been used *inter alia* in many practical exercises in evaluating poverty, and these empirical works—related to Bangladesh, India, Iran, Malaysia, United States, Brazil, and several other countries—have been done with much care and skill.[8] Despite my scepticism of the appropriateness of the so-called Sen measure and other indicators that diagnose poverty in terms of *low income*, I would not dispute the analytical and practical contribution made by these empirical works through the use of distribution-sensitivity in evaluating poverty.

The concentration on the income space is often hard to avoid given the comparatively greater availability of income statistics rather than other types of data.[9] *Within* that informational format, the traditional use of the head-count ratio as a measure of poverty can deflect anti-poverty policy by ignoring the greater misery of the *poorer* among the poor. Indeed, with the head-count ratio as the measure of poverty, any government faces a strong temptation to concentrate on the *richest* among the poor, since that is the way that the number of the poor—and the head-count ratio H—can be most easily reduced.[10] Recasting the empirical measurement of poverty in

[7] On the characteristics of the Gini coefficient, see *OEI*, ch. 2. On the properties of the Gini coefficient, Lorenz-curve comparisons, and related matters, see Graaff (1946, 1977, 1985), Kolm (1969), Atkinson (1970b), Newbery (1970), Sheshinski (1972), P. Dasgupta, Sen, and Starrett (1973), Sen (1974, 1976b), Pyatt (1976, 1987), Cowell (1977), Blackorby and Donaldson (1978, 1980), P. J. Hammond (1978), Yitzhaki (1979), Kakwani (1980b), Roberts (1980b), P. K. Sen (1986), Seidl (1986a).

[8] See Ahluwalia (1978), Alamgir (1978), Anand (1977, 1983), Bhatty (1974), Sastry (1977), Seastrand and Diwan (1975), Clark and Hemming (1981), Szal (1977), Dutta (1978), Fields (1979, 1980a), Fishlow (1980), Gaiha and Kazmi (1981), van Ginneken (1980), Kakwani (1980b, 1981, 1986, 1988), Sundaram and Tendulkar (1981), Osmani (1982), Pantulu (1980), Sastry (1980a, 1980b), Hemming (1984), Ray (1984b), Gaiha (1985), Babu (1986), and others. There have been a number of other important empirical studies in similar lines in more recent years.

[9] This applies even to the use of *income* as opposed to *expenditure* statistics. The case for using the latter on grounds of greater relevance is often very strong, but actual use is nevertheless restricted because of the difficulty of obtaining reliable expenditure information. On this see Atkinson (1989: ch. 1).

[10] On the relevance of this type of consideration for the Indian debates on poverty, see Sen (1973c), Ahluwalia (1978), Dutta (1978), S. R. Chakravarty (1981), L. Chakravarty (1986). The policy implications of the neglect of distributional issues in insensitive measures of deprivation is, in fact, a pervasive problem which crops up in different contexts. For example, if the extent of homelessness is judged just by the

a distribution-sensitive way has the effect of making *comparatively better* use of income data (despite the overall limitations of that income-based informational base).

The need for having distribution-sensitivity in measuring poverty seems to be fairly widely accepted by now, and various other distribution-sensitive measures of poverty have also been suggested in the theoretical literature, taking some other inequality measure D among the poor, and using other mathematical forms of combination.[11] I shall not comment on the relative merits of these different measures and assess the distinct ways of taking note of the three aspects of the problem of deriving an aggregate measure of poverty.[12] The major issue in the context of measuring poverty in the income space seems to me to be the need to pay attention to *all* the three aspects—particularly to incorporate distribution-sensitivity (rather than insisting that this incorporating be done in some very *specific* way).[13] And the primary issue in the more general context, to be addressed in the present study, is the questioning of the relevance of the income space itself for the measurement of poverty. That

number of people without a proper home, the temptation to deal with more easily remediable cases—irrespective of the extent of homelessness or the intensity of the misery resulting from it—can be very strong.

[11] See particularly Anand (1977, 1983), L. Taylor (1977), Drewnowski (1978), Hamada and Takayama (1978), Takayama (1979), Thon (1979), Blackorby and Donaldson (1980), Fields (1980a), Kakwani (1980a, 1980b, 1981), Sastry (1980a, 1980b), S. R. Chakravarty (1981, 1983a, 1983b), S. Clark, Hemming, and Ulph (1981), Osmani (1982), Kundu and Smith (1983), Foster, Greer, and Thorbecke (1984), Foster (1984), Ray (1984a), Bigman (1985, 1986), Lipton (1985), Cowell (1986), Donaldson and Weymark (1986), Jorgenson and Slesnick (1986), Seidl (1986a), Atkinson (1987, 1989), Lewis and Ulph (1987), Pyatt (1987), R. N. Vaughan (1987), Besley and Kanbur (1988), Buhmann *et al.* (1988), Foster and Shorrocks (1988a, 1988b, 1991), Ravallion and van de Walle (1988), Smeeding, Rainwater, and O'Higgins (1988), Bourguignon and Fields (1990), Pattanaik and Sengupta (1991), among other contributions.

[12] One issue that has received much attention is the insistence on 'separability' in poverty measures. Separability is certainly convenient property, and permits us to build up the overall poverty picture from the poverty measures applied to subgroups. The requirement has much cutting power. There is a helpful technical literature on this and related issues, including their implications (see Anand 1983; Foster 1984; Foster, Greer, and Thorbecke 1984; Cowell 1986; Foster and Shorrocks 1991). There remains a more general question as to whether it is sensible to assume that poverty indicators should be combinable in this way, which requires that the view of poverty for particular groups be, in some specific ways, insensitive to what happens to other groups, and that the whole picture does not introduce anything other than what is already there in the parts.

[13] See, however, the critical and comparative analyses presented by Foster (1984) and Seidl (1986a), and also the general methodological critique presented by Atkinson (1987, 1989). See also Sen (1981a, 1983d).

critical examination would apply to *all* the different measures that share this concentration on seeing poverty in terms of low income.

7.2. THE NATURE OF POVERTY

Consider two persons 1 and 2—person 1 has an income level somewhat lower than that of 2. But 2 has a kidney problem and needs to use a dialysis machine which costs him a lot, and he has also a much more impoverished life than person 1. Who is the poorer of the two—person 1 because his income is lower, or person 2 because his capability set is more restricted?

The question may sound like one of pure semantics. It might even be tempting to take the view that it does not matter at all whom we *call* 'poorer', as long as we define our terms clearly enough. That bit of philosophical 'nominalism' does make some sense, but the fact also remains that 'poverty' is a major evaluative concern in most societies, and how we identify poverty is a matter of some practical moment in the contexts in which questions of this kind are posed. So here we do have a substantive issue. While the term poverty is used in rather different ways, there are some clear associations that constrain the nature of the concept, and we are not entirely free to characterize poverty in any way we like.

The question can be given both *descriptive* and *policy* forms. In the first view, the identification of poverty is an acknowledgement of deprivation. It may lead to a policy recommendation also, but that is a derived feature, and the first exercise is one of deciding who are truly deprived as these things are judged in the society in question. The second view simply identifies poverty with a policy recommendation, viz. an assertion that something should be done by society to encounter these deficiencies.[14] In the second view poverty is primarily a matter of identifying the focus of public action, and its descriptive meaning is only derivative. In contrast, the first view makes the description primary and the policy conclusion derivative.

Again, it may be a mistake to spend much time on sorting out which of the two views to take. I have tried to argue elsewhere that there is a case for sticking to the first—primarily descriptive—view, so that diagnosis *precedes* policy choice.[15] This is also important in

[14] See Beckerman (1979) for a discussion of the policy-related view of poverty.
[15] The arguments are presented in Sen (1979e, 1981a). I have to confess that while I haven't changed my position on this, I don't now attach as much importance to the contrast as I then evidently did.

order to make sure that the non-availability of public resources to help eliminate severe deprivations should not make us redefine poverty itself. For example, if the state and the society lack the means to alleviate extreme economic hardship, that would be a conclusive reason against a policy recommendation to counter that deprivation through using the necessary—but non-available—funds.[16] But that fact in itself should not make us decide that there isn't much poverty around (as we would be obliged to say, *if* we were to define poverty entirely in terms of the recommended choice of policy).

A policy recommendation is contingent on feasibility, but the recognition of poverty has to go beyond that. One can argue that the first step is to *diagnose* deprivation, and related to that, to determine what we *should* do *if* we had the means. And then the next step is to make actual policy choices in line with our means. In this sense, the descriptive analysis of poverty has to be *prior* to the policy choice.

But how should that descriptive analysis of poverty proceed? Just because it is a primarily descriptive exercise, we should not make the mistake of thinking that the analysis must be somehow *independent* of the society in which poverty is being assessed. Even the demand of 'objectivity' in description does not really require *social invariance*, as it is sometimes supposed. What is seen as terrible deprivation can, of course, vary from society to society, but from the point of view of the social analyst these variations *are* matters of objective study.[17] We could, of course, debate about the exact ways in which normative judgements should take note of such social variations, but the primary exercise of diagnosing deprivation cannot but be sensitive to the way various types of hardships are viewed in the society in question. To deny that connection is not so much to be super-objective, but to be super-dense.

The existence of social variations does not, of course, rule out various agreements on what is to count as serious deprivation. Indeed, it can be argued that if we concentrate on certain basic general functionings and the corresponding capabilities, there may be much more agreement on their importance, than there would be if we concentrated on particular commodity bundles and particular ways of achieving those functionings. For example, there is likely to be

---

[16] This claim relates to the old dictum: 'ought implies can'. On this philosophical issue, see Hare (1952).

[17] This issue has been discussed in Sen (1980*b*).

more intercultural—and also interpersonal—agreement on the importance of having the capability to avoid acute hunger or severe undernourishment, than on the significance of having an adequate supply of particular food items (e.g. some specific types of meat or fish or grains or pulses) to serve those functionings. To take another type of examples, there may be more agreement on the need to be entertained, or to have the capability to take part in the life of the community, than on the form that entertainment must take, or on the particular way the life of the community may be shared.[18]

This is, in fact, one reason why poverty is better seen in terms of capability failure than in terms of the failure to meet the 'basic needs' of specified commodities. The 'basic needs' literature and the related studies on the 'quality of life' have been enormously helpful in drawing attention to deprivations of essential goods and services, and their crucial role in human living.[19] The underlying motivation can perhaps be more directly addressed in terms of achieving certain basic functionings and acquiring the corresponding capabilities.[20] In so far as the underlying reasoning of the basic-needs approach relates to giving people the *means* of achieving certain basic functionings, the problem of interpersonal variations in 'transforming' commodities into functionings—discussed earlier—can also be avoided by directly looking at the functioning space rather than at the commodity space.[21]

7.3. LOWNESS *VIS-À-VIS* INADEQUACY OF INCOMES

In line with the preceding reasoning, it is possible to argue for seeing poverty as the failure of basic capabilities to reach certain minimally acceptable levels.[22] The functionings relevant to this

---

[18] These issues are discussed in Sen (1980*b*, 1981*a*, 1983*d*). The basic point of social variation of form related to the same general functioning goes back, in fact, to Adam Smith (1776). There is some similarity here with the Aristotelian position on 'non-relative virtues', on which see Nussbaum (1988*b*).

[19] For an excellent discussion of the general approach, see Streeten *et al.* (1981). On related issues, see also Pant *et al.* (1962), Adelman and Morris (1973), Sen (1973*d*, 1981*a*), P. Bardhan (1974*b*, 1984), Adelman (1975), Grant (1978), Morris (1979), Chichilnisky (1980), P. Dasgupta (1986), Drèze and Sen (1989), UNDP (1990, 1991), Desai, Boltvinnik and Sen (1991).

[20] On this general question, see Sen (1984, 1985*b*), Streeten (1984), Stewart (1988), Griffin and Knight (1989).

[21] On these issues, see Griffin and Knight (1989).

[22] On this see Desai (1990) and Hossain (1990). See also Sen (1980*a*) and Griffin and Knight (1989).

analysis can vary from such elementary physical ones as being well-nourished, being adequately clothed and sheltered, avoiding preventable morbidity, etc., to more complex social achievements such as taking part in the life of the community, being able to appear in public without shame, and so on. These are rather 'general' functionings, but—as was discussed earlier—the specific form that their fulfilments may take would tend to vary from society to society.

This capability-based approach to poverty can be contrasted both (1) with the view of poverty as low utility, and (2) with seeing poverty in terms of low income (or, more generally, low holding of primary goods or of resources).[23] The analyses presented in the earlier chapters indicate why neither utility nor income (nor primary goods, nor resources) can be identified with well-being as such. But that fact is not decisive in determining the appropriate approach to poverty. In particular, since the concept of poverty has a well-recognized link with deprivation caused by economic problems, the approach of poverty as 'low income' needs further consideration.

It can be argued that poverty is not a matter of low well-being, but of the inability to pursue well-being precisely because of the lack of economic means. If Mr Richman has a high income and can buy whatever he needs, and still squanders the opportunities and ends up rather miserable, it would be odd to call him 'poor'. He had the means to live well and to lead a life without deprivation, and the fact that he managed nevertheless to generate some deprivation does not place him among the poor. This way of analysing the problem would seem to get one some distance towards seeing poverty in terms of income deprivation after all.

That line of reasoning certainly has some merit. It does indeed get us 'towards' seeing poverty in terms of income deprivation, but does not take us quite there. There are other distinctions to be considered. Perhaps the most important point to note is that the adequacy of the economic means cannot be judged independently of the actual possibilities of 'converting' incomes and resources into capability to function. The person with the kidney problem needing dialysis (in the example discussed earlier in this chapter) may have more income than the other person, but he is still short of economic means (indeed of income), *given* his problem in converting income and resources into functionings. If we want to identify poverty in terms of income, it cannot be adequate to look *only* at incomes (i.e. whether it is

[23] On related matters, see Goodin (1985, 1988).

generally low or high), independently of the capability to function derivable from those incomes. Income adequacy to escape poverty varies parametrically with personal characteristics and circumstances.[24]

The basic failure that poverty implies is one of having minimally adequate capabilities, even though poverty is also *inter alia* a matter of inadequacy of the person's economic means (the means to prevent the capability failure). Consider the example touched on earlier of the person with a high metabolic rate, or a large body size, or a parasitic disease that wastes nutrients. He is less able to meet minimal nutritional norms with the same level of income, compared with another person *without* those disadvantages. If he is to be seen as poorer than the second person, despite the fact that both have the same income, the reason for this lies in his greater capability failure (the focus of our concern). The same set of facts can also be seen as indicating the greater inadequacy of his income *given* his personal characteristics and circumstances. To have inadequate income is not a matter of having an income level below an externally fixed poverty line, but to have an income below what is adequate for generating the specified levels of capabilities for the person in question.

In the income space, the relevant concept of poverty has to be *inadequacy* (for generating minimally acceptable capabilities), rather than *lowness* (independently of personal characteristics).[25] A 'poverty line' that ignores individual characteristics altogether cannot do justice to our real concerns underlying poverty, viz. capability failure because of inadequate economic means. Often it will make sense to group individuals into particular categories (related to class, gender, occupational group, employment status, and so on).[26] If we choose to express poverty in the income space, then the incomes needed would have to be linked to the causal requirements of minimal capabilities.

This question relates to the fact that the primary concern in poverty analysis is with capability to function, rather than with achieved functionings. The example, discussed earlier, of the person with means who *fasts* out of choice, as opposed to another who *has to*

[24] On this, see also Himmelfarb (1984).
[25] Rowntree (1901, 1941) himself was much concerned with the issue of income inadequacy—and not just with its lowness—in his pioneering studies of poverty in Britain.
[26] The use of such categories is discussed in Ch. 8.

starve because of lack of means, is relevant here. Both may end up starving and fail to be adequately nourished, but the person without the means—and thus without the capability to be adequately nourished—is poor in a way that the fasting person is not. So the focus of attention of poverty analysis has to be capability as opposed to achievement (even though we may sometimes use information about achievement to try to *surmise* the capability enjoyed by a person).[27]

All this is close to the issue of the distinction between freedom and resources examined earlier (in Chapters 2 and 5). Resources *are* important for freedom, and income *is* crucial for avoiding poverty. But if our concern is ultimately with freedom, we cannot—given human diversity—treat resources as the same thing as freedom. Similarly, if our concern is with the failure of certain minimal capabilities because of lack of economic means, we cannot identify poverty simply as low income, dissociated from the interpersonally-variable connection between income and capability. It is in terms of capability that the adequacy of particular income levels has to be judged.

7.4. DO CONCEPTS MATTER?

The idea of 'income inadequacy', as discussed in the last section, goes well beyond that of 'low income' as such, since the former is sensitive to the conversion of income into capability in a way that the size of income as such cannot be. When the ranking of incomes goes opposite to the relative advantages in converting income into capability, the ordering of poverty and the identification of the poor may be very different if it is done entirely in terms of the size of income (as is the standard practice in most countries) compared with what it would be if the focus is on capability failure.

The problem is particularly serious with specific types of deprivation. For example, both because of biological reasons and social

[27] The fact that we are not classifying as 'poor' a person who has the capability to achieve good nourishment, but chooses not to, should not, of course, be taken to imply that such a person's deprivation should not command any sympathy or attention. As was discussed earlier (in Ch. 4), a person may give priority to non-well-being goals in his agency objectives, but that does not entail that *others* cannot have good reason to try to raise his low level of achieved well-being. Poverty is not the only reason for sympathetic regard from others. For example, while Mahatma Gandhi clearly had excellent reasons for fasting indefinitely in protest against the communal riots of 1947, his friends and well-wishers also had good reasons for trying to see that this did not lead to his fatal debilitation.

factors (especially as they operate with a resilient tradition of— explicit or implicit—sexism), women may have special disadvantages in converting income into particular functionings. To consider a variety of different types of cases, such disadvantages may apply to the capability of being nourished (e.g. because of the demands of pregnancy and neonatal care), achieving security (e.g. in single-parent families), having fulfilling work (e.g. because of stereotyping of 'women's jobs'), establishing one's professional reputation early on in one's career (e.g. because of the asymmetric demands of family life). The extent of deprivation may be underjudged if we concentrate only on the size of incomes, and the need to bring in capability failures explicitly can be particularly acute in such cases.

Similarly, the relationship between income and capability would be strongly affected by age (e.g. by the specific needs of the old and the very young), by location (e.g. by the special challenges to safety and security in urban living), by epidemiological atmosphere (e.g. vulnerability to diseases endemic in a region), and by many other parameters.[28] By focusing poverty study specifically on incomes as such, crucial aspects of deprivation may be entirely lost.[29]

Sometimes the same handicaps, such as age or disability or illness, that reduce one's ability to earn an income, can also make it harder to convert income into capability. Often, a high proportion of the poor in the advanced countries have such handicaps,[30] and the extent of poverty in such countries is substantially underestimated, since it overlooks the 'coupling' of income-*earning* handicap and income-*using* handicap in generating capability. For example, an old person has a much harder time in being free from disease, in leading a healthy life, in achieving mobility, in taking part in the life of the community, in seeing friends, and so on.[31] And these income-*using* disadvantages can tremendously compound the feature of low

[28] For analyses of some of the factors involved in the context of the United States, see the papers included in Danziger and Weinberg (1986). Illuminating analyses of different types of non-income variables influencing the extent of deprivation of the vulnerable in the USA can be found in Palmer, Smeeding, and Torrey (1988), Case and Katz (1990), and several other recent studies.

[29] In the 'Scandinavian studies on living conditions' the informational base has been widened to include important functionings (rather than just examining income and opulence), and the empirical works demonstrate how big a difference is made by this departure. On this, see Allardt (1981) and Erikson and Aberg (1987), and the literature cited there, and also Allardt (1992), Erikson (1992) and Ysander (1992).

[30] See Atkinson (1970a) and Townsend (1979).

[31] See Wedderburn (1961), Townsend (1979), Palmer, Smeeding, and Torrey (1988), Laslett (1991), among others.

earning power which is the only one that the traditional focus on income-based poverty analysis manages to capture.

7.5. POVERTY IN RICH COUNTRIES

Even the causes of the persistence of hunger in rich societies cannot be fully understood if we confine our attention only to the size of incomes. Hunger in the United States is associated with many parameters of which low income is only one.[32] The health aspects relate to the social environment, to the provision of medical care, to the pattern of family life, and a variety of other factors, and a purely income-based analysis of poverty cannot but leave that story half told.[33]

The extent of capability deprivation can be quite remarkably high in the world's most affluent countries. For example, a study by McCord and Freeman (1990), presented in *The New England Journal of Medicine*, indicates that men in the Harlem region of the prosperous city of New York have less chance of reaching the age of 40 or more than Bangladeshi men have. This is not because the residents of Harlem have lower incomes than the average Bangladeshi does. The phenomenon is more connected with problems of health care, inadequacy of medical attention, the prevalence of urban crime, and other such factors that affect the basic capabilities of the Harlem resident.

The problem is not confined only to 'pockets' of deprivation in a small number of places. There are systematic patterns of intense inequality in non-income features between different groups. For example, in an article in *The Journal of the American Medical Association*, Otten *et al.* (1990) show that in the age group between 35 and 55, African–Americans have 2.3 times the mortality rate as do whites in the United States, and that only about half their excess mortality can be explained by income differences. The need to go beyond the information on incomes to the pervasive diversities of social circumstances and characteristics is well illustrated by the nature of these terrible problems. The social environment is deeply

[32] On this, see School of Public Health, Harvard University (1985).

[33] For interesting empirical analyses related to this general issue in the context of the richer countries, see van Praag, Hagenaars, and van Weeren (1982) and Mack and Lansley (1985). See also the conceptual contributions to poverty study and its welfare-economic antecedents made by the Leiden School, e.g. van Praag (1968, 1978, 1991), Kapteyn and van Praag (1976).

influenced by the inadequacy of health facilities, the violent modes of inner-city living, the absence of social care, and such other factors. The lowness of income is only one factor among many that influence poverty in the United States.

The issue of food deprivation in rich America also raises a question of profound importance in understanding the nature of American poverty. Surprise is sometimes expressed at the fact there could be any actual *hunger* in a country as rich as the United States, where even the poorest groups tend to have much higher incomes than the middle-classes in many poorer countries who may not be particularly bothered by hunger as such. To some extent the difference may be due to the fact that money buys less of some types of commodities in the richer countries.[34] But even after corrections are made for these price differences, the paradoxical feature is still retained. Also, as it happens, food is not one of the items that are typically very much cheaper in the poorer countries than in the United States.

In explaining the apparent paradox, the capability perspective can help in two different ways. First, hunger and undernutrition are related both to food intake and to the ability to make nutritive use of that intake. The latter is deeply affected by general health conditions, and that in turn depends much on communal health care and public health provisions (a subject that will be further examined in the next section).[35] This is precisely where the civic problems of health delivery and inequalities in health care can precipitate capability failures in health and nutrition even when personal incomes are not that low in international standards.

Second, being poor in a rich society itself is a capability handicap for reasons that I have tried to discuss elsewhere.[36] *Relative* deprivation in the space of *incomes* can yield *absolute* deprivation in the space of *capabilities*. In a country that is generally rich, more income may be needed to buy enough commodities to achieve the *same social functioning*, such as 'appearing in public without shame'.[37] The same applies to the capability of 'taking part in the life of the community'.[38] These general social functionings impose commodity

---

[34] This relates to sharp differences in relative prices, on which see Usher (1968).

[35] On this, see Drèze and Sen (1989).

[36] See Sen (1983d), and also the exchange with Peter Townsend on this subject: Townsend (1985), Sen (1985c).

[37] This is an issue that Adam Smith had investigated with great clarity in the context of discussing the idea of 'necessary goods'; see Smith (1776: 351–2).

[38] On the importance of this achievement, see Townsend (1979).

requirements that vary with what *others* in the community standardly have.

While the rural Indian may have little problem in appearing in
public without shame with relatively modest clothing and can take
part in the life of the community without a telephone or a television,
the commodity requirements of these general functionings are much
more demanding in a country where people standardly use a bigger
basket of diverse commodities.[39] Not only does this make it more
expensive to achieve these *social functionings* themselves, but the
deflection of resources involved in pursuing these social functionings also drains the financial means that are potentially usable for
health and nutrition. The apparent paradox of hunger in the rich
countries is not hard to explain once our attention is shifted from
exclusive concentration on the space of incomes, so that we can take
note of the *conversion* of income and other resources into capabilities
of various types.

The distinction between 'low income' and 'capability failure' *does*
matter. A poverty analysis that concentrates only on incomes can be
quite remote from the main motivation behind our concern with
poverty (viz. the limitation of the *lives* that some people are forced to
live). It may also fail to provide empirical guidance regarding the
genesis and prevalence of deprivation.[40] Concentrating on the right
space is no less important for poverty study than it is for the general
investigation of social inequality.

[39] See Townsend (1979). Townsend interprets this aspect of poverty as requiring a
'thoroughgoing relativist' approach. On the other hand, it can be argued that while
this variability of commodity requirement shows the relativity of poverty in the space
of *commodities and incomes*, we are still concerned here with absolute deprivation in
the space of *capabilities* (e.g. not being able to take part in the life of the community).
This claim (see Sen 1983*d*) has led to a certain amount of heated—and not invariably
enlightening—debate (see Townsend 1985; Sen 1985*d*, Seidl 1986*a*; Desai and Shah
1988), but the main issue is fairly simple. The absolute-relative correspondence
relates to the variable commodity requirement for the *same* functioning (e.g. a much
larger need for commodities in richer countries to achieve the *same* functionings, such
as taking part in the life of the community, or—to go back to Adam Smith's
example—appearing in public without shame). While the minimally acceptable
capabilities to function may *also* vary from society to society, the variable commodity
requirement for the *same* capabilities does not, in itself, require that we take a
basically 'relativist' approach to poverty, provided we see poverty as capability
failure.

[40] On this question, see the results of the 'Scandinavian studies in living standards'
presented in Allardt (1981) and Erikson and Aberg (1987), and the literature cited
there. See also Allardt (1992), Erikson (1992) and Ysander (1992).

8

CLASS, GENDER AND OTHER GROUPS

8.1. CLASS AND CLASSIFICATION

As was discussed in the very first chapter of this monograph, the importance of the distinction between seeking equality in different *spaces* relates ultimately to the nature of human diversity. It is because we are so deeply diverse, that equality in one space frequently leads to inequality in other spaces. The force of the question 'equality of *what*?', thus, rests to a great extent on the empirical fact of our dissimilarity—in physical and mental abilities and disabilities, in epidemiological vulnerability, in age, in gender, and of course, in the social and economic bases of our well-being and freedom.

There are diversities of many different kinds. It is not unreasonable to think that if we try to take note of all the diversities, we might end up in a total mess of empirical confusion. The demands of practice indicate discretion and suggest that we disregard some diversities while concentrating on the more important ones. That bit of worldly wisdom is not to be scoffed at, and indeed, no serious study of inequality that is geared to practical reasoning and action can ignore the need to overlook a great deal of our immense range of diversities. The question in each context is: What are the significant diversities in *this* context?

In fact, general analyses of inequality must, in many cases, proceed in terms of groups—rather than specific individuals—and would tend to confine attention to *intergroup variations*.[1] In doing group analysis, we have to pick and choose between different ways of classifying people, and the classifications themselves select particu-

---

[1] A distinction has to be made between (1) an *intrinsic* interest in the inequality between different groups (viewed as *groups*), and (2) the *derivative* interest in group inequality because of what it says about inequality among individuals placed in different groups. Our focus here is on the latter. On the distinction between the two approaches and the ethical status of any *intrinsic* interest in group inequality, see among others Béteille (1983a, 1983b) and Loury (1987).

lar types of diversities rather than others. In the literature on inequality, the classification that has been, traditionally, most widely used has been that of economic class—either defined in terms of Marxian or some similar categories (mainly, concentrating on ownership of means of production and occupation), or seen in terms of income groups or wealth categories.[2]

The importance of this type of class-based classifications is obvious enough in most contexts. They also indicate why it is the case that equality in the space of, say, libertarian rights does not yield anything like equality of well-being, or equality of the overall freedoms to lead the lives that people may respectively value. They also draw attention to the importance of inequalities in wealth and income in generating unequal well-beings and living conditions, even when there is equality in *formal procedures* and in the allocation of some *specific facilities*—which are sometimes called, somewhat euphemistically, 'equality of opportunities'.[3] The crucial relevance of such class-based classifications is altogether undeniable in the context of general political, social, and economic analysis.

The class analysis is also central to the Marxian theory of 'exploitation'. The contrast between some people working hard and getting little income while others toil little and enjoy high income is one that has moved social critics to theorize the dichotomy in different ways. While Marx rejected Proudhon's diagnosis that property was 'theft', he did outline a system of accounting in terms of effective labour time that captured the contrast in a descriptively rich way.[4] But going further into production analysis, the theory of exploitation involved an identification of who is 'producing' what. Exploita-

---

[2] For examples of recent economic and social analyses making use of the ideas of class, income, and ownership, see Dalton (1925), Kuznets (1961, 1966, 1973), Lydall (1966), Atkinson (1972, 1975), Thurow (1975), Edwards, Reich, and Weisskopf (1986), Dahrendorf (1988). Recent analyses of Marxian class categories include such diverse contributors as Hobsbawm (1964), Miliband (1977), G. A. Cohen (1978, 1988), Kolakowski (1978), M. Cohen, Nagel, and Scanlon (1980), A. E. Buchanan (1982), Roemer (1982), Marglin (1984), Elster (1986), among many others.

[3] On the ambiguities of the concept of 'equal opportunities', see Thurow (1975), Le Grand (1982), Bayer, Caplan, and Daniels (1983), Béteille (1983a), Verba *et al.* (1987), Goodin (1988), Van Parijs (1990b, 1991). On the limits of what can be achieved by the standard imperatives of 'equality of opportunities' even in a country like the United States, see Jencks (1972).

[4] This was one of the uses to which Marx put the 'labour theory of value'. Indeed, both the major theories of value explored in the 19th cent.—the labour theory and the utility theory—paid much attention to descriptive richness, as opposed to just predictive usability. See Dobb (1937), Sen (1980b), Roemer (1982, 1986a).

tion was seen as the enjoyment of one person of the fruits of another's labour.

Diagnosis of who is producing what in an integrated system of production is not an easy task, and this is a difficulty that applies even to the later attempts—on the basis of neo-classical economic analysis—to attribute to each factor of production a definite share of the product. Such attribution plays a major part in normative theories of production-based 'desert', as reflected—in one form or another—in the writings of J. B. Clark (1902) and Peter Bauer (1981). Peter Bauer's attack on 'the unholy grail of equality' has many distinct features, but it turns crucially on the right of the 'producers' to enjoy the fruits of their production (as he puts it, 'it is by no means obvious why it should be unjust that those who produce more should enjoy higher income').[5]

The identification of who has produced what is, in fact, quite arbitrary in any integrated production structure. Production is an interdependent process involving the joint use of many resources, and there is in general no clear way of deciding which resource has produced what. The concept of the 'marginal product' of a resource is not really concerned with who has 'actually produced' what, but with guiding the allocation of resources by examining what would happen if one more unit of a resource were to be used (given all the other resources). To read in that *counterfactual* marginal story (what *would happen* if one more unit *were* applied, given everything else) an identification of who has 'in fact' produced what in the total output is to take the marginal calculus entirely beyond its purpose and depth.[6]

This problem of identification (who has produced what) applies to Marx's theory of exploitation as well—perhaps even more strongly, since the non-labour resources are treated in a very limited way. If that theory is to be seen not mainly as a significant description of the production process in terms of human work,[7] but as the usurping of one person's product by another, there remain many unanswered questions. Marx himself was fairly sceptical of this more

[5] Bauer (1981: 17). It was argued earlier—in Ch. 1—that despite Bauer's explicitly anti-egalitarian stand, his own theory insists on the *equal right* of the producers to enjoy what they have produced. We are not concerned with that particular issue here, but with the substantive content of the type of justice Bauer seeks.

[6] I have discussed this issue in Sen (1985*e*).

[7] See Dobb (1937) for the classic exposition of the view of labour theory—and also of utility theory—as rich description.

assertive diagnosis. Even though he did invoke it in many contexts, he refused to see it as the central distributive concern in his evaluative system (discussed most clearly in his 'Critique of the Gotha Program', Marx 1875).

In analysing the relation between economic opportunities and freedoms, the tradition of classification based on the so-called Marxian classes can be quite inadequate. There are many other diversities, and an approach to equality related to the fulfilment of needs or to ensuring freedoms has to go beyond purely class-based analysis. For example, even if inequalities based on property ownership are eliminated altogether, there can be serious inequalities arising from diversities in productive abilities, needs, and other personal variations.

The case for going beyond class analysis was, in fact, persuasively made by Marx (1875) himself in chastising the German Workers Party for taking for granted that equality in rewards for *work* would not conflict with equality in satisfying *needs*.

But one man is superior to another physically or mentally and so supplies more labour in the same time, or can labour for a longer time; and labour, to serve as a measure, must be defined by its duration or intensity, otherwise it ceases to be a standard of measurement. This equal right is an unequal right for unequal labour.[8]

Marx saw the insistence on equal reward for equal work— irrespective of needs—as an extension of a 'bourgeois right' seeing human beings only as producers (Marx 1875: 9). The diversities *within* the category of the working class made Marx insist on the need to seek other classifications. In fact, productivity differences constituted only one of Marx's concerns. He also focused attention on the necessity to address our manifold diversities, including differences in needs, and this led him to the well-known slogan 'from each according to his ability to each according to his needs'. An essential part of Marx's complaint was about the mistake of seeing human beings 'from one definite side only', in particular seeing people '*only as workers*, and nothing more seen in them, everything else being ignored'.[9]

As an illustration Marx had referred specifically to the fact that different workers have families of different size.[10] While it could be

[8] Marx (1875: 9).   [9] Marx (1875: 9). On this distinction, see also *OEI*, ch. 4.
[10] 'Further, one worker is married, and another not; one has more children than another and so on and so forth' (Marx 1875: 9).

argued that as far as the parents are concerned, the number of children are, at least partly, within their control (and therefore a subject on which their own responsibility must be accepted), that argument would not reduce at all the force of the claims of the children themselves.[11] The differential needs arising from unequal family size can be, to some extent, accommodated within the income-based approach by suitable normalization and by the use of 'equivalence scales'.[12] But the more general problem of need variations cannot be similarly handled. Equality of incomes, or—more generally—of primary goods or resources, can fail to yield equal satisfaction of needs, when needs vary interpersonally and so does the transformation of resources into need-fulfilment. In pursuing the demands of equality in the space of well-being, or need-fulfilment, we have to go beyond the income-based categories and also the so-called Marxian classes (indeed, as Marx himself had argued).

This argument is exactly parallel to the one, discussed earlier, of the variable conversion rates of incomes, primary goods, and resources into freedom to do, to be, and to live the way one would like. Pervasive human diversity is the source of both the problems and the reason for their respective importance. After acknowledging and taking on board the widespread relevance of the diversity of class, ownership, and occupation, we also have to go well beyond that to other diversities that influence the lives that we can lead and the freedoms we can enjoy.

Sometimes the other sources of disparity may be *partly* associated with class, but diverge from it in specific respects with influences of their own. For example, race and colour may have good statistical correlation with class in the United States or the United Kingdom, but the deprivation associated with being black is not *just* a matter of its class correlates. The way a person is viewed in a society with racial disparity may be deeply influenced by his or her visible racial characteristics, and that can act as a barrier to functioning possibili-

---

[11] This is not to deny that there is an 'incentive issue' also involved in offering larger social help for larger families, and problems of population policy cannot be ignored in this context. But that incentive argument has to be tempered by the concern for the well-being and capabilities of the disadvantaged members of the larger families among the poor.

[12] See Barten (1964), Muellbauer (1974*a*, 1974*b*, 1987), Pollak and Wales (1979, 1981), Deaton (1980, 1988), Deaton and Muellbauer (1980, 1986), Blackorby, Donaldson, and Auersperg (1981), Atkinson (1983, 1989), Jorgenson and Slesnick (1983, 1984*a*, 1984*b*, 1987), Blackorby and Donaldson (1984, 1988), Atkinson and Bourguignon (1987), Buhmann *et al.* (1988), among other contributions.

ties in many circumstances. Distinctions of caste similarly have influences of their own, despite being frequently correlated with class.[13] Race or caste can be a factor with far-reaching influence on many aspects of day-to-day living—varying from securing employment and receiving medical attention to being fairly treated by the police. Inequalities in the distribution of income and ownership will typically be *part* of the story, but by no means the whole of it.

8.2. GENDER AND INEQUALITY

One basis of classification that is particularly relevant in this context is gender. There are systematic disparities in the freedoms that men and women enjoy in different societies, and these disparities are often not reducible to differences in income or resources. While differential wages or payment rates constitute an important part of gender inequality in most societies, there are many other spheres of differential benefits, e.g. in the division of labour within the household, in the extent of care or education received, in liberties that different members are permitted to enjoy.[14]

Indeed, in the context of intrahousehold divisions, it is not easy to split up the total household income into the incomes going respectively to different members of the family. The sharing may take an unequal form, especially in relation to needs, but this is hard to translate into income differentials, which would be an odd concept to use in examining intrahousehold divisions.[15] Inequality inside the

---

[13] See Srinivas (1962) and Béteille (1981, 1983a, 1987, 1990).

[14] On different aspects of 'the gender gap', see Amsden (1980), Okin (1987, 1989), Bergmann (1986), Goldin (1989), Folbre *et al.* (1991), Nussbaum (1991a, 1991b), R. A. Putnam (1991), Annas (1992), O'Neill (1992), among other contributions.

[15] The use of 'household-equivalence scales' provides a way of making *inter*household comparisons, typically *assuming* no differential treatment *within* the household, even though that feature can to some extent be altered by discriminating analysis (see Muellbauer 1987; Deaton 1988; Blackorby and Donaldson 1988). But it is, in general, informationally limited to the extent that the observations do not directly include actual functionings (e.g. individual undernutrition or morbidity) and concentrates instead only on aggregate consumption patterns and commodity compositions of the household. However, sometimes the limitations of data regarding functionings can make this approach the best that can, in those circumstances, be used.

household is one of resource-*use* and of the *transformation* of the used resources into capability to function, and neither class of information is well captured by any devised notion of 'income distribution' within the family.

There is a lot of indirect evidence of differential treatment of women and men, and particularly of girls *vis-à-vis* boys, in many parts of the world, e.g. among rural families in Asia and North Africa.[16] The observed morbidity and mortality rates frequently reflect differential female deprivation of extraordinary proportions.

Even the crude ratio of women to men in the total population varies between only 0.93 and 0.96 in South Asia, West Asia, North Africa, and China. In contrast, partly because of the biological advantages that women seem to have over men (given symmetric care), the female–male ratio in the population tends to be much higher than unity (around 1.05 or so) in Europe and North America. It is, of course, quite possible that a part of the higher mortality rate of the males in the richer countries reflect social rather than biological factors.[17] For example, there is considerable evidence of greater incidence of death from violence for men in many societies, such as the USA. There are also some effects of higher male mortality due to war deaths. But there does seem to be a substantial biological component in the advantages in favour of women, *given* similar treatment.[18] The mortality differential *against* women in Asia and North Africa, thus, reflects quite a remarkable departure from what could be expected on the basis of biological potentials, given symmetric care (on this see Sen, 1989a). The higher mortality and morbidity of women *vis-à-vis* men in these countries reflect serious 'attainment inequality', in addition to exhibiting

---

[16] On this see, among many other contributions, Boserup (1970, 1987, 1990), Tinker and Bramsen (1976), A. Mitra (1980), Miller (1981), L. C. Chen, Huq, and D'Souza (1981), Rosenzweig and Schultz (1982), Buvinic, Lycette, and McGreevey (1983), Kynch and Sen (1983), Sen and Sengupta (1983), P. Bardhan (1984, 1987), Sen (1984, 1985d, 1988c, 1990c), Jain and Banerjee (1985), Kynch (1985), M. Chen (1986a, 1986b), Banister (1987), Harriss and Watson (1987), Das Gupta (1987), M. Vaughan (1987), A. Basu (1988), Behrman (1988, 1992), Behrman and Deolalikar (1988), Kumar (1989), Sen (1989a, 1990b), Tinker (1990a), Kanbur and Haddad (1990), Harriss (1990), Whitehead (1990).

[17] On the general issue of cultural influences on gender differences in demographic factors, see Johansson (1991).

[18] On this, see I. Waldron (1976, 1983). The biological advantages seem to apply even in the womb, with female foetuses having a lower rate of miscarriage than their male counterparts.

extraordinary extents of 'shortfall inequality', given the biological potential in the *opposite* direction.[19]

In the context of many developing countries, these are elementary and important aspects of gender inequality, and their assessment need not be derivative on any constructed concept of income inequality *within* the family. They reflect functioning differences and the corresponding disparities in the elementary capabilities to avoid escapable morbidity and preventable mortality. We are not concerned here with the causal factors underlying these gender inequalities,[20] but with the prior exercise of identifying the nature of the problem of gender inequality. Here a departure from the traditional perspective of income distribution towards direct accounting of functionings and capabilities can be an important step.[21]

Even when the gender differentials in morbidity and mortality are not so acute, there can be disparities in other important functionings and capabilities yielding substantial inequalities in freedoms.

[19] For example, if India had the African ratio (1.02) of females to males (not to take up the very high ratio of 1.05 or so of the long-lived European or North American population), rather than the ratio it does actually have (0.93), then—given the number of males in the country—there would have been nearly 30 million more women in India in the mid-1980s. The corresponding number of 'missing women' in China (*vis-à-vis* the African ratio) is close to 40 million (see Drèze and Sen 1989). To provide serious quantitative estimates of 'missing women', proper demographic models of births and deaths would have to be considered (with clear specification of the possible counterfactual scenarios), but we get some idea of the enormity of the problem from even these crude estimates of the millions involved (based on using the ratios obtaining in sub-Saharan Africa). For analyses of the different economic, social, and cultural factors underlying the problem of 'missing women', see Sen (1988*c*, 1989*a*) and Drèze and Sen (1989).

[20] I have tried to discuss them elsewhere, in Sen (1984, 1985*d*, 1989*a*, 1990*c*). For analyses of various aspects of this question, see also Boserup (1970, 1987, 1990), Gardiner, Himmelweit, and Mackintosh (1975), Banerjee (1979, 1982), Loutfi (1980), Manser and Brown (1980), McElroy and Horney (1981), Miller (1981, 1984), Rochford (1981), Young, Wolkowitz, and McCullagh (1981), Beneria (1982), Dixon (1982, 1983), Rosenzweig and Schultz (1982), Ahmed (1983), Buvinic, Lycette, and McGreevey (1983), Kynch and Sen (1983), Sen and Sengupta (1983), P. Bardhan (1984, 1987), Folbre (1984), K. Bardhan (1985), Jain and Banerjee (1985), Mazumdar (1985), Agarwal (1986, 1991), M. Chen (1986*a*, 1986*b*), Banister (1987), Behrman (1988), Das Gupta (1987), Harriss and Watson (1987), A. Basu (1988), Okin (1989), Harriss (1990), Papanek (1990), Tinker (1990*a*), Allen (1991), Folbre *et al.* (1991), among other contributions.

[21] This does not deny that differential earning power of women *vis-à-vis* men may affect the status of women (on this, see Boserup 1970; P. Bardhan 1984; Sen 1984, 1985*d*, 1990*c*, K. Bardhan 1985), or influence economic calculations underlying child care (on this see Rosenzweig and Schultz 1982). That is a separate issue requiring *causal* analysis of the role of income-earning power, and must be distinguished from the problem of *diagnosis* of gender inequality.

While anti-female bias in nutrition, morbidity, or mortality is much less present in sub-Saharan Africa,[22] there are often big gender differences in many other capabilities, such as being able to read and write, avoiding bodily mutilation, being free to pursue independent careers, or being in positions of leadership.

In terms of many social functionings, gender differences can be important also in the rich countries of Europe and North America, even though in terms of survival and mortality, women do have a relative advantage (at least in terms of attainment, if not in shortfall avoidance). I shall not have the opportunity of pursuing this question further here,[23] but I would argue that the question of gender inequality in the advanced societies—no less than in developing countries—can be understood much better by comparing those things that intrinsically matter (such as functionings and capabilities), rather than just the means like primary goods or resources. The issue of gender inequality is ultimately one of disparate freedoms.

8.3. INTERREGIONAL CONTRASTS

Before closing this chapter, I would like to discuss some empirical examples of interregional contrasts to illustrate the importance of the distinction between judging poverty by income and judging it by the capability to achieve some basic functionings.

Some of the most important functionings for living standard, including the most elementary one of being able to live long (without being grabbed by premature mortality), often diverge from real income per head in a really spectacular way. This is easily seen in making international comparisons of gross national product (GNP) per head and life expectancy at birth.[24] In terms of per capita GNP, South Africa ($2,470), Brazil ($2,540), Gabon ($2,960), and Oman

---

[22] On the relatively better nutritional situation of girls *vis-à-vis* boys in many parts of Africa, see Svedberg (1988, 1990). See also Deaton (1988).

[23] I have, elsewhere, tried to discuss the general question of gender inequality as unequal outcomes of 'co-operative conflicts' in the broad perspective of inequality or entitlements and capabilities; see Sen (1981a, 1985d, 1990c). See also Kynch and Sen (1983), Sen and Sengupta (1983), Bryceson (1985), Jain and Banerjee (1985), Kynch (1985), Tilly (1985), Vaughan (1985, 1987), Brannen and Wilson (1987), Wilson (1987), Aslanbeigui and Summerfield (1989), Drèze and Sen (1989), Papanek (1990), Tinker (1990a), UNDP (1990), Agarwal (1991), M. Chen (1991), Ahmad *et al.* (1991).

[24] The data on international comparisons are taken from the *World Development Report 1991* (World Bank 1991). See also UNICEF (1987, 1992), UNDP (1990, 1991) on related matters. The figures are in US dollars.

($5,220) have six or more times the per capita GNP of China ($350) and Sri Lanka ($430). But these relatively richer countries give their people significantly lower ability to survive premature mortality (with life expectancies varying between 53 and 66 years) than do the two lower-income countries (with life expectancies around 70 years or more). Costa Rica, which is also considerably poorer than the first four countries, offers not only a much higher life expectancy than those four (and other 'upper-middle-income countries'), but a life expectancy that is not significantly below those obtaining in the richest countries of Europe and North America (with ten or more times Costa Rica's GNP per head). For example, the USA with a GNP per head of $20,910 has a life expectancy at birth of 76 years, whereas Costa Rica with a GNP per head of only $1,780 has already achieved a life expectancy of 75 years.

As we move our attention from commodities and income to functionings and capabilities, the relative picture can change radically. The difference seems to relate to a great extent to differences in the social, educational, and epidemiological conditions. The achievements of China, Sri Lanka, and Costa Rica in quality of life has much to do with policies regarding communal health services, medical care, and basic education.[25] Thus, this distinction between deprivation of income and that of the capability to achieve elementary functionings, also has some relevance for public policy— both for development and for the removal of poverty and inequality.[26]

Another interesting exercise relates to contrasts *within* a large country, e.g. India. Among the Indian states, Kerala has one of the lower real incomes per head, but by a long margin the highest life expectancy at birth—over 70 years (compared with around 57 years for India as a whole).[27] Its infant mortality rate is, correspondingly,

[25] In the case of China, the big surge in life expectancy and decline in mortality rates took place *before* the economic reforms of 1979, and occurred actually in a period of very moderate economic growth and virtually stagnant food output per head. In contrast, in the post-reform period growth of GNP has been fast, but progress in life expectancy seems to have faltered a little. On this and related matters, see C. Riskin (1987) and Drèze and Sen (1989).

[26] Of course, life expectancy, literacy, and other common indicators of 'quality of life' are not, by themselves, anywhere near adequate in reflecting the overall picture of the capability to achieve valuable functionings, but they are important *parts* of the overall picture.

[27] The Sample Registration Survey for 1986–8 yields a figure of 73.2 years for females and 67.0 years for males for Kerala as a whole.

much lower than the Indian average.[28] Kerala also has a much higher level of general literacy (91 per cent, as opposed to the Indian average of 52 per cent), and particularly female literacy (87 per cent, compared with the national average of 39 per cent).[29] Indeed, Kerala's achievements for many crucially important functionings are not only very much better than those of the rest of India, but they have an edge in some fields—especially with respect to women—even over China and Sri Lanka. For example, the low female–male ratio that characterizes China as well as India as a whole (around 0.93), in contrast with the substantial *excess* of females over males in Europe, North America, and sub-Saharan Africa (discussed earlier in this chapter), does not apply to Kerala. The female–male ratio for Kerala is 1.04, which is very similar to the ratios around 1.05 in Europe and North America.[30]

If the value of average GNP is 'corrected' by taking note of distributional inequality, the income perspective is made somewhat more articulate. But even with this adjustment (i.e. even when distribution-corrected measures of real income are used), Kerala still remains one of the poorer Indian states.[31] Distributional corrections do not seem to eliminate adequately the deficiency of the income approach to explain the high capability levels in Kerala to escape premature mortality. The deficiency of the income approach is not adequately remedied by supplementing the average income figures

[28] However, Kerala does have a much higher self-reported morbidity rate than the rest of India (on this question and related issues, see Panikar and Soman 1984; Kumar 1987, 1989; Vaidyanathan 1987). This may, to some extent, reflect the low-income level of the Kerala population and possible nutritional deficiencies resulting therefrom. But to a great extent the higher self-reported morbidity seems to be a consequence of more *awareness* of health status on the part of the Kerala population, largely related to greater literacy and higher use of health services. Indeed, the self-reported morbidity rates are lowest in the least literate states of Bihar and Uttar Pradesh, which have very high mortality rates (combined with illiteracy). And as Murray and Chen (1990) have shown in a recent paper, using similar criteria of self-reporting of morbidity, the United States has even higher rates of reported ill-health than Kerala. Incidentally, this inverse connection between self-perception of illness and observed mortality rates also illustrates the pitfalls of going only by self-perception in judging well-being (discussed in Ch. 3).

[29] The Indian comparative data are taken from publications and working papers of the office of the Registrar General and Census Commissioner of India, including *Census of India 1991: Provisional Population Totals* (New Delhi: Government of India, 1991). The literacy data relate to the population aged 7 years or more.

[30] In fact, the ratios would possibly not be materially different if the effects of the differentially higher male mortality of Europeans and North Americans due to past wars were to be factored out.

[31] See Sen (1976*b*) and Bhattacharya, Chatterjee, and Pal (1988).

by considerations of inequality of incomes and commodity holdings.

The explanation of Kerala's success in the important space of basic capabilities has to be sought in the history of public policy involving education (including female literacy) and health services (including communal medical care), and to some extent, food distribution (including the use of public support of food consumption of the rural as well as the urban population), in contrast with the rest of India. There are also other factors involved, including a more favourable position of women in property rights and in inheritance among a substantial and influential section of Kerala's population, and the greater public activism connected with educational campaigns as well as politics in general. The history of public action in Kerala goes back a long time, with remarkable literacy campaigns in the native states of Travancore and Cochin in the nineteenth century.

This monograph does not, of course, provide the occasion to go into details of policy issues,[32] but it is important to emphasize that the evaluative perspective of the capability approach does draw our attention forcefully to examining and scrutinizing such policy questions. It also suggests the need to take a broad view of development efforts, going far beyond the focus on improving the national output and the distribution of incomes.

[32] These diverse matters (including the international comparisons and the regional contrasts within in India) have been discussed, with a focus on policy issues, in Drèze and Sen (1989).

9

THE DEMANDS OF EQUALITY

9.1. QUESTIONS OF EQUALITY

This monograph has had two rather different—though inter-related—objectives. The first aim is primarily methodological, the second mainly substantive.

The first set of issues is concerned with understanding the relevance and reach of the questions that can be legitimately asked about egalitarianism, in particular, 'why equality?' and 'equality of what?'. In that context, it is important to come to grips both (1) with the diversity of human beings (the fact that we differ from each other in personal characteristics as well as external circumstances), and (2) with the plurality of relevant 'spaces' in which equality can be judged (the multiplicity of variables—incomes, wealths, utilities, liberties, primary goods, capabilities—which can respectively serve as the sphere of comparison). The demands of equality in the different spaces do not coincide with each other precisely because human beings are so diverse. Equality in one space goes with substantial inequalities in others.

The second set of exercises relates to exploring a particular substantive approach to equality. While I began with methodological issues (Chapter 1), the bulk of the book has been concerned with substantive matters. The particular approach to equality that I have explored involves judging individual advantage by *the freedom to achieve*, incorporating (but going beyond) *actual achievements*. In many contexts, particularly in the assessment of individual well-being, these conditions can, I have argued, be fruitfully seen in terms of *the capability to function*, incorporating (but going beyond) the actual functionings that a person can achieve. The 'capability approach' builds on a general concern with freedoms to achieve (including the capabilities to function).

The capability approach points to the need to examine freedom to achieve in general and capabilities to function in particular. In addition to discussing the motivation underlying the capability approach, I have also tried to consider how we might address the difficulties in interpreting and defending this view (Chapters 2 and 3). I have gone on to examine the implications of this approach for assessing freedom and advantage (Chapter 4), for theories of justice (Chapter 5), for the welfare economics of inequality evaluation (Chapter 6), for the assessment of poverty in rich as well as poor countries (Chapter 7), and for analysing inequalities associated with categories such as class, gender, and other groups (Chapter 8).

In this final chapter I shall try to review and assess some of the general points that have emerged from the preceding analysis (even though there will be no attempt to 'summarize' the discussions presented, or 'list' the specific conclusions reached). I shall be particularly concerned with the interrelations between the methodological and substantive issues.

9.2. EQUALITY, SPACE AND DIVERSITY

It was argued, in Chapter 1, that the often-asked question 'why equality?' can be quite misleading. Every plausibly defendable ethical theory of social arrangements tends to demand equality in *some* 'space', requiring equal treatment of individuals in some significant respect—in terms of some variable that is important in that particular theory. The 'space' that is invoked does differ from theory to theory. For example, 'libertarians' are concerned with equal liberties; 'economic egalitarians' argue for equal incomes or wealths; utilitarians insist on equal weight on everyone's utilities in a consequentialist maximand; and so on. But in each system a demand for equality—in its own form—is incorporated as a foundational feature of that system. What really distinguishes the different approaches is the variation in their respective answers to the question 'equality of what?'. *That* question is truly central in understanding the distinctions between the diverse ethical approaches to social arrangements.

I have also argued that there are good reasons why all the major ethical theories of social organization tend to demand equality in some space—a space that has some basic importance in that theory. There is a connection here with the foundational need for the plausibility of a theory to extend equal consideration to all, in some crucial way (related to the structure of that theory).[1] This diagnosis does not, of course, suggest that we should 'do away' with the ques-

[1] I have examined some of the issues involved in this diagnosis in Sen (1985*a*).

tion 'why equality?'. Each specific theory of equality in *any* space does require a defence. But the nature, content, and demands of the query 'why equality?' can be understood and examined only by relating it to the central question 'equality of what?'.

Each approach has its own interpretation of what we have been calling 'basal equality'—equality in some individual feature that is taken to be basic in that particular conception of social justice and political ethics. That foundational concern leads to a particular way of interpreting the demands of symmetry and impartiality, and this in its turn disputes the case for insisting on equality in *other* spaces—seen as less basic in the light of that theory. For example, to demand equal entitlements to an extensive set of libertarian rights as a basic requirement of social organization (as is done by Nozick 1974) has the consequence of undermining any insistence on the equality of incomes, wealths, or utilities, as well. Similarly, if equal incomes are to be achieved, then we could not insist also on equality in utilities, or rights, or freedoms. An immovable object leaves little room, in principle, for any irresistible force.

Conflicts that *can* arise in principle need not, however, arise in practice. The need to determine conceptual priorities—important in principle—becomes momentous in practice because of the far-reaching diversities of human beings (the reach of these diversities was extensively discussed in the previous chapters). The demands of equality in different spaces tend to conflict, *in fact* (not just in principle), with each other. Thus, the choice of basal equality has tremendous practical importance in asserting some claims and denying others. The need for ensuring the fulfilment of basal demands, including basal equality, necessitates the tolerance of inequality in what are seen as the outlying 'peripheries'.

9.3. PLURALITY, INCOMPLETENESS AND EVALUATION

The demands of equality can take various forms, and a certain amount of plurality of concerns is inescapable in the evaluation of basal equality itself. This can introduce some ambiguities in characterizing the conditions under which equality can be taken to be complete (or 'full'), and—perhaps more importantly—in ranking alternative possibilities in terms of their *extents* of inequality (i.e. in judging the respective 'distances' from full equality). The source of these problems lies in what may be called 'internal plurality', relating to: (1) the heterogeneity of the space in terms of which basal equality is defined, and (2) the different ways in which 'distances' may be measured and inequalities compared in the distributions even of a *homogeneous* variable.

Some of the basal variables certainly have much heterogeneity within their own respective categories.[2] For example, the liberty that is championed by libertarians would inevitably involve different types of rights, covering different spheres and taking various forms (such as 'claims', 'immunities', 'powers', etc.).[3] Similarly, primary goods are of different types. Different capabilities are distinct from each other. Even utilities are diverse.[4]

It is also possible for an ethical theory to include more than one type of variables in the category of basal significance. We may be concerned both with liberties and with levels of well-being. We may attach intrinsic importance both to well-being and to agency. We may value freedom as well as achievement.[5] Indeed, pluralist proposals make up much of practical ethics, even though descriptive homogeneity evidently appeals to many moral philosophers (utilitarians among them).[6]

There are also different ways of evaluating equality in the *same* homogeneous space, using distinct methods of *measuring* inequality. Variations in inequality indicators in a *given* space (e.g. coefficient of variation, Gini coefficient, standard deviation of logarithms, measures of entropy) have been extensively discussed in the literature.[7] The ideas underlying the discipline of measurement vary greatly among the different measures, and while many of these ideas have good reasons behind them, they often conflict with each other.

Different features of basal equality can, therefore, suggest different rankings of particular situations. Sometimes the plurality

[2] This question was discussed in the specific context of the heterogeneity of functionings in Ch. 3.

[3] See Kanger (1957, 1972, 1985), Lindahl (1977), Raz (1986).

[4] The claim that different types of utilities have different status in human well-being and in social relevance can be traced back to Aristotle and was emphasized also by John Stuart Mill (1859, 1861).

[5] In the previous chapters I have discussed the force of these considerations seen severally and jointly (Chs. 2–4).

[6] The belief that ethical pluralism lacks sophistication is of respectable ancestry (going back at least to John Stuart Mill), but it is not particularly sound for that reason (or any other). I have tried to discuss this question in Sen (1985*a*). On related matters, see B. Williams (1973*a*, 1985), Nagel (1979), Hurley (1989).

[7] It was one of the main subjects of *OEI*. Helpful accounts of the literature can be found in Cowell (1977), Foster (1985), and Lambert (1989).

arising from these sources may be reduced through scrutinized exclusion of the claims of particular elements in the initial plurality. At other times the plurality can be lessened through 'combining' or 'uniting' the considerations by some procedure of evaluative weighting. But even after all these reductions are carried out, there may remain some residual plurality, with consequent ambiguities in the ordering of equalities and inequalities.

The presence of ambiguities of this type is, in fact, a central problem in decision theory and in social choice theory, and can arise in many different contexts. Several lines of analysis have, in fact, been proposed to address the demands of reasoned decision despite residual ambiguity (or 'unresolved conflicts').[8] One simple line of—relatively unambitious—reasoning, which was much used in my earlier book on inequality (*OEI*), involves separating out a *shared partial ranking* in which all the desirable features move together. An 'intersection' partial ordering places x above y if and only if x is better than y according to *all* the desirable features.

In the context of the capability approach, the problems of selection and weighting of different functionings and capabilities were discussed earlier (in Chapter 3). There are various analytical and logistic issues involved in evaluating functioning vectors (and capability sets consisting of such vectors), but the techniques of 'dominance' and of 'intersection' are not only consistent and cogent, they can also, typically, take us quite a substantial distance.[9]

The use of 'intersections' does not, of course, obviate the necessity of thoroughly scrutinizing the claims of each allegedly 'desirable feature'. But when the different criteria that survive scrutiny actually conflict in ranking two alternatives, the pair has to be left unranked. Sometimes further analysis or more information may permit us to cut down the 'pluralities' that have to be accommodated. When that occurs, the intersection partial ordering can be correspondingly *extended*—ordering pairs that could not be ranked earlier.[10] In this sense an intersection partial ordering would typically be tentative, and always open to extension if and when reasons are found to cut down the relevant pluralities (through scrutinized elimination of some features, or weighted combining of distinct aspects). The

---

[8] Some of the problems involved are discussed in Sen (1970*a*, 1982*a*), Suzumura (1983), and Levi (1986). See also the literature on 'fuzzy' sets and preferences.

[9] I have tried to discuss the scope and range of the 'intersection' analysis in Sen (1970*a*, 1970*b*, 1985*b*).

[10] On this general question, see Sen (1970*a*, 1970*b*, 1982*a*).

distinction between 'foundational' and 'pragmatic' incompleteness discussed in Chapter 3 is relevant in this context.[11]

The need to admit incompleteness in inequality evaluation is inescapable, and there is much to be said for addressing that question explicitly rather than in grudgingly implicit ways. The incompleteness may be due to the nature of the concept itself (e.g. the idea of equality may *incorporate* substantial ambiguities), or because of the absence of information (e.g. data may be lacking that would permit some comparisons to be made), or due to the need to respect residual disagreements among the parties involved (e.g. this would relate to the acceptance of plurality as a part of an approach to fairness and justice). To 'complete' partial orderings *arbitrarily* for the sake of decisiveness, or convenience, or order, or some other worthy concern, may be a very misleading step to take. Even when the partial ranking is quite extensively incomplete, the case against 'forcing' completeness may be quite strong. Babbling is not, in general, superior to being silent on matters that are genuinely unclear or undecided.

However, one consequence of adopting such a 'partial ranking' view of interpersonal comparisons and of the assessment of equality is to admit the possibility that in many situations no clear judgement can be made as to whether there is more equality in situation a than in situation b.[12] Those who see equality as a clear, articulate, and decisive arbitrator of every social or political dispute would find this position particularly unattractive. I don't share that disappointment, for reasons that I have discussed (in Chapters 1–4).[13] Nor do I see that arbitrarily completing a partial order does much justice to the idea of equality, or—for that matter—helps to ensure that the demands of equality would receive attention when it *does* have something clear and compelling to say. There is even a real danger of undermining the concern for reducing inequality by an over-ambitious programme of trying to catch all the little gaps that may be detectable in some very particular scaling but which would be hard to see in terms of other plausible views. A more solid founda-

---

[11] See Sect. 3.4. Different reasons for accepting some foundational incompleteness has been discussed in Chs. 1–4.

[12] It must, however, be emphasized that in identifying *poverty* and social *deprivation* much can be fruitfully said even with a list of levels of capabilities that are taken to be minimally necessary, and this does not require anything like an ordering of different bundles of capabilities. On this, see Sen (1984) and Hossain (1990).

[13] Also in Sen (1970a, 1973a).

tion can be built for the rejection of substantial inequalities—visible from different angles—by not lumping them together with more fine-tuned presumptions.

9.4. DATA, OBSERVATIONS AND EFFECTIVE FREEDOMS

The limits of practical calculations are also set by data restrictions, and this can be particularly hard on the representation of capability sets, as opposed to observed functioning achievements. When the data simply do not exist to calculate the extents of the respective capability sets, there is no option but to settle for the chosen functioning combination as the basis for forming a view of the opportunities that were actually enjoyed.[14] In many situations, practical compromises would have to be made, at least partially. But even when the pragmatic acceptance of limitations of data availability force us to set our sights lower than the full representation of capability sets, it is important to keep the underlying motivations clearly in view and to see practical compromises as the best we can do under the circumstances.

It is also relevant to note here that even for assessing freedom, the perspective of 'effective freedom' as opposed to 'freedom as control' can permit some limited comparisons of freedoms (in the form of counterfactual choice) on the basis of observed outcomes. The argument was outlined in Chapter 4, and it involved defending references to freedom in such expressions as 'freedom from hunger' or 'freedom from malaria'. I have argued that these uses of the term freedom need not illustrate just loose talk (as they are often taken to be), since an important concept of freedom is, in fact, involved in these outcome-based judgements of freedom. If that argument is accepted, then the observed functionings can, in particular circumstances, tell us something not merely about well-beings achieved, but also about freedoms enjoyed. For the main theses of this monograph, it is not, of course, necessary that there be general acceptance of the relevance of this view of effective freedom and of counterfactual choice (giving it the limited but important role for which I have tried to argue). But if that view *is* accepted, then there would be a bit more articulation on some aspects of freedom and inequality than would otherwise be possible on the basis of available data.

---

[14] There may, of course, be various degrees of data unavailability, and the choice need not take an 'either-or' form.

9.5. AGGREGATION, EGALITARIANISM AND EFFICIENCY

The understanding of 'internal plurality' *within* the demands of
basal equality has to be supplemented by the recognition of claims
other than those of basal equality in general. No matter which space
is chosen for the assessment of equality, a conflict can arise between
aggregative considerations (e.g. generally enhancing individual advantages, no matter how distributed) and *distributive* ones (e.g.
reducing disparities in the distribution of advantages). Considerations of 'efficiency'—much discussed in economics—reflect a
common element in aggregative concerns.[15] When it is expressed in
the form of a demand that no dominant improvement (enhancing the
position of each) should be left undone, there is an appeal to a
particularly non-controversial part of our aggregative moral
sentiments.

In economics, the demands of efficiency frequently take the special
form of 'Pareto optimality', which is defined in the particular space
of utilities. It is a weak condition of unimprovability, demanding
that there remains no possibility of any change that raises the utilities
of all.[16] Pareto efficiency is almost certainly the most widely used
criterion in modern welfare economics, and its acceptability is
typically taken to be entirely non-controversial. Disputations on
the acceptability of Pareto efficiency as a necessary condition of
social optimality relates to the status of the utility space itself.[17]
They rarely take the form of questioning the case for carrying out
dominant improvements in what would be accepted as the relevant
space (enhancing the position of each in that space). The question is
whether utilities constitute the relevant space. What is disputed in

[15] Note that this part of the aggregative consideration can be used even when there
is interpersonal incomparability in the variable in question (e.g. individual utilities
are non-comparable).

[16] A stronger version ('strong Pareto optimality') is also used, particularly in
welfare economics, and it demands that no possible improvement could raise the
utility of one, without reducing the utility of any.

[17] The acceptability of Pareto optimality as a necessary condition has to be distinguished from any claim regarding its sufficiency as a criterion of social optimality.
Even though Pareto optimality is sometimes treated implicitly as if it were *sufficient*,
the more common—and certainly the more explicit—claim is in favour of its *necessity* for social optimality. Given its complete neglect of distributive issues, sufficiency
would be a most unplausible claim for Pareto optimality (except in specialized
contexts, such as consensual constitutionality, on which see J. M. Buchanan and
Tullock 1962). What is being discussed in the text here is not the obvious limitation of
the sufficiency claims in favour of Pareto optimality, but the inadequacy of that
criterion viewed *even* as a necessity condition.

particular is the alleged priority of the space of utilities (or of fulfilment of desires) on which Pareto optimality concentrates, and this involves arguing for the need to accommodate the rival claims of other considerations such as liberties or freedoms.[18]

Aggregative considerations can make us move in a different direction from equality in general. In concentrating on the programme of explaining the far-reaching role of basal equality, we must not overlook the plurality of ethical concerns that take us beyond equality altogether.[19] The distinction between aggregative and distributive considerations has often been discussed in the specific context of assessing *results* (e.g. the conflict between increasing total income and reducing distributional inequalities in incomes, or between raising aggregate utility and decreasing interpersonal utility differences). But similar contrasts hold in other spaces as well, which may not involve any particular concentration on results as such. For example, there may be a conflict between promoting some rights in general (irrespective of distribution) and seeking a more equal distribution of those rights. Indeed, the aggregative–distributive dichotomy is one of the more pervasive issues in social evaluation. Equality—no matter how broadly defined—can hardly be the only concern in any basal space, and aggregative considerations (including the demands of efficiency) tend to have an irreducible status.

However, in integrating these distinct considerations, we also have to note that the aggregating concerns themselves may give a crucial role to equality in their formulation. In carrying out aggregation, there are questions of what to include and what weights to attach, and here equality is often invoked as a demand on the discipline of aggregation. Indeed, it is precisely in giving equal weight to each person in the utilitarian aggregative maximand that utilitarianism adopts a firmly egalitarian stand—a stand the significance of which has been particularly emphasized by such utilitarian analysts as Harsanyi (1955, 1982) and Hare (1963, 1981, 1982). Giving equal weight on the utilities of each person in the aggregate maximand makes utilitarianism an egalitarian approach in a very specific way—specialized not just through the choice of a particular space (viz. utilities), but also through the form that the requirement of

[18] On this and related issues, see Sen (1970*a*, 1979*a*, 1983*a*, 1992*a*).

[19] This plurality goes beyond the multiplicity of focus that may be part and parcel of basal equality itself ('internal plurality'), discussed in Sect. 9.3.

equality takes in that space (viz. giving equal weight to all in the aggregate objective, rather than, say, promoting the equality of utility levels).[20] The demands of equality can be imposed in different ways, and it can have a role even in the formulation of what may initially appear to be a purely aggregative exercise.

Thus, the demands of equality may come up in many distinct contexts, in quite different ways. But it is also clear that not all the issues to be settled can be resolved simply by the demands of equality even in their most diverse forms. For example, while equality may influence the form of the aggregative objective (e.g. insisting on an unweighted sum as the proper maximand), the demand to *maximize* that aggregate objective is not—in itself—a demand of equality. We have to recognize the variety and extensive reach of the demands of equality, without seeking in it a completeness of considerations that cannot possibly be there.

9.6. ALTERNATIVE DEFENCES OF INEQUALITY

When competing with aggregative considerations, the demands of equality may often be substantially compromised in the endorsed arrangements. This recognition does not contradict the persistent relevance and reach of egalitarian values. Indeed, the pursuit of equality can be properly evaluated only within a broader context in which other demands are not arbitrarily ignored.

In the context of reasoned judgement of social arrangements, inequality in terms of any variable (e.g. incomes, capabilities) may be defended by using one of, at ~~best~~, three different types of arguments without generally disputing the relevance of equality for social arrangements: (1) 'the wrong space' argument, (2) the 'incentive' argument, and (3) 'operational asymmetry' argument.

'The wrong space' argument takes the form of claiming that the variable in question (i.e. income, or capability, or whatever) is not the right one in terms of which equality should be sought. It does not provide, so it is suggested (usually implicitly), the right space for the demands of equality. Indeed, in this class of arguments, the need for equality in some *other* space may be *inter alia* asserted, such as

[20] Meade (1976) provides a welfare-economic analysis in which the claims of equal weight in the maximand *as well as* equality in the individual levels achieved receive competing attention, in the space of utilities. See also Mirrlees (1971, 1986), Phelps (1973), Mueller (1979), Atkinson and Stiglitz (1980), Roberts (1980a), Drèze and Stern (1987), Starrett (1988).

equality of libertarian rights (Nozick 1974), equal rights to enjoy what one has 'produced' (Bauer 1981), equal and impartial treatments in terms of some procedures (Gauthier 1986), equal weighting of utilities in the aggregate maximand (Bentham 1789; Harsanyi 1955; Hare 1981), and so on. And because of these demands—including demands of equality—in the *other* space, equality cannot be insisted on in the particular space in dispute (e.g. incomes, or capabilities, or utility levels, or some other field favoured by the 'egalitarians').

I have discussed the nature of this argument and its implications quite extensively earlier on in this monograph (in Chapter 1 and also earlier on in this concluding chapter), and I shall not elaborate it further here. Nor am I discussing here why many of these claims may be disputable.[21] Indeed, the plausibility of valuing equality in terms of capabilities (with which a lot of this monograph has been concerned) is itself an argument against insisting, unconditionally, on equality in other spaces.

The other two arguments are related to each other in bringing in non-equality considerations in the space in question. They dispute the demands of the pursuit of equality in that space not by airing the superior claims of another space, but by pointing to the conflict between equality and efficiency (in a general sense) in that space itself. It may be accepted that inequality in that space may be a bad thing, but that badness (it is claimed) may be outweighed by its efficiency advantages. Attempts to eliminate that inequality would lead to worse consequences, e.g. worsening of the position of all (or most people).

Efficiency-based critiques of equality can take at least two distinct forms, and in the list presented earlier, these were put down as two different arguments (as they indeed are): the 'incentive' argument and the 'operational asymmetry' argument. The incentive argument, which has perhaps been more discussed in the literature, concentrates on the need to give people the incentive to do the right thing for the promotion of the objectives. Inequality may, thus, play a functionally useful role in encouraging work, enterprise, and investment.[22]

[21] I have presented arguments against the claims of Nozick (1974) and Bauer (1981), among other claims, in Sen (1982*b*, 1985*e*).

[22] Unequal outcomes may also be associated with the willingness to take risky but useful decisions. However, the relation between riskiness and inequalities in income distribution is more complex than is often presumed; on this see Kanbur (1979).

It is often taken for granted that the objectives must be of the 'aggregative' type (in the sense of promoting individual achievements irrespective of distribution, e.g. seeking Pareto improvement, or maximizing the sum-total). But the demands of efficiency can, in fact, be related to any type of objectives—distributive as well as aggregative.[23] There are issues of efficiency in the promotion of equality itself along with other objectives.[24] The incentive argument, applied to individuals, deals with the need to provide motivation and encouragement to individuals so that their choices and actions are conducive to the promotion of overall objectives.[25] These goals could be purely aggregative, or include distributive goals as well.

The incentive argument has been invoked, for a very long time, in disputing the immediate claims of equality. Egalitarian policies have been criticized on the ground that they hinder the pursuit of social goals, and this can happen even when these goals include equality as well. Incentive-based critiques of egalitarianism have had a fair amount of practical airing in recent years, e.g. in discussing what went wrong with egalitarian policies in Maoist China, or in criticizing redistributive features of 'welfare state' policies.[26]

The third line of argument also relates to the tension between equality and efficiency, but it concentrates specifically on aggregative objectives and the need to have inequality in promoting them because of the necessity of operational asymmetry. The need for such asymmetry can arise from differences in people's skills and abilities. For example, it may be argued that giving more power and capabilities of particular types (e.g. in running governments, taking business decisions) to the more able and skilled would help every-

---

[23] On this and related issues, see Le Grand (1990, 1991).

[24] If 'efficiency' is taken to mean wasteless, productive promotion of objectives (no matter what these objectives are), then the subject-matter of efficiency can encompass the promotion of equality itself, if that were among the chosen objectives. But the inclusion of equality among the objectives to be promoted does not rule out the possibility that a no-nonsense pursuit of equality may lead to less overall achievement.

[25] Simple but illuminating examples of the conflict between distributive concerns and incentive demands can be found in the literature on optimum income taxes; see e.g. Mirrlees (1971), Stern (1976), Sadka (1977), Seade (1977).

[26] There is also a basic issue of individual incentives in the operation of *political* processes (including legislation and administration) which govern the objectives pursued by state policy; on this see Buchanan and Tullock (1962) and Buchanan (1975, 1985).

one, but this would obviously be accompanied by inequality of those powers and capabilities. This 'operational asymmetry' argument applies particularly to inequalities in some specific space, e.g. powers and capabilities, and may or may not be directly relevant to other spaces (such as utilities).[27]

Another variant of the 'operational asymmetry' argument focuses on the possibility that the need for asymmetric treatment arises from the *social* role of asymmetry (e.g. a few people have to take operational decisions to avoid confusion). In this view, efficiency of operation would require that *some* people should have more authority or power than others. Asymmetric treatment may be necessary, in this view, even if the people who are in authority are no more talented than others are. Similarly, indivisibilities in the economic opportunities, which could not be shared given the nature of technology, may lead to operational asymmetry on grounds of aggregative objectives. The operational asymmetry arguments need not focus on the individual incentive problem as such, but on the social role of asymmetries, e.g. those related to the use of differences in skills, or to the need for authority or discipline, or the presence of indivisibilities.[28]

9.7. INCENTIVES, DIVERSITY AND EGALITARIANISM

In the economic literature on resource allocation, the 'incentive' argument in particular has been very extensively explored.[29] How does the emphasis on the diversity of human beings—one of the

---

[27] Indeed, a variant of the 'operational asymmetry' argument may yield the odd result in the utility space that the more productive should have *lower* total utilities. If some people are more productive than others, and can generate more output through the same amount of work (and the same loss of leisure) than others can, then a system of total utility maximization might require that these more productive people should work *harder* and end up having less utility than others because of harder work and smaller leisure. On this, see Mirrlees (1971, 1974), and also Roemer (1985). See also Atkinson and Stiglitz (1980) and Tuomala (1984, 1990).

[28] Arguments for asymmetric treatment can arise also in other circumstances and may *inter alia* involve incentive problems (without being entirely reducible to it). See Stiglitz's (1982) discussion of the difficulty of having 'horizontal equity' along with aggregative objectives. The particular case he deals with is that of utilitarianism, and he considers cases in which 'social welfare (as measured by the sum of utilities) is higher if individuals who have the same tastes and the same endowments are treated differently' (p. 2).

[29] See Atkinson and Stiglitz (1980), Auerbach and Feldstein (1987), and Starrett (1988).

recurrent themes in this monograph—affect the incentive argument? It is arguable that an explicit recognition of some types of deeper human diversities and their roles in inequality evaluation may have the effect of restraining the force of the incentive problem. At least, the incentive problem may have to be stated somewhat differently from the way it is often posed, especially in popular accounts.

In many economic models (e.g. in welfare economics or in public finance), the disparity between the achievements of different persons arises typically from differences in efforts and in other *decision variables* of the individuals, and not from any antecedent diversity in productive ability (though there may be differences in tastes, e.g. for responding to risk or to financial rewards). These differences are clearly related to problems of motivations and opportunities, and in that context the incentive argument has—rightly—figured fairly ubiquitously in that literature.[30] There is much to be learned from such analysis.

If, on the other hand, human diversities of particular types— rather than differences in decisions—are an important factor behind unequal achievement or freedom, then the incentive argument, in its straightforward form, may not directly apply. For example, to the extent that gender or age is responsible for inequality of capabilities, the policy response may take the form of providing special help to members of the more deprived gender or age categories. Since it is impossible to change one's age rapidly, and particularly hard to change one's sex, the special treatments may not generate incentive problems of the standard kind.[31] It is, of course, possible to lie about one's age or gender, but that may not always be easy nor convincing. In general, the possibility of incentive distortions may be a good deal less with egalitarian policy in this case than in the standard economic models involving individuals whose fortunes diverge because of their own *chosen* levels of application.

Similarly, if individuals suffering from diseases are offered special medical or other facilities, the incentive problem may be relatively light, since people do not typically wish to cultivate

---

[30] This holds not only for the market mechanism, but also for allocation under other institutional arrangements. For the relevance of such considerations for resource allocation in economies with peasants or collectives, see Putterman (1986).

[31] See, in the context, Sen (1973*a*), Akerlof (1978, 1984), and Atkinson (1991*c*).

diseases, nor do they usually have much use for the specific medical and other facilities that may be on offer. To the extent that free or heavily subsidized medical facilities may make people take less precaution, there would of course be an incentive effect here too (since the difference here would be caused by a choice variable, to wit, being careless), but in most circumstances and with most illnesses people are reluctant to take such risk just because the treatment itself would be free or inexpensive. The different genetic and environmental risks of illness can be dealt with by providing special medical facilities without having terrible incentive problems.[32]

Egalitarian policies to undo the inequalities associated with human diversity are much less problematic from the point of view of incentives than policies to undo inequality arising from differences in effort and application, on which much of the incentive literature has tended to focus. Thus, the importance of human diversity in inequality evaluation, with which we have been much concerned in much of this monograph, may also have some considerable bearing on the nature and force of the incentive problem in pursuing egalitarian policy (particularly in the context of moving towards less inequality of elementary capabilities). This is not a trivial issue, in so far as antecedent diversities (e.g. in gender, age, class) are among the central factors behind unequal freedoms that people have in the world in which we live.

9.8. ON EQUALITY AS A SOCIAL CONCERN

This monograph has been much concerned with exploring capabilities as the basis of judging individual advantage. I have tried to emphasize that this capability perspective can be used not just for evaluating equality, but also for assessing efficiency. Efficiency in the capability space, if defined analogously to the usual definitions of 'economic efficiency' (characterized in terms of the utility space), would require that no one's capability can be further enhanced

[32] For a private insurance company, there will of course be considerable incentive to find out who are genetically more prone to illness, since excluding them would enhance profits. If, however, it is accepted that there are good social arguments for providing medical coverage for those who are genetically more prone to disease, then that policy initiative need not run into a severe barrier of incentive problems. The 'incentive compatibility' in this case contrasts with the problems that arise when the differences are not due to basic human diversities, but mainly the result of choice of actions.

while maintaining the capability of everyone else at least at the same level.[33]

The explicit acceptance of aggregative concerns as an integral part of social evaluation does make a difference to the way equality itself may be assessed. The demands of equality cannot be clearly interpreted or understood without taking adequate note of efficiency considerations. The point is not merely that the demands of equality have to be ultimately weighed against the force of competing demands, when present. It is also that the interpretation of the demands that equality makes has to be assessed in the light of the other considerations (e.g. aggregative concerns) that are *inter alia* recognized. The explicit admittance of other concerns avoids the overburdening of equality with unnecessary loads. This general point may be illustrated with a couple of examples.

First, as was argued earlier (in Chapter 6, Section 6.2), the case for 'attainment equality' as opposed to 'shortfall equality' may be severely weakened if no weight is to be given to aggregative considerations, but that in the presence of aggregative concerns, movements towards attainment equality may have much that is commendable. When person A's potentials permit a maximal achievement of x, compared with a general maximal achievement of, say, $2x$ for all others (the difference may be related, for example, to some physical disability that person A has), a demand for equality as the only consideration would tend to have the effect of levelling down everyone else (without disabilities) to x. Under those circumstances, shortfall equality would seem to have some comparative merit, and its programme of equating everyone's achievements as a *proportion* of their respective maximal values would be distinctly less extremist.

On the other hand, that programme would not yield a patently just solution either. Person A is disadvantaged in having a lower maximal achievement, and it is not clear why priority should not be given to helping A to move as close to x as possible, even at the cost

[33] Note that this definition of efficiency takes note of the possibility of incompleteness in the ranking of individual capabilities. Given extensive incompleteness, the requirement that no one's capability be actually *reduced* would have been more easily passed. Due to incomparabilities, a change can fail to keep a person at a level that is judged to be giving him at least the same overall capability without actually leading to a decidable *reduction* of capability. This distinction can be particularly important in policy judgements, e.g. in assessing the efficiency of competitive market equilibria in terms of capabilities (on this, see Sen 1992b).

of some people having a lower proportionate achievement *vis-à-vis* their own higher maximal $2x$. What the situation demands is a respect for attainment equality, without losing sight of aggregative considerations, including the demands of efficiency. If the problem is thus reformulated, person A will have preferential treatment in being helped to move to his maximal achievement x, without all others being dragged down to x (from their respective maximal potential of $2x$). The admittance of aggregative and efficiency considerations, thus, removes from the sphere of equality a load that it cannot comfortably carry, under either interpretation of equality. No less importantly, the case for giving weight to attainment equality comes into its own once that is combined with a concern for efficiency as well. The *ad hoc* case for shortfall equality would then be cut back to size.[34]

A second example is chosen from Rawls's (1990) defence of using primary goods as the basis of the Difference Principle in his 'justice as fairness'. He is responding here particularly to a claim (made in Sen 1980a) that it is more fair to use capabilities in judging individual advantage.[35] Rawls argues against equating people's capabilities in influencing public policy, and reasserts the fairness and justice of a system in which influential offices are filled through open competition.[36] While people will have the same opportunity to compete for these offices which are open to all (and thus, in some sense, enjoy the same holding of these primary goods in terms of opportunities), they will end up having unequal capabilities. Rawls points out that when individuals differ in 'moral and intellectual capacities and skills', there is nothing unfair or unjust in people with greater skills occupying influential positions and offices.[37] This links with the 'operational asymmetry' argument discussed in the last section.

Let me begin by accepting the substantive conclusion of Rawls that there may be no injustice in having a selection system for offices and positions of responsibility that favours the more skilled. The

[34] For a fuller discussion of this rather complex issue, see Sect. 6.2 in Ch. 6.

[35] See also Ch. 5 above.

[36] Rawls (1971) demands equality in the distribution of primary goods unless unequal divisions are advantageous for all. But the specification of primary goods tends to concentrate on the opportunities (e.g. 'holding positions open', p. 61). 'All social values—liberty and opportunity, income and wealth, and the bases of self-respect—are to be distributed equally unless an unequal distribution of any, or all, of these values is to everyone's advantage' (p. 62).

[37] Rawls (1990), Lecture 5, Sect. 3: 'Primary Goods and Interpersonal Comparisons'.

important question is: *why* do we agree with this conclusion? This is the case, I would argue, *not* because there is any intrinsic superiority in more skilful people having more office-related capabilities than others. The case for merit-based selection of officers and influential positions relates, ultimately, to the efficiency of such a system. Being born with lower mental skills is not a fault for which a person should be penalized (for reasons that John Rawls, more than anyone else, has taught us to understand). Indeed, if we *could* have had equality in the holding of influential offices and positions without inefficiency and loss of advantages in general, justice would have (I would argue) demanded that we consider opting for it. What makes us accept the inequality involved in this case is precisely the impossibility of achieving that hypothetical position.

There *is* a significant inequality in the arrangements under discussion—an inequality that can be understood in terms of differences in capabilities and powers that different people would end up having. The argument that such an inequality may nevertheless be acceptable is best understood in terms of its efficiency advantages, and not through denying that there is any real inequality here, since everyone had the same opportunity of competing for offices. A significant inequality has to be acknowledged first, before it is examined as to whether it is justified or not. Justifying the inequality in capabilities in the case discussed would take the form of arguing that eliminating it would tend to pull down many people's capabilities quite substantially and that would be inefficient and unacceptable. The justification is contingent on the aggregative consideration working this way.

The contingent acceptability of the social arrangement that Rawls defends does not, therefore, show that focusing on primary goods is a fairer or better way of judging individual advantage than capabilities. What it really suggests is that demands of equality of individual advantages have to be supplemented by considerations of efficiency in generating these advantages.

Rawls himself has outlined the need to consider the demands of efficiency in his second principle of justice. But the use he can make of efficiency considerations is somewhat limited by the insistence on the extremism of giving total priority to the interests of the worst off.[38] This priority makes it harder to justify inequalities through aggregative considerations, since the focus has to be, lexicographically, on the worst-off group only. The demands of Rawls's maximin

[38] On this, see Sen (1970*a*, 1977*b*).

formula is more easily fulfilled when we have a characterization of individual advantages (in the form of holding primary goods) that does not record inequalities that would be readily recorded in the space of capabilities. But that absence of recording does make the political scrutiny informationally poorer. There are good reasons, instead, for recording significant inequalities in capabilities, and examining whether they can or cannot be justified by efficiency arguments.

So far I have not disputed the substantive claim of Rawls that there is no unfairness or injustice in allocating offices through open competition, with the more skilled being actually selected (as long as everyone has the same opportunity to be educated and to compete). Basing the justification of such inequalities explicitly on their efficiency advantages makes it necessary to scrutinize the causal connections related to the claims of efficiency. I do not doubt that in many circumstances the procedure that Rawls supports (and which I tentatively accepted earlier on) would prove to be just right. If, on the other hand, it turns out that a system by which offices and influential positions go to people who do better in open competition creates a kind of 'meritocracy' that is not so efficient and which leads to people of less favoured groups being unequally treated (in the exercise of those offices and positions), then that justification would no longer obtain.

In the political debates that raged in India through 1990 on the proposal of the then Prime Minister V. P. Singh that more than half the influential jobs in civil service be reserved for members of lower castes and other disadvantaged groups (the disputes were crucial to V. P. Singh's eventual loss of parliamentary majority and the fall of his government), the presumed efficiency advantages of selection through open competition was severely questioned. It is not my purpose here to argue that V. P. Singh's scepticism of the efficiency advantages was correct or incorrect, but only that the justice of the open-competition arrangement must be sensitive to the answer that we give to that question. The issue cannot be settled by a prior fixation of the distributive pattern of primary goods (e.g. in the form of none of the offices being reserved for the socially immobile underprivileged). The justice of the arrangements must be sensitive to the respective impacts of the different systems on aggregative and distributive aspects of people's effective freedoms and capabilities. Such an analysis could, of course, fully support Rawls's recommendation, but if it did, then that would indeed be a powerful reason for that recommendation.

9.9. RESPONSIBILITY AND FAIRNESS

John Rawls (1971) and other modern theorists of justice (such as Ronald Dworkin 1981) have tended to stress the need to see each person as being peculiarly responsible for matters over which she has control. In contrast, responsibility is not attributed—nor credit given—to a person for something she could not have changed (such as having rich or poor parents, or having or lacking natural gifts). The lines are sometimes hard to draw, but there is much plausibility in that general differentiation. The analysis presented in this book has made a good deal of use of that distinction.

Indeed, the criticism of Rawls's theory of 'justice as fairness' from the capability perspective arose partly from our attempt to take direct note of a person's difficulties—naturally or socially generated—in converting 'primary goods' into actual freedoms to achieve (see Chapter 5). A person less able or gifted in using primary goods to secure freedoms (e.g. because of physical or mental disability, or varying proneness to illness, or biological or conventional constraints related to gender) is disadvantaged compared with another more favourably placed in that respect even if both have the same bundle of primary goods. A theory of justice, I have argued, must take adequate note of that difference. It is for this reason that the approach presented here both draws on and criticizes the Rawlsian theory—it draws on Rawls's illuminating analysis of fairness and of responsibility to criticize his theory's particular dependence on the holding of primary goods (as opposed to the freedoms and capabilities the persons respectively enjoy).

The distinction is of significance on another contentious issue, viz. the choice between achievements and freedoms to judge a person's relative situation. In dealing with responsible adults, it is more appropriate to see the claims of individuals on the society (or the demands of equity or justice) in terms of *freedom to achieve* rather than *actual achievements*. If the social arrangements are such that a responsible adult is given no less freedom (in terms of set comparisons) than others, but he still wastes the opportunities and ends up worse off than others, it is possible to argue that no unjust inequality may be involved. If that view is taken, then the direct relevance of capability (as opposed to achieved functionings) will be easy to assert.

It is, however, important to be clear about some qualifications that must apply to the preceding argument. For one thing, the issue is quite different in the presence of uncertainties. The predicament of a person due to adverse happenings over which he has no control can scarcely be dismissed on grounds of personal responsibility.

That responsibility argument is more applicable when the person himself willingly takes a risk and ends up losing the gamble, since there will be more scope here for invoking the person's own responsibility. But even here the picture may be made more complicated by the difficulty of getting adequate information that would permit a person to make intelligent decisions in risky situations. For example, the collapse of a well-known insurance company or a well-regarded bank can hardly be seen as an occasion for hard-headed dismissal (with no special quarter being given to the unfortunate victims) on the grounds that the victims themselves had *chosen* the insurance company or the bank.[39] In fact, the case for concentrating on freedoms to achieve as opposed to actual achievements depends quite heavily on the knowledge and the ability of the persons to understand and intelligently choose from the alternatives they really do have.

A closely related issue concerns the way in which capability accounting must take note of the real freedoms that people *in fact* (not just 'in principle') enjoy. If social conditioning makes a person lack the courage to choose (perhaps even to 'desire' what is denied but what would be valued *if* chosen), then it would be unfair to undertake the ethical assessment *assuming* that she does have that effective choice. It is a matter of concentrating on the real freedoms actually enjoyed, taking note of *all* the barriers—including those from 'social discipline'.

Indeed, an overdependence on what people 'manage to desire' is one of the limiting aspects of utilitarian ethics, which is particularly neglectful of the claims of those who are too subdued or broken to have the courage to desire much.[40] It would be particularly unfortunate to err in the same way in the capability accounting. There is,

---

[39] Interestingly, the British and the American public responses to such collapses have been quite different, as illustrated by the enormous protectiveness with which the 'Savings & Loans' crises have been dealt with in the USA, compared with the relatively smaller compensations offered to the unlucky depositors of the busted-up Bank of Credit and Commerce International (BCCI). Even the legal frameworks of protection of depositors are quite different in the two countries, and involve rather disparate views of responsibility.

[40] This issue is discussed in Sen (1985*a*).

however, no need to err in that way, since the capabilities to be accounted are those that people do *actually* have (and not those that they *could have had* if they were less influenced by 'social discipline'). This question is of particular importance in dealing with entrenched inequalities that are supported by the victims' conditioned acceptance of comparative deprivation (e.g. women's acceptance of subjugated roles in traditional social arrangements).[41]

9.10. CAPABILITY, FREEDOM AND MOTIVATIONS

The 'capability approach' has something to offer both to the evaluation of *well-being* and to the assessment of *freedom*. Considering the former connection first, the capability approach to well-being differs from the more traditional concentration on economic opulence (in the form of real income, consumption levels, etc.) in two distinct respects: (1) it shifts the focus from the space of *means* in the form of commodities and resources to that of functionings which are seen as *constitutive* elements of human well-being; and (2) it makes it possible—though not obligatory—to take note of the *set* of alternative functioning vectors from which the person can choose. The 'capability set' can be seen as the overall freedom a person enjoys to pursue her well-being.

If the ability to choose between substantively important alternatives is seen as valuable in leading a worthwhile life, then the capability set has a further role: it can be directly influential in the determination of a person's well-being. An alternative combination x of functionings can, then, be seen as going with a certain freedom to choose from a set S, to which x belongs. If the well-being that a person gets from what she *does* is dependent on *how* she came to do it (in particular, whether she chose that functioning herself), then her well-being depends not just on x, but on the choice of x from the set S.[42]

There are complex problems involved in these issues (discussed in Chapters 3 and 4). The crucial question here, in the context of well-being, is whether freedom to choose is valued only instrumentally, or is also important in itself. The capability approach is broad

---

[41] On this question, see Kynch and Sen (1983), Sen (1985*d*, 1990*c*), Laden (1991*b*).
[42] The analysis of well-being, then, has to be related to the pair (x, S), and not just to x.

enough to permit both the rival—but interrelated—characterizations of well-being, and can be used in either way.

It is important to emphasize that even if freedom to choose is valued only instrumentally in the determination of individual *well-being*, the extent of freedom enjoyed by each person can, nevertheless, be directly important for a good society. Indeed, whether or not freedom enters *individual* well-being, individual freedom can be seen as being constitutive of the goodness of *the society* which we have reasons to pursue.[43]

Our interest in equality of freedoms can, therefore, be related to different evaluative foundations. In this monograph I have not particularly focused on the relative merits of these diverse ethical underpinnings,[44] but it is useful to keep in view the different foundational reasons for which we may wish to attach importance to the equality of freedoms. The perspective provided by the capability approach can be used to analyse and assess equality of freedoms in relation to each of these distinct motivations.

Much the same plurality applies also to the approach of seeing poverty as capability failure. This can be linked to various underlying concerns, such as guaranteeing minimal individual well-being or providing minimal individual freedoms, and these in turn can be related to more foundational demands of good—or right—social arrangements. The case for reorienting poverty analysis from *low incomes* to *insufficient basic capabilities* can be, ultimately, connected with these alternative foundational concerns.

No matter what exact foundational structure we opt for, the reorientation from an income-centred to a capability-centred view gives us a better understanding of what is involved in the challenge of poverty.[45] It provides clearer guidance on the priorities of anti-poverty policy and also helps us to understand better the genesis of poverty in apparently unlikely circumstances (e.g. in the rich coun-

---

[43] A related but different line of ethical analysis takes the form of making individual freedoms the subject-matter of the 'rightness' of social arrangements, without necessarily invoking any prior notion of the social good. That way of seeing the problem has distinctly Kantian roots (Kant 1788). On the relevance of the Kantian foundations for these and related issues, see particularly Rawls (1971, 1988a); see also O'Neill (1989, 1992), and Korsgaard (1992).

[44] See, however, Sen (1982b, 1985a).

[45] A probing empirical study, done by Schokkaert and Van Ootegem (1990), of the perception of poverty by the Belgian unemployed indicates that the unemployed themselves may see poverty precisely as lack of substantive freedom.

tries of Europe and America). The wisdom of focusing on poverty as lack of freedom is consistent with a variety of foundational concerns.

This monograph has been aimed at examining the nature and reach of the demands of equality. While the analysis has been mainly conceptual, it has some direct bearing on matters of practical concern. The analysis has been very substantially motivated by that connection.

References

ACKERMAN, B. A. (1980). *Social Justice in the Liberal State* (New Haven, Conn.: Yale University Press).

—— (1984). 'The Storrs Lectures: Discovering the Constitution', *Yale Law Journal*, 93.

—— (1988). 'Neutralities,' mimeographed, Yale Law School.

ADELMAN, I. (1975). 'Development Economics—A Reassessment of Goals,' *American Economic Review*, Papers and Proceedings, 65.

—— and MORRIS, C. T. (1973). *Economic Growth and Social Equity in Developing Countries* (Stanford, Calif.: Stanford University Press).

AGARWAL, B. (1986). 'Women, Poverty and Agricultural Growth in India', *Journal of Peasant Studies*, 13.

—— (1991). 'Social Security and the Family: Coping with Seasonality and Calamity in Rural India', in Ahmad *et al.* (1991).

AHLUWALIA, M. S. (1974). 'Income Inequality: Some Dimensions of the Problem', in Chenery *et al.* (1974).

—— (1978). 'Rural Poverty and Agricultural Performance in India', *Journal of Development Studies*, 14.

AHMAD, E., and HUSSAIN, A. (1991). 'Social Security in China: A Historical Perspective', in Ahmad *et al.* (1991).

—— Drèze, J., Hills, J., and SEN, A. (1991) (eds.). *Social Security in Developing Countries* (Oxford: Clarendon Press).

AHMED, I. (1983). 'Technology and Rural Women in the Third World', *International Labour Review*, 122.

AHOOJA-PATEL, K. (1980) (ed.). *Women at Work* (Geneva: ILO).

AIGNER, D. J., and HEINS, A. J. (1967). 'A Social Welfare View of the Measurement of Income Inequality', *Review of Income and Wealth*, 13.

AKERLOF, G. (1978). 'The Economics of "Tagging"', *American Economic Review*, 68.

—— (1984). *An Economic Theorist's Book of Tales* (Cambridge: Cambridge University Press).

ALAMGIR, M. (1978). *Bangladesh: A Case of Below Poverty Level Equilibrium Trap* (Dhaka: Bangladesh Institute of Development Studies).

—— (1980). *Famine in South Asia—The Political Economy of Mass Starvation in Bangladesh* (Cambridge, Mass.: Oelgeschlager, Gunn and Hain).

ALDRICH, J. (1977). 'The Dilemma of a Paretian Liberal: Some Consequences of Sen's Theory', *Public Choice*, 30.

ALLARDT, E. (1981). 'Experiences from the Comparative Scandinavian Welfare Study, with a Bibliography of the Project', *European Journal of Political Research*, 9.

ALLARDT, E. (1992). 'Having, Loving, Being: An Alternative to the Swedish Model of Welfare Research', in Nussbaum and Sen (1992).

ALLEN, T. (1988). 'The Impossibility of the Paretian Liberal and its Relevance to Welfare Economics', *Theory and Decision*, 24.

—— (1991). 'Economic Development and the Feminization of Poverty', in Folbre *et al.* (1991).

AMIEL, Y., and COWELL, F. (1989). 'Measurement of Income Inequality: Experimental Test vs. Questionnaire', Discussion Paper TIDI/140, STICERD, London School of Economics.

AMSDEN, A. H. (1980) (ed.). *The Economics of Women and Work* (Harmondsworth: Penguin).

ANAND, S. (1977). 'Aspects of Poverty in Malaysia', *Review of Income and Wealth*, 23.

—— (1983). *Inequality and Poverty in Malaysia* (New York: Oxford University Press).

—— and HARRIS, C. (1990). 'Food and Standard of Living: An Analysis Based on Sri Lankan Data', in Drèze and Sen (1990), vol. 1.

—— —— (1992). 'Issues in the Measurement of Undernutrition', in Osmani (1992*a*).

—— and KANBUR, R. (1984). 'Inequality and Development: A Reconsideration', in Nissen (1984).

—— —— (1986). 'Inequality and Development: A Critique', mimeographed, St Catherine's College, Oxford, and Warwick University.

—— —— (1990). 'Public Policy and Basic Needs Provision: Intervention and Achievement in Sri Lanka', in Drèze and Sen (1990), vol. 3.

ANCKAR, D., and BERNDTSON, E. (1984) (eds.). *Essays on Democratic Theory* (Tampere: Finnpublishers).

ANNAS, J. (1992). 'Women and the Quality of Life: Two Norms or One?', in Nussbaum and Sen (1992).

APFFEL MARGLIN, F., and MARGLIN, S. A. (1990) (eds.). *Dominating Knowledge: Development, Culture, Resistance* (Oxford: Clarendon Press).

ARCHIBALD, G. C., and DONALDSON, D. (1979). 'Notes on Economic Inequality', *Journal of Public Economics*, 12.

ARISTOTLE. *The Nicomachean Ethics*, English trans. in Ross (1980).

ARNESON, R. (1989*a*). 'Equality and Equality of Opportunity for Welfare', *Philosophical Studies*, 56.

—— (1989*b*). 'Paternalism, Utility and Fairness', *Revue Internationale de Philosophie*, 43.

—— (1990*a*). 'Liberalism, Distributive Subjectivism, and Equal Opportunity for Welfare', *Philosophy and Public Affairs*, 19.

—— (1990*b*). 'Primary Goods Reconsidered', *Nous*, 24.

—— (1990*c*). 'Neutrality and Utility', *Canadian Journal of Philosophy*, 20.

—— (1991). 'A Defence of Equal Opportunity for Welfare', forthcoming in *Philosophical Studies*.

ARROW, K. J. (1951). *Social Choice and Individual Values* (New York: Wiley).

—— (1963). *Social Choice and Individual Values*, 2nd extended edn. (New York: Wiley).

—— (1977). 'Extended Sympathy and the Possibility of Social Choice', *American Economic Review*, 67.

—— (1982a). 'Risk Perception in Psychology and Economics', *Economic Inquiry*, 20.

—— (1982b). 'Why People Go Hungry', *New York Review of Books*, 29 (15 July).

—— (1983). 'Behaviour under Uncertainty and its Implications for Policy', in B. P. Stigum and F. Wenstop (eds.), *Foundations of Utility and Risk Theory with Applications* (Dordrecht: Reidel).

—— (1991) (ed.). *Markets and Welfare* (London: Macmillan).

—— and INTRILIGATOR, M. (1986). *Handbook of Mathematical Economics*, iii (Amsterdam: North-Holland).

ARTICLE 19 (1990). *Starving in Silence: A Report on Famine and Censorship*, ed. Frances D'Souza (London: Article 19).

ASAHI, J. (1987). 'On Professor Sen's Capability Theory', mimeographed, Tokyo.

ASLANBEIGUI, N., and SUMMERFIELD, G. (1989). 'Impact of the Responsibility System on Women in Rural China: An Application of Sen's Theory of Entitlements', *World Development*, 17.

ASPREMONT, C. D' (1985). 'Axioms for Social Welfare Ordering', in Hurwicz, Schmeidler, and Sonnenschein (1985).

—— and GEVERS, L. (1977). 'Equity and the Informational Basis of Collective Choice', *Review of Economic Studies*, 46.

AHTISAARI, M. (1991). 'Amartya Sen's Capability Approach to the Standard of Living', Jonathan Lieberson Memorial Prize Essay, mimeographed, Columbia University.

ATKINSON, A. B. (1970a). *Poverty in Britain and the Reform of Social Security* (Cambridge: Cambridge University Press).

—— (1970b). 'On the Measurement of Inequality', *Journal of Economic Theory*, 2. (Repr. in Atkinson 1983.)

—— (1972). *Unequal Shares* (London: Allen Lane, The Penguin Press).

—— (1975). *The Economics of Inequality* (Oxford: Clarendon Press).

—— (1983). *Social Justice and Public Policy* (Brighton: Wheatsheaf and Cambridge, Mass.: MIT Press).

—— (1987). 'On the Measurement of Poverty', *Econometrica*, 5.

—— (1989). *Poverty and Social Security* (New York: Harvester Wheatsheaf).

—— (1991a). 'The Social Safety Net', mimeographed, STICERD, London School of Economics.

—— (1991b). 'What is Happening to the Distribution of Income in the

UK?', Keynes Lecture, British Academy.

—— (1991*c*). 'On Targeting', mimeographed, STICERD, London School of Economics.

ATKINSON A. B. and BOURGUIGNON, F. (1982). 'The Comparison of Multi-dimensional Distributions of Economic Status', *Review of Economic Studies*, 49.

———— (1987). 'Income Distribution and Differences in Needs', in Feiwel (1987).

—— and STIGLITZ, J. E. (1980). *Lectures on Public Economics* (London: McGraw-Hill).

AUERBACH, A., and FELDSTEIN, M. (1987). *Handbook of Public Economics* (Amsterdam: North-Holland).

AUSTEN-SMITH, D. (1979). 'Fair Rights', *Economic Letters*, 4.

—— (1982). 'Restricted Pareto and Rights', *Journal of Economic Theory*, 26.

BABU, S. C. (1986). 'Identifying the Poor—A Development Approach: Case Study of a South Indian Village', unpub. manuscript, Iowa State University.

BALL, S. W. (1987). 'Choosing between Choice Models of Ethics: Rawlsian Equality, Utilitarianism, and the Concept of Persons', *Theory and Decision*, 22: 3.

BANERJEE, N. (1979). 'Women in Urban Labour Market', *Labour Capital and Society*, 12.

—— (1982). *Unorganised Women Workers: The Calcutta Experience* (Calcutta: Centre for Studies in Social Sciences).

BANISTER, J. (1987). *China's Changing Population* (Stanford, Calif.: Stanford University Press).

BARDHAN, K. (1985). 'Women's Work, Welfare and Status', *Economic and Political Weekly*, 20 (21–8 Dec.).

BARDHAN, P. (1974*a*). 'On the Incidence of Poverty in Rural India in the Sixties', in Srinivasan and Bardhan (1974).

—— (1974*b*). 'On Life and Death Questions', *Economic and Political Weekly*, 9 (Special Number).

—— (1984). *Land Labour and Rural Poverty: Essays in Development Economics* (New York: Columbia University Press).

—— (1987). 'On the Economic Geography of Sex Disparity in Child Survival in India', mimeographed, University of California, Berkeley.

—— (1988). 'Sex Disparity in Child Survival in Rural India', in Srinivasan and Bardhan (1988).

BARNES, J. (1980). 'Freedom, Rationality and Paradox', *Canadian Journal of Philosophy*, 10.

BARRY, B. (1986). 'Lady Chatterly's Lover and Doctor Fischer's Bomb Party: Liberalism, Pareto Optimality and the Problem of Objectional Preferences', in Elster and Hylland (1986).

BARTEN, A. P. (1964). 'Family Composition, Prices and Expenditure Patterns', in P. Hart *et al.* (eds.), *Econometric Analysis for National Economic Planning* (London: Butterworth).

BASU, A. (1988). *Culture, the Status of Women and Demographic Behaviour* (New Delhi: National Council of Applied Economic Research).

—— *et al.* (1986). 'Sex Bias in Intrahousehold Food Distribution: Roles of Ethnic and Socioeconomic Characteristics', *Current Anthropology*, 27.

BASU, K. (1979). *Revealed Preference of Governments* (Cambridge: Cambridge University Press).

—— (1984). 'The Right to Give Up Rights', *Economica*, 51.

—— (1987a). 'Achievements, Capabilities and the Concept of Well-Being', *Social Choice and Welfare*, 4.

—— (1987b). 'Axioms for Fuzzy Measures of Inequality', *Mathematical Social Sciences*, 14.

—— (1989). 'A Theory of Association: Social Status, Prices and Markets', *Oxford Economic Papers*, 41.

BATRA, R., and PATTANAIK, P. (1972). 'On Some Suggestions for Having Non-Binary Social Choice Functions', *Theory and Decision*, 3.1–11.

BAUER, P. T. (1981). *Equality, the Third World and Economic Delusion* (Cambridge, Mass.: Harvard University Press).

BAUMOL, W. J. (1986). *Superfairness* (Cambridge, MA: MIT Press).

BAYER, R., CAPLAN, A. L., and DANIELS, N. (1983) (eds.). *In Search of Equity: Health Needs and the Health Care System* (New York: Plenum Press).

BECKER, G. S. (1965). 'A Theory of the Allocation of Time', *Economic Journal*, 75.

—— (1981). *A Treatise on the Family* (Cambridge, Mass.: Harvard University Press).

BECKERMAN, W. (1979). *The Impact of Income Maintenance Programmes on Poverty in Four Developing Countries* (Geneva: ILO).

—— and CLARK, S. (1982). *Poverty and Social Security in Britain since 1961* (Oxford: Clarendon Press).

BEDAU, H. A. (1971) (ed.). *Justice and Equality* (Englewood Cliffs, NJ: Prentice-Hall).

BEHRMAN, J. R. (1988). 'Intrahousehold Allocation of Nutrients in Rural India: Are Boys Favoured? Do Parents Exhibit Inequality Aversion?' *Oxford Economic Papers*, 40.

—— (1992). 'Intrahousehold Allocation of Nutrients and Gender Effects: A Survey of Structural and Reduced-form Estimates', in Osmani (1992a).

—— and DEOLALIKAR, A. B. (1988). 'Health and Nutrition', in Chenery and Srinivasan (1988).

—— POLLAK, R., and TAUBMAN, P. (1989). 'Family Resources, Family Size, and Access to Financing for College Education', *Journal of Political Economy*, 97.

BEITZ, C. R. (1986). 'Amartya Sen's *Resources, Values and Development*', *Economics and Philosophy*, 2.

BELLMAN, R. E., and ZADEH, L. A. (1970). 'Decision Making in a Fuzzy Environment', *Management Science*, 17.

BENERIA, O. (1982) (ed.). *Women and Development: The Sexual Division of Labour in Rural Societies* (New York: Praeger).

BENTHAM, J. (1789). *An Introduction to the Principles of Morals and Legislation* (London: Payne). (Republished Oxford: Clarendon Press, 1907.)

BENTZEL, R. (1970). 'The Social Significance of Income Distribution Statistics', *Review of Income and Wealth*, 16.

BERGMAN, B. (1986). *The Economic Emergence of Women* (New York: Basic Books).

BERGSON, A. (1938). 'A Reformulation of Certain Aspects of Welfare Economics', *Quarterly Journal of Economics*, 52.

—— (1966). *Essays in Normative Economics* (Cambridge, Mass.: Harvard University Press).

BERLIN, I. (1955–6). 'Equality as an Ideal', *Proceedings of the Aristotelian Society*, 56.

—— (1969). *Four Essays on Liberty*, 2nd edn. (London: Oxford University Press).

BERNHOLZ, P. (1974). 'Is a Paretian Liberal Really Impossible?', *Public Choice*, 19.

—— (1980). 'A General Social Dilemma: Profitable Exchange and Intransitive Group Preferences', *Zeitschrift für Nationalökonomie*, 40.

BESLEY, T. (1989). 'Ex Ante Evaluation of Health Status and the Provision for Ill-Health', *Economic Journal*, 99.

—— and KANBUR, R. (1988). 'Food Subsidies and Poverty Alleviation', *Economic Journal*, 98.

BÉTEILLE, A. (1969) (ed.). *Social Inequality* (Harmondsworth: Penguin Books).

—— (1977). *Inequality among Men* (Oxford: Blackwell).

—— (1981). *The Backward Classes and the New Social Order* (Delhi: Oxford University Press).

—— (1983a). *The Idea of Natural Inequality and Other Essays* (Delhi: Oxford University Press).

—— (1983b) (ed.). *Equality and Inequality* (Delhi: Oxford University Press).

—— (1987). 'Equality as a Right and as a Policy', *LSE Quarterly*, 1.

—— (1990). 'Distributive Justice and Institutional Well-Being', text of V. T. Krishnamachari Lecture, mimeographed, Delhi School of Economics.

BEUS, J. DE (1989). *Markt, Democratie en Vrijhe* (Market, Democracy and Freedom) (Amsterdam: Tjeenk Willink, Zwolle), in Dutch.

BEZEMBINDER, TH., and VAN ACKER, P. (1979). 'A Note on Sen's Partial

Comparability Model', mimeographed, Department of Psychology, Katholieke Universiteit, Nijmegen.

—————— (1986). 'Factual versus Representational Utilities and their Interdimensional Comparisons', mimeographed, Department of Psychology, Katholieke Universiteit, Nijmegen.

BHARGAVA, A. (1991). 'Malnutrition and the Role of Individual Variation with Evidence from India and the Phillippines', mimeographed, Department of Economics, University of Houston.

BHATTACHARYA, N., and CHATTERJEE, G. S. (1988). 'A Further Note on Between-States Variation in Level of Living in Rural India', in Srinivasan and Bardhan (1988).

—— and PAL, P. (1988). 'Variations in Levels of Living across Regions and Social Groups', in Srinivasan and Bardhan (1988).

BHATTY, I. Z. (1974). 'Inequality and Poverty in Rural India', in Srinivasan and Bardhan (1974).

BHATTY, Z. (1980). 'Economic Role and the Status of Women: A Case Study of Women in the Beedi Industry in Allahabad', ILO working paper.

BHUIYA, A., *et al.* (1986). 'Socioeconomic Determinants of Child's Nutritional Status: Boys versus Girls', *Food and Nutrition Bulletin*, 8.

BIGMAN, D. (1985). 'Aggregate Poverty Measures and the Aggregation of Individual Poverty: A Reconsideration of Sen's Axiomatic Approach', unpub. manuscript, The Hebrew University of Jerusalem.

—— (1986). 'On the Measurement of Poverty and Deprivation', Working Paper No. 8602, The Center for Agricultural Economics Research, The Hebrew University of Jerusalem.

BINMORE, K., and DASGUPTA, P. (1987) (eds.). *The Economics of Bargaining* (Oxford: Blackwell).

BISWAS, T. (1987). 'Distributive Justice and Allocation by the Market: On the Characterization of a Fair Market Economy', *Mathematical Social Sciences*, 14.

BLACKORBY, C. (1975). 'Degrees of Cardinality and Aggregate Partial Ordering', *Econometrica*, 43.

—— and DONALDSON, D. (1977). 'Utility versus Equity: Some Plausible Quasi-Orderings', *Journal of Public Economics*, 7.

—————— (1978). 'Measures of Relative Equality and their Meaning in Terms of Social Welfare', *Journal of Economic Theory*, 18.

—————— (1980). 'Ethical Indices for the Measurement of Poverty', *Econometrica*, 48.

—————— (1984). 'Ethically Significant Ordinal Indexes of Relative Inequality', *Advances in Econometrics*, 3.

—————— (1988). 'Adult-Equivalence Scales and the Economic Implementation of Interpersonal Comparisons of Well-Being', mimeographed, University of British Columbia.

——— and AUERSPERG, M. (1981). 'A New Procedure for the Measurement of Inequality within and among Population Subgroups', *Canadian Journal of Economics*, 14.

BLACKORBY, C., DONALDSON, D., and WEYMARK, J. (1984). 'Social Choice with Interpersonal Utility Comparisons: A Diagrammatic Introduction', *International Economic Review*, 25.

——— (1990). 'A Welfarist Proof of Arrow's Theorem', *Recherches économiques de Louvain*, 56.

BLAIR, D. H. (1988). 'The Primary-Goods Indexation Problem in Rawls' *Theory of Justice*', *Theory and Decision*, 24.

BLAU, J. H. (1975). 'Liberal Values and Independence', *Review of Economic Studies*, 42.

BLAXTER, K., and WATERLOW, J. C. (1985) (eds.). *Nutritional Adaptation in Man* (London: John Libbey).

BLISS, C. J. (1992). 'Life-Style and the Standard of Living', in Nussbaum and Sen (1992).

BORDA, J. C. (1781). 'Mémoire sur les élections au scrutin', *Mémoires des l'Académie Royale des Sciences*, English trans. by A. de Grazia, *Isis*, 44 (1953).

BOS, D., ROSE, M., and SEIDL, C. (1986) (eds.). *Welfare and Efficiency in Public Economics* (Berlin: Springer-Verlag).

BOSERUP, E. (1970). *Women's Role in Economic Development* (London: Allen and Unwin).

——— (1987). 'Inequality between the Sexes', in J. Eatwell, M. Milgate, and P. Newman (eds.), *The New Palgrave: A Dictionary of Economics*, ii (London: Macmillan).

——— (1990). 'Economic Change and the Roles of Women', in Tinker (1990*a*).

BOURGUIGNON, F. (1979). 'Decomposable Income Inequality Measures', *Econometrica*, 47.

——— (1990). 'Growth and Inequality in the Dual Model of Development', *Review of Economic Studies*, 57.

——— and FIELDS, G. (1990). 'Poverty Measures and Anti-Poverty Policy', *Recherches économiques de Louvain*, 56.

BRAITHWAITE, R. B. (1955). *Theory of Games as a Tool for the Moral Philosopher* (Cambridge: Cambridge University Press).

BRANDT, R. B. (1979). *A Theory of the Good and the Right* (Oxford: Clarendon Press).

BRANNEN, J., and WILSON, G. (1987) (eds.). *Give and Take in Families* (London: Allen and Unwin).

BRENKERT, C. G. (1980). 'Freedom and Private Property in Marx', in M. Cohen, Nagel, and Scanlon (1980).

——— (1983). *Marx's Ethics of Freedom* (London: Routledge).

BREYER, F. (1977). 'The Liberal Paradox, Decisiveness over Issues, and Domain Restrictions', *Zeitschrift für Nationalökonomie*, 37.

—— and GARDNER, R. (1980). 'Liberal Paradox, Game Equilibrium and Gibbard Optimum', *Public Choice*, 35.

—— and GIGLIOTTI, G. A. (1980). 'Empathy and the Respect for the Right of Others', *Zeitschrift für Nationalökonomie*, 40.

BROCK, D. (1992). 'Quality of Life Measures in Health Care and Medical Ethics', in Nussbaum and Sen (1992).

BRODER, I. E., and MORRIS, C. T. (1983). 'Socially Weighted Real Income Comparisons: An Application to India', *World Development*, 11.

BROOME, J. (1978). 'Choice and Value in Economics', *Oxford Economic Papers*, 30.

—— (1987). 'What's the Good of Equality?' in J. Hey (ed.), *Current Issues in Macroeconomics* (London: Macmillan).

—— (1988). 'What is Wrong with Poverty', *London Review of Books*, 10 (19 May).

BROWN, M., and CHUANG, C. F. (1980). 'Intra-Household Power and Demand for Shared Goods', mimeographed, SUNY, Buffalo.

BRYCESON, D. F. (1985). *Women and Technology in Developing Countries* (Santo Domingo: United Nations).

BUCHANAN, A. E. (1982). *Marx and Justice* (London: Methuen).

BUCHANAN, J. M. (1975). *The Limits of Liberty* (Chicago: University of Chicago Press).

—— (1984). 'On the Ethical Limits of Taxation', *Scandinavian Journal of Economics*, 86.

—— (1986). *Liberty, Market and the State* (Brighton: Wheatsheaf Books).

—— and TULLOCK, G. (1962). *The Calculus of Consent* (Ann Arbor, Mich.: University of Michigan Press).

BUHMANN, B., RAINWATER, L., SCHMAUS, G., and SMEEDING, T. M. (1988). 'Equivalence Scales, Well-Being, Inequality and Poverty: Sensitivity Estimates across Ten Countries using the Luxembourg Income Study Data Base', *Review of Income and Wealth*, 34.

BURMAN, S. (1979) (ed.). *Fit Work for Women* (London: Croom Helm).

BUVINIC, M., LYCETTE, M., and McGREEVEY, W. (1983) (eds.). *Women and Poverty in the Third World* (Baltimore: Johns Hopkins Press).

CAMPBELL, D. E. (1976). 'Democratic Preference Functions', *Journal of Economic Theory*, 12.

—— (1989). 'Equilibrium and Efficiency with Property Rights and Local Consumption Externalities', *Social Choice and Welfare*, 6.

CASE, A., and KATZ, L. (1990). 'The Company You Keep: Effects on Family and Neighborhood on Disadvantaged Youth', mimeographed, Harvard University.

CASSEN, R. (1978). *India: Population, Economy, Society* (London: Macmillan).

CHAKRAVARTY, L. (1986). 'Poverty Studies in the Context of Agricultural Growth and Demographic Pressure (Case of Post-Independence India)', mimeographed, Indraprastha College, Delhi University.

CHAKRAVARTY, S. (1969). *Capital and Development Planning* (Cambridge, Mass.: MIT Press).

CHAKRAVARTY, S. R. (1981). 'On Measurement of Income Inequality and Poverty', Ph.D. thesis (Indian Statistical Institute, Calcutta).

—— (1983a). 'Ethically Flexible Measures of Poverty', *Canadian Journal of Economics*, 16.

—— (1983b). 'Measures of Poverty Based on Income Gap', *Sankhya*, 45.

—— (1984). 'Normative Indices for Measuring Social Mobility', *Economics Letters*, 15.

—— (1988). 'Extended Gini Indices of Inequality', *International Economic Review*, 29.

—— (1990). 'Distributional Implications of Minimum Sacrifice Principle', mimeographed, Indian Statistical Institute.

—— and CHAKRABORTY, A. B. (1984). 'On Indices of Relative Deprivation', *Economics Letters*, 14.

—— and DUTTA, B. (1987). 'A Note on Measures of Distance between Income Distributions', *Journal of Economic Theory*, 41.

—— and ROY, T. (1985). 'Measurement of Fuzziness: A General Approach', *Theory and Decision*, 19.

—— DUTTA, B., and WEYMARK, D. (1985). 'Ethical Indices of Income Mobility', *Social Choice and Welfare*, 2.

CHAPMAN, B. (1983). 'Rights as Constraints: Nozick vs. Sen', *Theory and Decision*, 15.

CHEN, L. C. (1986). 'Primary Health Care in Developing Countries: Overcoming Operational, Technical and Social Barriers', *Lancet*, 2.

—— HUQ, E., and D'SOUZA, D. (1981). 'Sex Bias in the Family Allocation of Food and Health Care in Rural Bangladesh', *Population and Development Review*, 7.

CHEN, M. (1986a). *A Quiet Revolution: Women in Transition in Rural Bangladesh* (Dhaka: BRAC).

—— (1986b). 'Poverty, Gender and Work in Bangladesh', *Economic and Political Weekly*, 21 (1 Feb.).

—— (1991). 'A Matter of Survival: Women's Right to Work in India and Bangladesh', paper presented at the WIDER conference on 'Human Capabilities: Women, Men and Equality', 14–16 August.

CHENERY, H. B., and SRINIVASAN, T. N. (1988) (eds.). *Handbook of Development Economics*, i (Amsterdam: North-Holland).

—— AHLUWALIA, M. S., BELL, C. L. G., DULOY, J. H., and JOLLY, R. (1974) (eds.). *Redistribution with Growth* (Oxford: Clarendon Press).

CHICHILNISKY, G. (1980). 'Basic Needs and Global Models', *Alternatives*, 6.

CHIPMAN, J. (1985). 'The Theory of Measurement of Income Distribution', *Advances in Econometrics*, 4.

CLARK, J. B. (1902). *Distribution of Wealth* (London: Macmillan).

CLARK, S., and HEMMING, R. (1981). 'Aspects of Household Poverty in Britain', *Social Policy and Administration*, 15.

—————— and ULPH, D. (1981). 'On Indices for the Measurement of Poverty', *Economic Journal*, 91.

CLEMHOUT, A. (1979). 'A Life-Cycle Theory of Marriage and Divorce: A Pareto Optimal Differential Game Model', in P. Liu and J. F. Sutinen (eds.), *Control Theory in Mathematical Economics* (New York: Marcel Dekker).

CLEMHOUT, S., and WAN, H. Y., JR. (1979). 'Symmetric Marriage, Household Decision Making and Impact on Fertility', Working Paper 152, Cornell University.

COHEN, G. A. (1978).

—— (1986). 'Self-Ownership, World Ownership, and Equality', *Social Philosophy and Policy*, 3.

—— (1988). *History, Labour and Freedom: Themes from Marx* (Oxford: Clarendon Press).

—— (1989). 'On the Currency of Egalitarian Justice', *Ethics*, 99.

—— (1990). 'Equality of What? On Welfare, Goods and Capabilities', *Recherches économiques de Louvain*, 56.

—— (1992). 'Equality of What? On Welfare, Resources and Capabilities', in Nussbaum and Sen (1992).

COHEN, M., NAGEL, T. and SCANLON, T. (1980) (eds.). *Marx, Justice and History* (Princeton, NJ: Princeton University Press).

COLANDER, D. (1984) (ed.). *Neoclassical Political Economy* (Boston: Ballinger Press).

COOPER, T. C. (1971). 'Poverty', unpub. manuscript, St Hugh's College, Oxford.

COUGHLIN, P. C. (1986). 'Libertarian Concessions of the Private Pareto Rule', *Economica*, 53.

COWELL, F. A. (1977). *Measuring Inequality* (New York: Wiley).

—— (1980). 'On the Structure of Additive Inequality Measures', *Review of Economic Studies*, 47.

—— (1985). 'Measures of Distributional Change: An Axiomatic Approach', *Review of Economic Studies*, 52.

—— (1986). 'Poverty Measures, Inequality and Decomposability', in Bos, Rose, and Seidl (1986).

—— (1988). 'Social Welfare Functions and Income Inequality', London School of Economics.

—— and KUGA, K. (1981). 'Inequality Measurement: An Axiomatic Approach', *European Economic Review*, 15.

CROCKER, D. A. (1983). *Praxis and Democratic Socialism* (Brighton: Harvester Press).

—— (1991a). 'Toward Development Ethics', *World Development*, 19.

—— (1991*b*). 'Functioning and Capability: The Foundations of Sen's Development Ethic', IDEA Montclair Workshop, mimeographed, Colorado State University.

CROCKER, L. (1980). *Positive Liberty* (London: Martinus Nijhoff).

CULYER, A. J. (1986). 'The Scope and Limits of Health Economics', in Gérard Gäfgen (ed.), *Ökonomie des Gesundheitswesens* (Berlin: Dunker and Humbolt).

DAHLBY, B. G. (1987). 'Interpreting Inequality Measures in a Harsanyi Framework', *Theory and Decision*, 22.

DAHRENDORF, R. (1988). *The Modern Social Conflict: An Essay on the Politics of Liberty* (London: Weidenfeld & Nicolson).

DALTON, H. (1920). 'The Measurement of the Inequality of Incomes', *Economic Journal*, 30.

—— (1925). *Inequality of Incomes* (London: Routledge).

DANIELS, H. (1983). 'Health Care Needs and Distributive Justice', in Bayer, Caplan, and Daniels (1983).

DANIELS, N. (1975) (ed.). *Reading Rawls* (Oxford: Blackwell).

DANZIGER, S. H., and WEINBERG, D. H. (1986). *Fighting Poverty: What Works and What Doesn't* (Cambridge, Mass.: Harvard University Press).

DAS, V., and NICHOLAS, R. (1981). '"Welfare" and "Well-Being" in South Asian Societies', ACLS–SSRC Joint Committee on South Asia (New York: SSRC).

DAS GUPTA, M. (1987). 'Selective Discrimination against Female Children in Rural Punjab, India', *Population and Development Review*, 13.

DASGUPTA, B. (1977). *Village Society and Labour Use* (Delhi: Oxford University Press).

DASGUPTA, P. (1980). 'Decentralization and Rights', *Economica*, 47.

—— (1982). *The Control of Resources* (Oxford: Blackwell).

—— (1986). 'Positive Freedom, Markets and the Welfare State', *Oxford Review of Economic Policy*, 2.

—— (1988). 'Lives and Well-Being', *Social Choice and Welfare*, 5.

—— (1989). 'Power and Control in the Good Polity', in A. Hamlin and Pettit (1989).

—— (1990). 'Well-Being and the Extent of its Realization in Poor Countries', *Economic Journal*, 100.

—— and HAMMOND, P. (1980). 'Fully Progressive Taxation', *Journal of Public Economics*, 13.

—— and HEAL, G. (1979). *Economic Theory and Exhaustible Resources* (London: James Nisbet and Cambridge: Cambridge University Press).

—— and RAY, D. (1990). 'Adapting to Undernutrition: Clinical Evidence and its Implications', in Drèze and Sen (1990), vol. 1.

—— SEN, A. K., and STARRETT, D. (1973). 'Notes on the Measurement of Inequality', *Journal of Economic Theory*, 6.

DAVIDSON, D. (1986). 'Judging Interpersonal Interests', in Elster and Hylland (1986).

DEATON, A. (1980). 'The Measurement of Welfare: Theory and Practical Guidelines', LSMS Working Paper 7, The World Bank.

—— (1987). 'The Allocation of Goods within the Household: Adults, Children and Gender', mimeographed, Princeton University.

—— (1988). 'Household Behavior in Developing Countries', Occasional Paper No. 1, Economic Growth Center, Yale University.

—— and MUELLBAUER, J. (1980). *Economics and Consumer Behaviour* (Cambridge: Cambridge University Press).

———— (1986). 'On Measuring Child Costs with Applications to Poor Countries', *Journal of Political Economy*, 94.

DEB, R. (1989). 'Rights as Alternative Game Forms: Is There a Difference of Consequence', mimeographed, Southern Methodist University.

DELBONO, F. (1986). Review article on *Commodities and Capabilities*, *Economic Notes* (Siena), 15.

DE LEONARDO, O., MAURIE, D., and ROTELLI, F. (1986). 'Deinstitutionalization, Another Way: The Italian Mental Health Reform', *Health Promotion*, 1.

DEN HARTOG, A. P. (1973). 'Unequal Distribution of Food within the Household', *FAO Newsletter*, 10: 4 (Oct.–Dec.).

DESAI, M. J. (1984). 'A General Theory of Poverty', *Indian Economic Review*, 19.

—— (1988). 'The Economics of Famine', in Harrison (1988).

—— (1990). 'Poverty and Capability: Towards an Empirically Implementable Measure', mimeographed, London School of Economics.

—— and SHAH, A. (1988). 'An Econometric Approach to the Measurement of Poverty', *Oxford Economic Papers*, 40.

—— BOLTVINNIK, J., and SEN, A. K. (1991). *Social Progress Index* (Bogota: UNDP).

DIEWERT, W., and MONTMARQUETTE, C. (1983) (eds.). *Price Level Measurement* (Ottawa: Statistics Canada).

DIXON, R. (1982). 'Mobilizing Women for Rural Employment in South Asia: Issues of Class, Caste and Patronage', *Economic Development and Cultural Change*, 30.

—— (1983). 'Land Labour and the Sex Composition of the Agricultural Labour Force: An International Comparison', *Development and Change*, 14.

DOBB, M. H. (1937). *Political Economy of Capitalism* (London: Routledge).

DONALDSON, D., and ROEMER, J. E. (1987). 'Social Choice in Economic Environments with Dimensional Variation', *Social Choice and Welfare*, 4.

—— and WEYMARK, J. A. (1980). 'A Single-Parameter Generalization of the Gini Indices of Inequality', *Journal of Economic Theory*, 22.

———— (1986). 'Properties of Fixed-Population Poverty Indices', *International Economic Review*, 27.

DREWNOWSKI, J. (1978). 'The Affluence Line', *Social Indicators Research*, 5.

DRÈZE, J., and SEN, A. (1989). *Hunger and Public Action* (Oxford: Clarendon Press).

———— (1990). *The Political Economy of Hunger*, 3 vols. (Oxford: Clarendon Press).

—— and STERN, N. H. (1987). 'The Theory of Cost Benefit Analysis', in Auerbach and Feldstein (1987).

D'SOUZA, F. (1988). 'Famine: Social Security and an Analysis of Vulnerability', in Harrison (1988).

—— (1990). 'Preface', in Article 19 (1990).

DUTTA, B. (1978). 'On the Measurement of Poverty in Rural India', *Indian Economic Review*, 15.

—— (1980). 'Intersectoral Disparities and Income Distribution in India: 1960–61 to 1973–74', *Indian Economic Review*, 15.

—— and RAY, D. (1989). 'A Concept of Egalitarianism under Participation Constraints', *Econometrica*, 57.

DWORKIN, G. (1982). 'Is More Choice Better than Less?' *Midwest Studies in Philosophy*, 7.

DWORKIN, R. (1978). *Taking Rights Seriously*, 2nd edn. (London: Duckworth).

—— (1981). 'What is Equality? Part 1: Equality of Welfare', and 'What is Equality? Part 2: Equality of Resources', *Philosophy and Public Affairs*, 10.

—— (1985). *A Matter of Principle* (Cambridge, Mass.: Harvard University Press).

—— (1987). 'What is Equality? III: The Place of Liberty', *Iowa Law Review*, 73.

DYSON, T. (1987). 'Excess Female Mortality in India: Uncertain Evidence on a Narrowing Differential', mimeographed, London School of Economics.

EBERT, U. (1987). 'Size and Distribution of Incomes as Determinants of Social Welfare', *Journal of Economic Theory*, 41.

—— (1988). 'Measurement of Inequality: An Attempt at Unification and Generalization', *Social Choice and Welfare*, 5.

EDGEWORTH, F. Y. (1881). *Mathematical Psychics* (London: Kegan Paul).

EDWARDS, R. C., REICH, M., and WEISSKOPF, T. (1986) (eds.). *The Capitalist System* (Englewood Cliffs, NJ: Prentice-Hall).

EICHHORN, W. (1988*a*) (ed.). *Measurement in Economics: Theory and Applications in Economic Indices* (Heidelberg: Physica-Verlag).

—— (1988*b*). 'On a Class of Inequality Measures', *Social Choice and Welfare*, 5.

—— and GEHRIG, W. (1982). 'Measurement of Inequality in Economics', in B. Korte (ed.), *Modern Applied Mathematics—Optimization and Operations Research* (Amsterdam: North-Holland).

ELSTER, J. (1979). *Ulysses and the Sirens* (Cambridge: Cambridge University Press).

—— (1986). *Making Sense of Marx* (Cambridge: Cambridge University Press).

—— and HYLLAND, A. (1986) (eds). *Foundations of Social Choice Theory* (Cambridge: Cambridge University Press).

ERIKSON, R. (1992). 'Descriptions of Inequality: The Swedish Approach to Welfare Research', in Nussbaum and Sen (1992).

—— and ABERG, R. (1987). *Welfare in Transition: A Survey of Living Conditions in Sweden (1968–81)* (Oxford: Clarendon Press).

—— HANSEN, E. J., RINGEN, S., and UUSITALO, H. (1986). *The Scandinavian Model: The Welfare State and Welfare Research* (New York: Sharpe).

EVANS, M. (1982) (ed.). *The Woman Question: Readings on the Subordination of Women* (London: Fontana).

FARMER, A. (1988). *The Developing World* (Dublin: Development Education Support Centre).

FARRELL, M. J. (1976). 'Liberalism in the Theory of Social Choice', *Review of Economic Studies*, 43.

FEIWEL, G. R. (1987) (ed.). *Arrow and the Foundations of the Theory of Economic Policy* (London: Macmillan).

FEREJOHN, J. A. (1978). 'The Distribution of Rights in Society', in Gottinger and Leinfellner (1978).

FIELDS, G. S. (1979). 'A Welfare Economic Approach to Growth and Distribution in the Dual Economy', *Quarterly Journal of Economics*, 93.

—— (1980a). *Poverty, Inequality and Development* (Cambridge: Cambridge University Press).

—— (1980b). 'Reply', *American Economic Review*, 70.

—— (1990). 'Do Inequality Measures Measure Inequality?' mimeographed, Cornell University.

—— and FEI, J. C. H. (1978). 'On Inequality Comparisons', *Econometrica*, 46.

—— and JAKUBSON, G. H. (1990). 'The Inequality–Development Relationship in Developing Countries', mimeographed, Cornell University.

FINE, B. J. (1975a). 'A Note on Interpersonal Aggregation and Partial Comparability', *Econometrica*, 43.

—— (1975b). 'Individual Liberalism in a Paretian Society', *Journal of Political Economy*, 83.

—— (1985). 'A Note on the Measurement of Inequality and Interpersonal Comparability', *Social Choice and Welfare*, 1.

FISHER, F. M. (1956). 'Income Distribution, Value Judgments and Welfare', *Quarterly Journal of Economics*, 70.

—— (1986). 'Household Equivalence Scales and Interpersonal Comparisons', mimeographed, MIT.

—— (1987). 'Household Equivalence Scales and Interpersonal Comparisons', *Review of Economic Studies*, 54.

—— and SHELL, K. (1972). *The Economic Theory of Price Indices* (New York: Academic Press).

FISHKIN, J. S. (1983). 'Can There Be a Neutral Theory of Justice?' *Ethics*, 93.

FISHLOW, A. (1980). 'Who Benefits from Economic Development? Comment', *American Economic Review*, 70.

FLOUD, R. (1992). 'Anthropometric Measures of Nutritional Status in Industrial Societies: Europe and North America since 1750', in Osmani (1992*a*).

—— and WACHTER, K. W. (1982). 'Poverty and Physical Stature: Evidence on the Standard of Living of London Boys 1770–1870', *Social Science History*, 6.

FOGEL, R. W. (1986). 'Nutrition and the Decline in Mortality since 1700: Some Additional Preliminary Findings', Working Paper 182, National Bureau of Economic Research, Cambridge, Mass.

—— (1992). 'Second Thoughts on the European Escape from Hunger: Crop Yields, Price Elasticities, Entitlements and Mortality Rates', in Osmani (1992*a*).

—— ENGERMAN, S. L., and TRUSSELL, J. (1982). 'Exploring the Use of Data on Height: The Analysis of Long Term Trends in Nutrition, Labour Welfare and Labour Productivity', *Social Science History*, 6.

FOLBRE, N. (1984). 'Cleaning House: New Perspectives on Household and Economic Development', mimeographed, New School for Social Research.

—— BERGMANN, B., AGARWAL, B., and FLORO, M. (1991) (eds.). *Women's Work in the World Economy* (London: Macmillan).

FOLEY, D. (1967). 'Resource Allocation in the Public Sector', *Yale Economic Essays*, 7.

FOSTER, J. (1984). 'On Economic Poverty: A Survey of Aggregate Measures', *Advances in Econometrics*, 3.

—— (1985). 'Inequality Measurement', in H. P. Young (ed.), *Fair Allocation* (Providence, RI: American Mathematical Society).

—— GREER, J., and THORBECKE, E. (1984). 'A Class of Decomposable Poverty Measurement', *Econometrica*, 42.

—— MAJUMDAR, M. K., and MITRA, T. (1988). 'Inequality and Welfare in Exchange Economies', CAE Discussion Paper No. 88–09, Cornell University.

—— and SHORROCKS, A. F. (1988*a*). 'Poverty Orderings', *Econometrica*, 56.

—— —— (1988*b*). 'Poverty Orderings and Welfare Dominance', *Social Choice and Welfare*, 5.

—— —— (1991). 'Subgroup Consistent Poverty Indices', *Econometrica*, 59.

FOUNTAIN, J. (1980). 'Bowley's Analysis of Bilateral Monopoly and Sen's Liberal Paradox in Collective Choice Theory: A Note', *Quarterly Journal of Economics*, 95.

FOXLEY, A., and RACZYNSKI, D. (1984). 'Vulnerable Groups in Recessionary Situations: The Case of Children and the Young in Chile', *World Development*, 12.

FRANK, R. H. (1985). *Choosing the Right Pond: Human Behavior and the Quest for Status* (New York: Oxford University Press).

FRANKFURT, H. (1987). 'Equality as a Moral Ideal', *Ethics*, 98.

FRIED, C. (1978). *Right and Wrong* (Cambridge, Mass.: Harvard University Press).

FUCHS, V. R. (1983). *How We Live: An Economic Perspective on Americans from Birth to Death* (Cambridge, Mass.: Harvard University Press).

GAERTNER, W. (1985). 'Justice Constrained Libertarian Claims and Pareto Efficient Collective Decisions', *Erkenntnis*, 23.

—— (1986). 'Pareto, Independent Rights Exercising and Strategic Behavior'. *Journal of Economics*, 46.

—— (1988). 'Review of Commodities and Capabilities', *Journal of Economics*, 48.

—— (1992). 'Comment on Cohen and Sen', in Nussbaum and Sen (1992).

—— and KRÜGER, L. (1981). 'Self-Supporting Preferences and Individual Rights: The Possibility of Paretian Liberalism', *Economica*, 48.

———— (1983). 'Alternative Libertarian Claims and Sen's Paradox', *Theory and Decision*, 15.

—— PATTANAIK, P., and SUZUMURA, K. (1992). 'Individual Rights Revisited', forthcoming in *Economica*.

GAIHA, R. (1985). 'Poverty, Technology and Infrastructure in Rural India', *Cambridge Journal of Economics*, 9.

—— and KAZMI, N. A. (1981). 'Aspects of Poverty in Rural India', *Economics of Planning*, 17.

GALBRAITH, J. K. (1952). *American Capitalism: The Concept of Countervailing Power* (Cambridge, Mass.: Riverside Press).

—— (1958). *The Affluent Society* (Boston: Houghton Mifflin).

—— (1967). *The New Industrial State* (Boston: Houghton Mifflin).

GAMBETTA, D. (1987) (ed.). *Trust and Agency* (Oxford: Blackwell).

GÄRDENFORS, P. (1981). 'Rights, Games and Social Choice', *Nous*, 15.

—— and PETTIT, P. (1989). 'The Impossibility of a Paretian Loyalist', *Theory and Decision*, 27.

GARDINER, J., HIMMELWEIT, S., and MACKINTOSH, M. (1975). 'Women's Domestic Labour', *Bulletin of the Conference of Socialist Economists*.

GARDNER, R. (1980). 'The Strategic Inconsistency of Paretian Liberalism', *Public Choice*, 35.

GASTWIRTH, J. L. (1975). 'The Estimation of a Family of Measures of Economic Inequality', *Journal of Econometrics*, 3.

GAUTHIER, D. (1986). *Morals by Agreement* (Oxford: Clarendon Press).

GEVERS, L. (1979). 'On Interpersonal Comparability and Social Welfare Orderings', *Econometrica*, 47.

GIBBARD, A. (1974). 'A Pareto-Consistent Libertarian Claim', *Journal of Economic Theory*, 7.

—— (1979). 'Disparate Goods and Rawls's Difference Principle: A Social Choice Theoretic Treatment', *Theory and Decision*, 11.

—— (1986). 'Interpersonal Comparisons: Preference, Good, and the Intrinsic Reward of a Life', in Elster and Hylland (1986).

GIGLIOTTI, G. A. (1988). 'The Conflict between Naive and Sophisticated Choice as a Form of the "Liberal Paradox"', *Theory and Decision*, 24.

GLANTZ, M. H. (1976). *The Political Economy of Natural Disaster* (New York: Praeger).

GLOVER, J. (1977). *Causing Death and Saving Lives* (Harmondsworth: Penguin Books).

GOLDIN, C. (1989). *Understanding the Gender Gap: An Economic History of American Women* (New York: Oxford University Press).

GOLDSCHMIDT-CLERMONT, L. (1982). *Unpaid Work in the Household* (Geneva: ILO).

GOODIN, R. E. (1982). *Political Theory and Public Policy* (Chicago: University of Chicago Press).

—— (1985). *Protecting the Vulnerable* (Chicago: University of Chicago Press).

—— (1986). 'Laundering Preferences', in Elster and Hylland (1986).

—— (1987). 'Egalitarianism, Fetishistic and Otherwise', *Ethics*, 98.

—— (1988). *Reasons for Welfare: The Political Theory of the Welfare State* (Princeton, NJ: Princeton University Press).

GOPALAN, C. (1983). 'Measurement of Undernutrition: Biological Considerations', *Economic and Political Weekly*, 19 (9 Apr.).

GORMAN, W. M. (1956). 'The Demand for Related Goods', Journal Paper J 3129, Iowa Experimental Station, Ames, Ia.

—— (1976). 'Tricks with Utility Functions', in M. J. Artis and A. R. Nobay (eds.), *Essays in Economic Analysis* (Cambridge: Cambridge University Press).

GOSLING, J. C. B. (1969). *Pleasure and Desire* (Oxford: Clarendon Press).

GOTTINGER, H. W., and LEINFELLNER, W. (1978) (eds.). *Decision Theory and Social Ethics* (Dordrecht: Reidel).

GOUGUEN, J. A. (1967). 'L-Fuzzy Sets', *Journal of Mathematical Analysis and Applications*.

GRAAFF, J. DE V. (1946). 'Fluctuations in Income Concentration', *South African Journal of Economics*, 14.

—— (1957). *Theoretical Welfare Economics* (Cambridge: Cambridge University Press).

—— (1977). 'Equity and Efficiency as Components of General Welfare', *South African Journal of Economics*, 45.

—— (1979). 'Tastes, Values and the Foundations of Normative Economics', paper read at the 6th Interlaken Seminar on Analysis and Ideology.

—— (1985). 'Normative Measurement Theory', unpub. manuscript.

GRANT, J. P. (1978). *Disparity Reduction Rates in Social Indicators* (Washington, DC: Overseas Development Council).

GRAY, J. (1983). *John Stuart Mill's Doctrine of Liberty: A Defence* (London: Routledge and Kegan Paul).

GREEN, E. T. (1980). 'Libertarian Aggregation of Preferences: What the "Coase Theorem" Might Have Said', Social Science Working Paper No. 315, California Institute of Technology.

GRIFFIN, J. (1981). 'Equality: On Sen's Weak Equity Axiom', *Mind*, 50.

—— (1982). 'Modern Utilitarianism', *Revue internationale de philosophie*, 36.

—— (1986). *Well-Being* (Oxford: Clarendon Press).

GRIFFIN, K. (1978). *International Inequality and National Poverty* (London: Macmillan).

—— and KNIGHT, J. (1989) (eds.). *Human Development in the 1980s and Beyond, Journal of Development Planning*, 19 (Special Number).

GUTMANN, A. (1980). *Liberal Equality* (Cambridge: Cambridge University Press).

—— (1983). 'For and Against Equal Access to Health Care', in Bayer, Caplan, and Daniels (1983).

GUTTAMACHER, A. F. (1957). *Pregnancy and Birth* (New York: Viking Press).

GWATKIN, D. R., WILCOX, J. R., and WRAY, J. D. (1980). 'The Policy Implications of Field Experience in Primary Health and Nutrition', *Social Science and Medicine*, 14C.

HAGENAARS, A. J. M., and DE VOS, K. (1989). 'A Comparison between the Poverty Concepts of Sen and Townsend', mimeographed.

—— and VAN PRAAG, B. M. S. (1983). 'A Synthesis of Poverty Line Definitions', Report P3.01, Center for Research in Public Economics, Leiden University.

HAHN, F. H. (1971). 'Equilibrium with Transaction Costs', *Econometrica*, 39.

—— and HOLLIS, M. (1979) (eds.). *Philosophy and Economic Theory* (Oxford: Clarendon Press).

HAKSAR, V. (1979). *Equality, Liberty and Perfectionism* (Oxford: Clarendon Press).

HAMADA, K., and TAKAYAMA, N. (1978). 'Censored Income Distributions and the Measurement of Poverty', *Bulletin of International Statistical Institute*, 47.

HAMLIN, A. (1986). *Ethics, Economics and the State* (Brighton: Wheatsheaf Books).

—— (1989). 'Rights, Indirect Utilitarianism, and Contractarianism', *Economics and Philosophy*, 5.

—— and PETTIT, P. (1989) (eds.). *The Good Polity: Normative Analysis of the State* (Oxford: Blackwell).

HAMMOND, P. J. (1976a). 'Equity, Arrow's Conditions and Rawls' Difference Principle', *Econometrica*, 44.

—— (1976b). 'Why Ethical Measures of Inequality Need Interpersonal Comparisons', *Theory and Decision*, 7.

—— (1977). 'Dual Interpersonal Comparisons of Utility and the Welfare Economics of Income Distribution', *Journal of Public Economics*, 6.

—— (1978). 'Economic Welfare with Rank Order Price Weighting', *Review of Economic Studies*, 45.

—— (1981). 'Liberalism, Independent Rights and the Pareto Principle', in J. Cohen (ed.), *Proceedings of the 6th International Congress of Logic, Methodology and Philosophy of Science* (Dordrecht: Reidel).

—— (1982). 'Utilitarianism, Uncertainty and Information', in Sen and Williams (1982).

—— (1985). 'Welfare Economics', in G. Feiwel (ed.), *Issues in Contemporary Microeconomics and Welfare* (Albany, NY: SUNY Press).

—— (1986). 'Consequentialist Social Norms for Public Decisions', in Heller, Starr, and Starrett (1986).

HAMMOND, R. J. (1951). *History of the Second World War: Food* (London: HMSO).

HAMPSHIRE, S. (1982). 'Morality and Convention', in Sen and Williams (1982).

HANSSON, B. (1977). 'The Measurement of Social Inequality', in R. Butts and J. Hintikka (eds.), *Foundational Problems in the Special Sciences* (Dordrecht: Reidel).

HANSSON, S. O. (1988). 'Rights and the Liberal Paradoxes', *Social Choice and Welfare*, 5.

HARE, R. M. (1952). *The Language of Morals* (Oxford: Clarendon Press).

—— (1963). *Freedom and Reason* (Oxford: Clarendon Press).

—— (1981). *Moral Thinking: Its Levels, Methods and Point* (Oxford: Clarendon Press).

—— (1982). 'Ethical Theory and Utilitarianism', in Sen and Williams (1982).

HAREL, A., and NITZAN, S. (1987). 'The Libertarian Resolution of the Paretian Liberal Paradox', *Journal of Economics*, 47.

HARMAN, G. (1977). *The Nature of Morality* (New York: Oxford University Press).

HARRISON, G. A. (1988). *Famines* (Oxford: Clarendon Press).

HARRISS, B. (1977). 'Paddy Milling: Problems in Policy and Choice of Technology', in B. F. Farmer (ed.), *The Green Revolution* (London: Billing).

—— (1990). 'The Intrafamily Distribution of Hunger in South Asia', in Drèze and Sen (1990), vol. 1.

—— and WATSON, E. (1987). 'The Sex-Ratio in South Asia', in J. H. Momsen and J. Townsend (eds.), *Geography of Gender in the Third World* (London: Hutchinson).

HARSANYI, J. C. (1955). 'Cardinal Welfare, Individualistic Ethics and Inter-personal Comparisons of Utility', *Journal of Political Economy*, 63.

—— (1982). 'Morality and the Theory of Rational Behaviour', in Sen and Williams (1982).

HART, H. L. A. (1961). *The Concept of Law* (Oxford: Clarendon Press).

—— (1973). 'Rawls on Liberty and its Priority', *University of Chicago Law Review*, 40. (Repr. in Daniels 1975.)

HART, K. (1987). 'Commoditization and the Standard of Living', in Sen *et al.* (1987).

HAUSMAN, D. M., and McPHERSON, M. S. (1991). 'Taking Morality Seriously: Economics and Contemporary Moral Philosophy', mimeo-graphed, University of Wisconsin and Williams College.

HAWTHORN, G. (1987). 'Introduction', in Sen *et al.* (1987).

HAYEK, F. A. (1960). *The Constitution of Liberty* (London: Routledge and Kegan Paul).

—— (1967). *Studies in Philosophy, Politics, and Economics* (Chicago: University of Chicago Press).

HELLER, W. P., STARR, R. M., and STARRETT, D. A. (1986) (eds.). *Social Choice and Public Decision Making: Essays in Honor of Kenneth J. Arrow* (Cambridge: Cambridge University Press).

HELM, D. (1986). 'The Assessment: The Economic Borders of the State', *Oxford Review of Economic Policy*, 2.

HELPMAN, E., and SADKA, E. (1978). 'Optimal Taxation of Full Income', *International Economic Review*, 19.

HEMMELL, V., and SINDBJERG, P. (1984). *Women in Rural China: Policy towards Women before and after the Cultural Revolution* (Copenhagen: Scandinavian Institute of Social Studies and Humanities Press).

HEMMING, R. (1984). *Poverty and Incentives: The Economics of Social Security* (Oxford: Clarendon Press).

HICKS, J. R. (1939). *Value and Capital* (Oxford: Clarendon Press).

—— (1940). 'The Valuation of the Social Income', *Economica*, 7.

HILPINEN, R. (1971) (ed.). *Deontic Logic: Introductory and Systematic Readings* (Dordrecht: Reidel).

HIMMELFARB, G. (1984). *The Idea of Poverty* (London: Faber & Faber).

HIRSCH, F. (1977). *Social Limits to Growth* (London: Routledge).

HIRSCHMAN, A. O. (1958). *The Strategy of Economic Development* (New Haven, Conn.: Yale University Press).

—— (1982). *Shifting Involvement* (Princeton, NJ: Princeton University Press).

HOBSBAWM, E. (1964). *Labouring Men* (London: Weidenfeld and Nicolson).

—— (1989). *Politics for a Rational Left* (London: Verso).

HONDERICH, T. (1985) (ed.). *Morality and Objectivity: A Tribute to J. L. Mackie* (London: Routledge and Kegan Paul).

Hossain, I. (1990). *Poverty as Capability Failure* (Helsinki: Swedish School of Economics).

Houthakker, H. S. (1950). 'Revealed Preference and the Utility Function', *Economica*, 17.

Hull, C. H. (1899) (ed.). *The Economic Writings of Sir William Petty* (Cambridge: Cambridge University Press).

Hurley, S. (1985). 'Objectivity and Disagreement', in Honderich (1985).

—— (1989). *Natural Reasons* (Oxford: Clarendon Press).

Hurwicz, L., Schmeidler, D., and Sonnenschein, H. (1985) (eds.). *Social Goals and Social Organisation: Essays in Memory of Elisha Pazner* (Cambridge: Cambridge University Press).

Hussain, A., Liu, H., and Liu, X. (1989). 'Compendium of Literature on the Chinese Social Security System', mimeographed, London School of Economics.

Hutchens, R. M. (1986). 'Segregation Curves, Lorenz Curves and Inequality in the Distribution of People across Groups', New York School of Industrial and Labor Relations, Cornell University.

Hylland, A. (1986). 'The Purpose and Significance of Social Choice Theory: Some General Remarks and Application to the "Lady Chatterley Problem"', in Elster and Hylland (1986).

Isenman, P. (1980). 'Basic Needs: The Case of Sri Lanka', *World Development*, 7.

Iyengar, N. S. (1989). 'Recent Studies of Poverty in India', *Journal of Quantitative Economics*, 5.

Jain, D. (1985). 'The Household Trap: Report on a Field Survey of Female Activity Patterns', in Jain and Banerjee (1985).

—— and Banerjee, N. (1985). *Tyranny of the Household: Investigative Essays on Women's Work* (New Delhi: Vikas).

Jasso, G. (1981). 'Who Gains and Who Loses under Alternative Income Distribution Regimes that have Identical Magnitudes of the Gini Coefficient', *Proceedings of the Social Statistics Section of the American Statistical Association*, 1981.

Jayawardena, K. (1986). *Feminism and Nationalism in the Third World* (London: Zed Books).

Jayawardena, L. (1974). 'Sri Lanka', in Chenery *et al.* (1974).

Jencks, C. (1972). *Inequality* (New York: Basic Books).

Johansson, S. R. (1991). 'Mortality, Welfare and Gender: Continuity and Change in Explanations for Male/Female Mortality Differences over Three Centuries', *Continuity and Change*.

Jorgenson, D. W., and Slesnick, D. T. (1983). 'Individual and Social Cost of Living Indexes', in Diewert and Montmarquette (1983).

—————— (1984a). 'Inequality in the Distribution of Individual Welfare', *Advances in Econometrics*, 3.

—————— (1984*b*). 'Aggregate Consumer Behaviour and the Measurement of Inequality', *Review of Economic Studies*, 51.

—————— (1986). 'Redistribution Policy and the Elimination of Poverty', discussion paper, Harvard Institute of Economic Research.

—————— (1987). 'Aggregate Consumer Behaviour and Household Equivalence Scales', *Journal of Business and Economic Statistics*, 5.

——— LAU, L. J., and STOKER, T. M. (1980). 'Welfare Comparison under Exact Aggregation', *American Economic Review*, 70.

KAKWANI, N. (1980*a*). *Income, Inequality and Poverty* (New York: Oxford University Press).

——— (1980*b*). 'On a Class of Poverty Measures', *Econometrica*, 48.

——— (1981). 'Welfare Measures: An International Comparison', *Journal of Development Economics*, 8.

——— (1986). *Analysing Redistribution Policies* (Cambridge: Cambridge University Press).

——— (1988). 'Income Inequality, Welfare and Poverty in a Developing Economy with Applications to Sri Lanka', *Social Choice and Welfare*, 5.

——— (1992). 'Measuring Undernutrition with Variable Calorie Requirements', in Osmani (1992*a*).

——— and SUBBARAO, K. (1990). 'Rural Poverty in India, 1973–86', Working Paper WPS 526, The World Bank.

KALAI, E., and SMORDINSKY, M. (1975). 'Other Solutions to Nash's Bargaining Problem', *Econometrica*, 43.

KANBUR, R. [S. M. R.] (1979). 'Of Risk Taking and Personal Distribution of Income', *Journal of Political Economy*, 87.

——— (1982*a*). 'Entrepreneurial Risk Taking, Inequality and Public Policy', *Journal of Political Economy*, 87.

——— (1982*b*). 'The Measurement and Decomposition of Inequality and Poverty: A Selective Survey', in F. van der Ploeg (ed.), *Handbook of Applicable Mathematics: Economics* (Chichester: John Wiley and Sons).

——— (1987). 'The Standard of Living: Uncertainty, Inequality and Opportunity', in Sen *et al.* (1987).

——— and HADDAD, L. (1990). 'How Serious is the Neglect of Intrahousehold Inequality', *Economic Journal*, 100.

——— and STROMBERG, J. O. (1986). 'Income Transitions and Income Distribution Dominance', *Journal of Economic Theory*, 96.

KANEKO, M., and NAKAMURA, M. (1979). 'The Nash Social Welfare Function', *Econometrica*, 47.

KANGER, S. (1957). *New Foundations for Ethical Theory* (Stockholm). (Repr. in Hilpinen 1971.)

——— (1972). 'Law and Logic', *Theoria*, 32.

——— (1985). 'On Realization of Human Rights', *Acta Philosophica Fennica*, 38.

KANT, I. (1785). *Fundamental Principles of Metaphysics of Ethics*, English trans. by T. K. Abbott (London: Longmans, 1907).

—— (1788). *Critique of Practical Reason*, English trans. by L. W. Beck (New York: Liberal Arts Press, 1956).

KAPTEYN, A., and VAN PRAAG, B. M. S. (1976). 'A New Approach to the Construction of Family Equivalent Scales', *European Economic Review*, 7.

KARNI, E. (1978). 'Collective Rationality, Unanimity and Liberal Ethics', *Review of Economic Studies*, 45.

KELLY, J. S. (1976a). 'The Impossibility of a Just Liberal', *Economica*, 43.

—— (1976b). 'Rights-Exercising and a Pareto-Consistent Libertarian Claim', *Journal of Economic Theory*, 13.

—— (1978). *Arrow Impossibility Theorems* (New York: Academic Press).

KELSEY, D. (1985). 'The Liberal Paradox: A Generalization', *Social Choice and Welfare*, 1.

KELSEY, D. (1988). 'What is Responsible for the "Paretian Epidemic"', *Social Choice and Welfare*, 5.

KERN, L. (1978). 'Comparative Distribution Ethics: An Extension of Sen's Examination of the Pure Distribution Problem', in Gottinger and Leinfellner (1978).

KHAN, Q. M. (1985). 'A Model of Endowment Constrained Demand for Food in an Agricultural Economy with Empirical Application to Bangladesh', *World Development*, 13.

KOLAKOWSKI, L. (1978). *Main Currents of Marxism: Its Origin, Growth and Dissolution* (Oxford: Clarendon Press).

KOLM, S. CH. (1969). 'The Optimal Production of Social Justice', in Margolis and Guitton (1969).

—— (1976). 'Unequal Inequalities', *Journal of Economic Theory*, 12.

—— (1977). 'Multidimensional Egalitarianism', *Quarterly Journal of Economics*, 91.

KOOPMANS, T. C. (1964). 'On the Flexibility of Future Preferences', in M. W. Shelley and J. L. Bryan (eds.), *Human Judgments and Optimality* (New York: Wiley).

KORNAI, J. (1988). 'Individual Freedom and the Reform of Socialist Economy', *European Economic Review*, 32.

KORSGAARD, C. (1992). 'Comments on Cohen and Sen', in Nussbaum and Sen (1992).

KRELLE, W., and SHORROCKS, A. F. (1978) (eds.). *Personal Income Distribution* (Amsterdam: North-Holland).

KREPS, D. (1979). 'A Representation Theorem for "Preference for Flexibility"', *Econometrica*, 47.

KRISHNAJI, N. (1987). 'Poverty and the Sex Ratio: Some Data and Speculations', *Economic and Political Weekly*, 22.

KUMAR, B. G. (1987). 'Poverty and Public Policy: Government Intervention and Levels of Living in Kerala, India', D.Phil. thesis (Oxford).

—— (1989). 'Gender, Differential Mortality and Development: The Experience of Kerala', *Cambridge Journal of Economics*, 13.

KUMAR, A. K. S. (1992). 'Maternal Capabilities and Child Survival in Low Income Regions: Economic Analysis of Infant Mortality Differentials in India', Ph.D. dissertation, Harvard University.

KUNDU, A., and SMITH, T. E. (1983). 'An Impossibility Theorem on Poverty Indices', *International Economic Review*, 24.

KUZNETS, S. (1961). *Six Lectures on Economic Growth* (New York: Free Press of Glencoe).

—— (1966). *Modern Economic Growth* (New Haven, Conn.: Yale University Press).

—— (1973). *Population, Capital and Growth: Selected Essays* (London: Heinemann).

KYNCH, J. (1985). 'How Many Women are Enough? Sex Ratios and the Right to Life', *Third World Affairs 1985* (London: Third World Foundation).

—— and SEN, A. K. (1983). 'Indian Women: Well-Being and Survival', *Cambridge Journal of Economics*, 7.

LADEN, T. (1991*a*). 'Games, Fairness and Rawls's *A Theory of Justice*, *Philosophy and Public Affairs*, 20.

—— (1991*b*). 'Freedom, Preference and Objectivity: Women and the Capability Approach', mimeographed, Department of Philosophy, Harvard University.

LAMBERT, P. J. (1985). 'Social Welfare and the Gini Coefficient Revisited', *Mathematical Social Sciences*, 9.

—— (1989). *The Distribution and Redistribution of Income* (Oxford: Basil Blackwell).

—— and WEALE, A. (1981). 'Equality, Risk-Aversion and Contractarian Social Choice', *Theory and Decision*, 13.

LANCASTER, K. J. (1966). 'A New Approach to Consumer Theory', *Journal of Political Economy*, 74.

—— (1971). *Consumer Demand: A New Approach* (New York: Columbia University Press).

LARMORE, C. (1987). *Patterns of Moral Complexity* (Cambridge: Cambridge University Press).

LASLETT, P. (1991). *A Fresh Map of Life: The Emergence of the Third Age* (Cambridge, Mass.: Harvard University Press).

LE BRETON, K., and TRANNOY, A. (1987). 'Measures of Inequality as an Aggregation of Individual Preferences about Income Distribution: The Arrowian Case', *Journal of Economic Theory*, 41.

—————— and URIARTE, J. R. (1985). 'Topological Aggregation of Inequality Preorders', *Social Choice and Welfare*, 2.

LE GRAND, J. (1982). *The Strategy of Equality: Redistribution and the Social Services* (London: Allen and Unwin).

—— (1984). 'Equity as an Economic Objective', *Journal of Applied Philosophy*, 1.

—— (1990). 'Equity versus Efficiency: The Elusive Trade-off', *Ethics*, 10.

—— (1991). *Equity and Choice* (London: Harper Collins).

LEHNING, P. B. (1989). 'Liberalism and Capabilities: Some Remarks on the Neutrality Debate', mimeographed, Rotterdam University.

LETWIN, W. (1983) (ed.). *Against Equality* (London: Macmillan).

LEVI, I. (1982). 'Liberty and Welfare', in Sen and Williams (1982).

—— (1986). *Hard Choices* (Cambridge: Cambridge University Press).

LEWIS, G. W., and ULPH, D. T. (1987). 'Poverty, Inequality and Welfare', Discussion Paper 87/188, University of Bristol.

LINDAHL, L. (1977). *Position and Change: A Study of Law and Logic* (Dordrecht: Reidel).

LINDBECK, A. (1988). 'Individual Freedom and Welfare State Policy', *European Economic Review*, 32.

LIPTON, M. (1983). 'Poverty, Undernutrition and Hunger', World Bank Staff Working Paper (Washington, DC: The World Bank).

—— (1985). 'A Problem in Poverty Measurement', *Mathematical Social Sciences*, 10.

LITTLE, I. M. D. (1950). *A Critique of Welfare Economics* (Oxford: Clarendon Press).

LOPEZ, A. D., and RUZICKA, L. T. (1983) (eds.). *Sex Differences in Mortality* (Canberra: Department of Demography, Australian National University).

LOURY, G. (1987). 'Why Should We Care about Group Inequality?' *Social Philosophy and Policy*, 5.

LOUTFI, M. F. (1980). *Rural Women: Unequal Partners in Development* (Geneva: ILO).

LUCAS, G. R. (1990). 'African Famine: New Economic and Ethical Perspectives', *Journal of Philosophy*, 87.

LUCAS, J. R. (1965). 'Against Equality', *Philosophy*, 40.

—— (1980). *On Justice* (Oxford: Clarendon Press).

LUCE, R. D., and RAIFFA, H. (1957). *Games and Decisions* (New York: Wiley).

LUKER, W. (1986). 'Welfare Economics, Positivist Idealism and Quasi-Experimental Methodology', mimeographed, University of Texas at Austin.

LUKES, S. (1985). *Marxism and Morality* (Oxford: Clarendon Press).

—— (1990). 'Equality and Liberty: Must They Conflict?', mimeographed, European University Institute.

LYDALL, H. F. (1966). *The Structure of Earnings* (Oxford: Clarendon Press).

MAASOUMI, E. (1986). 'The Measurement and Decomposition of Multi-dimensional Inequality', *Econometrica*, 54.

—— (1989). 'Continuously Distributed Attributes and Measures of Multivariate Inequality', *Journal of Econometrics*, 42.

McCord, C., and Freeman, H. P. (1990). 'Excess Mortality in Harlem', *New England Journal of Medicine*, 322 (18 Jan.).

McDowell, J. (1981). 'Non-Cognitivism and Rule Following', in S. H. Holtzman and C. M. Leigh (eds.), *Wittgenstein: To Follow a Rule* (London: Routledge and Kegan Paul).

—— (1985). 'Values and Secondary Qualities', in Honderich (1985).

McElroy, M. B., and Horney, M. J. (1981). 'Nash-Bargained Household Decisions: Toward a Generalization of the Theory of Demand', *International Economic Review*, 22.

MacIntyre, I. D. A. (1987). '"The Liberal Paradox: A Generalisation" by D. Kelsey', *Social Choice and Welfare*, 4.

—— (1988). 'Justice, Liberty, Unanimity and the Axioms of Identity', *Theory and Decision*, 24.

Mack, J., and Lansley, S. (1985). *Poor Britain* (London: Allen and Unwin).

Mackie, J. L. (1978a). *Ethics: Inventing Right and Wrong* (Harmondsworth: Penguin).

—— (1978b). 'Can There be a Rights-Based Moral Theory?' *Midwest Studies in Philosophy*, 3.

—— (1986). 'The Combination of Partially-Ordered Preferences', in J. L. Mackie, *Persons and Values* (Oxford: Clarendon Press).

McLean, I. (1980). 'Liberty, Equality and the Pareto Principle', *Analysis*, 40.

MacLeod, A. M. (1984). 'Distributive Justice, Contract and Equality', *Journal of Philosophy*, 81.

McMurrin, S. M. (1980) (ed.). *Tanner Lectures on Human Values*, i (Salt Lake City: University of Utah Press and Cambridge: Cambridge University Press).

McPherson, M. S. (1982). 'Mill's Moral Theory and the Problem of Preference Change', *Ethics*, 92.

—— (1984). 'Limits of Self-Seeking: The Role of Morality in Economic Life', in Colander (1984).

Majumdar, T. (1969). 'Revealed Preference and the Demand Theorem in a Not Necessarily Competitive Market', *Quarterly Journal of Economics*, 83.

Manser, M., and Brown, M. (1980). 'Marriage and Household Decision Making: A Bargaining Analysis', *International Economic Review*, 21.

Marcus, R. B. (1980). 'Moral Dilemmas and Consistency', *Journal of Philosophy*, 1977.

Marglin, S. A. (1984). *Growth, Distribution and Prices* (Cambridge, Mass.: Harvard University Press).

Margolis, J., and Guitton, H. (1969) (eds.). *Public Economics* (London: Macmillan).

Marx, K. (1844). *The Economic and Philosophic Manuscript of 1844*, English trans. (London: Lawrence and Wishart).

MARX, K. (with F. ENGELS) (1845–46). *The German Ideology*, English trans. (New York: International Publishers, 1947).

—— (1857–58). *Grundrisse: Foundations of the Critique of Political Economy*, English trans. by M. Nicolaus (Harmondsworth: Penguin Books, 1973).

—— (1867). *Capital*, vol. I, English trans. (London: Allen and Unwin, 1938).

—— (1875). *Critique of the Gotha Program*, English trans. (New York: International Publishers, 1938).

MASKIN, E. (1978). 'A Theorem on Utilitarianism', *Review of Economic Studies*, 45.

—— (1979). 'Decision-Making under Ignorance with Implications for Social Choice', *Theory and Decision*, 11.

MAZUMDAR, V. (1985). *Emergence of Women's Questions in India and the Role of Women's Studies* (New Delhi: Centre for Women's Development Studies).

MEADE, J. E. (1955). *Trade and Welfare* (Oxford: Oxford University Press).

—— (1965). *Efficiency, Equity and the Ownership of Property* (Cambridge, Mass.: Harvard University Press).

—— (1976). *The Just Economy* (London: Allen and Unwin).

MEEKS, G. (1991) (ed.). *Thoughtful Economic Man* (Cambridge: Cambridge University Press).

MEHRAN, F. (1976). 'Linear Measures of Economic Equality', *Econometrica*, 44.

MEYER, M. (1987). 'Multidimensional Correlation and the Measurement of Ex-Post Inequality under Uncertainty', unpub. manuscript, St John's College, Oxford.

MEZZETTI, C. (1987). 'Paretian Efficiency, Rawlsian Justice and the Nozick Theory of Right', *Social Choice and Welfare*, 4.

MIES, M. (1982). *The Lace Makers of Nasrapur: Indian Housewives Produce for the World Market* (London: Zed Press).

MILIBAND, R. (1977). *Marxism and Politics* (Oxford: Clarendon Press).

MILL, J. S. (1859). *On Liberty* (London). (Republished Harmondsworth: Penguin, 1974.)

—— (1861). *Utilitarianism* (London).

MILLER, B. (1981). *The Endangered Sex: Neglect of Female Children in Rural North India* (Ithaca, NY: Cornell University Press).

—— (1982). 'Female Labor Participation and Female Seclusion in Rural India: A Regional View', *Economic Development and Cultural Change*, 30.

—— (1984). 'Child Survival and Sex Differential in the Treatment of Children', *Medical Anthropology*, 8.

MINCER, J. (1962). 'Labor Force Participation of Married Women', in H. G. Lewis (ed.), *Aspects of Labour Economics* (Princeton, NJ: Princeton University Press). (Repr. in Amsden 1980.)

—— and POLOCHEK, S. (1974). 'Family Investments in Human Capital Earnings of Women', *Journal of Political Economy*, 82. (Repr. in Amsden 1980.)

MIRRLEES, J. (1971). 'An Exploration in the Theory of Optimum Income Taxation', *Review of Economic Studies*, 38.

—— (1974). 'Notes on Welfare Economics, Information and Uncertainty', in M. Baleh, D. McFadden, and S. Wu (eds.), *Essays on Economic Behaviour under Uncertainty* (Amsterdam: North-Holland).

—— (1982). 'The Economic Uses of Utilitarianism', in Sen and Williams (1982).

—— (1986). 'The Theory of Optimal Taxation', in Arrow and Intriligator (1986).

MITRA, A. (1980). *Implications of Declining Sex Ratio in India's Population* (Bombay: Allied Publishers).

MOOKHERJEE, D., and SHORROCKS, A. (1982). 'A Decomposition Analysis of the Trends in UK Income Inequality', *Economic Journal*, 92.

MORRIS, M. D. (1979). *Measuring the Conditions of the World's Poor: The Physical Quality of Life Index* (Oxford: Pergamon Press).

MOULIN, H. (1989). 'Welfare Bounds and Fair Allocation of Private Goods', mimeographed, Virginia Polytechnic Institute.

—— (1990). 'Interpreting Common Ownership', *Recherches économiques de Louvain*, 56.

MUELLBAUER, J. (1974*a*). 'Household Composition, Engel Curves and Welfare Comparisons between Households: A Duality Approach', *European Economic Review*, 5.

—— (1974*b*). 'Inequality Measures, Prices and Household Composition', *Review of Economic Studies*, 41.

—— (1978). 'Distributional Aspects of Price Comparisons', in R. Stone and W. Peterson (eds.), *Economic Contributions to Public Policy* (London: Macmillan).

—— (1987). 'Professor Sen on the Standard of Living', in Sen *et al.* (1987).

MUELLER, D. C. (1979). *Public Choice* (Cambridge: Cambridge University Press).

MURRAY, C. and CHEN, L. (1990). 'Health Transitions: Patterns and Dynamics', mimeographed, Center for Population Studies, Harvard University.

MUSGRAVE, R. (1959). *The Theory of Public Finance* (New York: McGraw-Hill).

NAGEL, T. (1979). *Mortal Questions* (Cambridge: Cambridge University Press).

—— (1980). 'The Limits of Objectivity', in McMurrin (1980).

—— (1986). *The View from Nowhere* (New York: Oxford University Press).

NASH, J. F. (1950). 'The Bargaining Problem', *Econometrica*, 18.

NEWBERY, D. M. G. (1970). 'A Theorem on the Measurement of Inequality', *Journal of Economic Theory*, 2.

NG, Y.-K. (1971). 'The Possibility of a Paretian Liberal: Impossibility Theorems and Cardinal Utility', *Journal of Political Economy*, 79.

—— (1979). *Welfare Economics* (London: Macmillan).

NISSEN, H. P. (1984) (ed.). *Towards Income Distribution Policies* (Tilburg: European Association of Development Research and Training Institute).

NORDHAUS, W., and TOBIN, J. (1972). 'Is Growth Obsolete?', in *National Bureau of Economic Research, Economic Growth: Fiftieth Anniversary Colloquium* (New York: NBER).

NOZICK, R. (1973). 'Distributive Justice', *Philosophy and Public Affairs*, 3.

—— (1974). *Anarchy, State and Utopia* (Oxford: Blackwell).

—— (1989). *The Examined Life* (New York: Simon & Schuster).

NURMI, H. (1984). 'On Taking Preferences Seriously', in Anckar and Berndtson (1984).

—— (1987). *Comparing Voting Systems* (Dordrecht: Reidel).

NUSSBAUM, M. C. (1985). *Fragility of Goodness: Luck and Ethics in Greek Tragedy and Philosophy* (Cambridge: Cambridge University Press).

—— (1988*a*). 'Nature, Function, and Capability: Aristotle on Political Distribution', *Oxford Studies in Ancient Philosophy* (supplementary volume).

—— (1988*b*). 'Non-Relative Virtues: An Aristotelian Approach', *Midwest Studies in Philosophy*, 13; revised version in Nussbaum and Sen (1991).

—— (1991*a*). 'Human Functioning and Social Justice: In Defence of Aristotelian Essentialism', paper presented at the WIDER conference on 'Human Capabilities: Women, Men and Equality', 14–16 Aug.

—— (1991*b*). 'Emotions and Women's Capabilities', paper presented at the WIDER conference on 'Human Capabilities: Women, Men and Equality', 14–16 Aug.

—— and SEN, A. K. (1992) (eds.). *The Quality of Life* (Oxford: Clarendon Press).

NYGRAD, F., and SANDSTROM, A. (1981). *Measuring Income Inequality* (Stockholm: Almqvist and Wiksell International).

OKIN, S. M. (1987). 'Justice and Gender', *Philosophy and Public Affairs*, 16 (Winter).

—— (1989). *Justice, Gender and Family* (New York: Basic Books).

OKUN, A. (1975). *Equality and Efficiency: The Big Tradeoff* (Washington: Brookings).

O'NEILL, O. (1986). *Faces of Hunger* (London: Allen and Unwin).

—— (1989). *Constructions of Reason: Explorations of Kant's Practical Philosophy* (Cambridge: Cambridge University Press).

—— (1992). 'Justice, Gender and International Boundaries', in Nussbaum and Sen (1992).

OSMANI, S. R. (1978). 'On the Normative Measurement of Inequality', *Bangladesh Development Studies*, 6.

—— (1982). *Economic Inequality and Group Welfare* (Oxford: Clarendon Press).

—— (1990*a*). 'Nutrition and the Economics of Food: Implications of Some Recent Controversies', in Drèze and Sen (1990), vol. 1.

—— (1990*b*). 'Freedom and the Choice of Space', mimeographed, WIDER, Helsinki.

—— (1992*a*) (ed.). *Nutrition and Poverty* (Oxford: Clarendon Press), forthcoming.

—— (1992*b*). 'Undernutrition: Measurement and Implications', in Osmani (1992*a*).

—— (1992*c*). 'Comments', in Nussbaum and Sen (1992).

OTTEN, M. W., TEUTSCH, S. M., WILLIAMSON, D. F., and MARKS, J. S. (1990). 'The Effect of Known Risk Factors in the Excess Mortality of Black Adults in the United States', *Journal of the American Medical Association*, 263 (9 Feb.).

PADMANABHA, P. (1982). 'Trends in Morality', *Economic and Political Weekly*, 17 (7 Aug.).

PALMER, J., SMEEDING, T., and TORREY, B. (1988). *The Vulnerable: America's Young and Old in the Industrial World* (Washington, DC: Urban Institute Press).

PANIKAR, P. G. K., and SOMAN, C. R. (1984). *Health Status of Kerala* (Trivandrum: Centre for Development Studies).

PANT, P., *et al.* (1962). *Perspective of Development 1961–1976. Implications of Planning for a Minimum Level of Living* (New Delhi: Planning Commission of India).

PANTULU, Y. V. (1980). 'On Sen's Measure of Poverty', mimeographed, Sardar Patel Institute of Economic and Social Research.

PAPANEK, H. (1990). 'To each less than she needs, from each more than she can do: Allocations, Entitlements and Value', in Tinker (1990*a*).

PARFIT, D. (1984). *Reasons and Persons* (Oxford: Clarendon Press).

PATTANAIK, P. K. (1988). 'On the Consistency of Libertarian Values', *Economica*, 55.

—— and SENGUPTA, M. (1991). 'A Note on Sen's Normalization Axiom for a Poverty Measure', mimeographed.

—— and XU, Y. (1990). 'On Ranking Opportunity Sets in Terms of Freedom of Choice', *Recherches économiques de Louvain*, 56.

PAYNE, P. R. (1985). 'Nutritional Adoption in Man: Social Adjustments and their Nutritional Implications' in Blaxter and Waterlow (1985).

—— and LIPTON, M., with LONGHURST, R., NORTH, J., and TREAGUST, S. (1988). 'How Third World Rural Households Adapt to Dietary Energy Stress', mimeographed, International Food Policy Research Institute, Washington, DC.

PAZNER, E. A., and SCHMEIDLER, D. (1974). 'A Difficulty in the Concept of Fairness', *Review of Economic Studies*, 41.

PEACOCK, A. T., and ROWLEY, C. K. (1972). 'Welfare Economics and the

Public Regulation of Natural Monopoly', *Journal of Political Economy*, 80.

PEN, J. (1971). *Income Distribution: Facts, Theories, Policies* (New York: Praeger).

PERELLI-MINETTI, C. R. (1977). 'Nozick on Sen: A Misunderstanding', *Theory and Decision*, 8.

PETTY, W. (1676). *Political Arithmetick*. (Republished in Hull 1899.)

PHELPS, E. S. (1973) (ed.). *Economic Justice* (Harmondsworth: Penguin).

—— (1977). 'Recent Developments in Welfare Economics: Justice et équité', in M. D. Intriligator, *Frontiers of Quantitative Economics*, iii (Amsterdam: North-Holland). (Repr. in Phelps 1980.)

—— (1980). *Studies in Macroeconomic Theory*, ii. *Redistribution and Growth* (New York: Academic Press).

PIGOU, A. C. (1952). *The Economics of Welfare*, 4th edn. with eight new appendices (London: Macmillan).

PLOTT, C. (1978). 'Rawls' Theory of Justice: An Impossibility Result', in Gottinger and Leinfellner (1978).

POGGE, T. W. (1989). *Realizing Rawls* (Ithaca, NY: Cornell University Press).

POLLAK, R. A., and WALES, T. J. (1979). 'Welfare Comparisons and Equivalent Scales', *American Economic Review*, 69.

———— (1981). 'Demographic Variables in Demand Analysis', *Econometrica*, 49.

PRESTON, S., KEYFITZ, N., and SCHOEN, R. (1972). *Causes of Death: Life Tables of National Populations* (New York: Seminar Press).

PUTNAM, H. (1987). *The Many Faces of Realism* (La Salle, Ill.: Open Court).

—— (1992). 'Objectivity and the Science/Ethics Distinction', in Nussbaum and Sen (1992).

PUTNAM, R. A. (1991). 'Why Not a Feminist Theory of Justice?' paper presented at the WIDER conference on 'Human Capabilities: Women, Men and Equality', 14–16 Aug.

PUTTERMAN, L. (1986). *Peasants, Collectives, and Choice* (Greenwich, Conn.: JAI Press).

PYATT, G. (1976). 'On the Interpretation and Disaggregation of Gini Coefficients', *Economic Journal*, 86.

—— (1987). 'Measuring Welfare, Poverty and Inequality', *Economic Journal*, 97.

RAE, D. (1981). *Equalities* (Cambridge, Mass.: Harvard University Press).

RAM, N. (1990). 'An Independent Press and Anti-Hunger Strategies: The Indian Experience', in Drèze and Sen (1990), vol. 1.

RAMACHANDRAN, V. K. (1990). *Wage Labour and Unfreedom in Agriculture* (Oxford: Clarendon Press).

RAMSEY, F. P. (1928). 'A Mathematical Theory of Saving', *Economic Journal*, 38.

—— (1978). *Foundations: Essays in Philosophy, Logic, Mathematics and Economics* (London: Routledge).

RAVALLION, M. (1987). *Markets and Famines* (Oxford: Clarendon Press).

—— and VAN DE WALLE, D. (1988). 'Poverty Orderings of Food Pricing Reforms', Discussion Paper 86, Development Economics Research Centre, University of Warwick.

RAWLS, J. (1958). 'Justice as Fairness', *Philosophical Review*, 67.

—— (1971). *A Theory of Justice* (Cambridge, Mass.: Harvard University Press).

—— (1982). 'Social Unity and Primary Goods', in Sen and Williams (1982).

—— (1985). 'Justice as Fairness: Political not Metaphysical', *Philosophy and Public Affairs*, 14.

—— (1987). 'The Idea of an Overlapping Consensus', *Oxford Journal of Legal Studies*, 7.

—— (1988a). 'Priority of Right and Ideas of the Good', *Philosophy and Public Affairs*, 17.

—— (1988b). 'Reply to Sen', mimeographed, Harvard University.

—— (1988c). 'The Domain of the Political and Overlapping Consensus', mimeographed, Harvard University.

—— (1990). 'Political Liberalism', to be published by Columbia University Press.

—— FRIED, C., SEN, A., and SCHELLING, T. (1987). *Liberty, Equality, and Law*, ed. S. McMurrin (Cambridge: Cambridge University Press; and Salt Lake City: University of Utah Press).

RAY, R. (1984a). 'A Class of Decomposable Poverty Measures: A Correction and a Modified Poverty Measure', unpub. manuscript, University of Manchester.

—— (1984b). 'On Measuring Poverty in India: A Synthesis of Alternative Measures', unpub. manuscript, University of Manchester.

RAZ, J. (1986). *The Morality of Freedom* (Oxford: Clarendon Press).

REDDY, S. (1988). 'An Independent Press Working against Famine: The Nigerian Experience', *Journal of Modern African Studies*, 26.

REGAN, D. H. (1983). 'Against Evaluator Relativity: A Response to Sen', *Philosophy and Public Affairs*, 12.

RILEY, J. (1986). 'Generalized Social Welfare Functionals: Welfarism, Morality and Liberty', *Social Choice and Welfare*, 3.

—— (1987). *Liberal Utilitarianism: Social Choice Theory and J. S. Mill's Philosophy* (Cambridge: Cambridge University Press).

—— (1989a). 'Rights to Liberty in Purely Private Matters: Part I', *Economics and Philosophy*, 5.

—— (1989b). 'Rights to Liberty in Purely Private Matters: Part II', *Economics and Philosophy*, 6.

RINGEN, S. (1984). 'Towards a Third Stage in the Measurement of Poverty', unpub. manuscript, The Swedish Institute for Social Research, University of Stockholm.

—— (1987). *The Possibility of Politics: A Study of the Economy of the Welfare State* (Oxford: Clarendon Press).

RISKIN, C. (1987). *China's Political Economy* (Oxford: Clarendon Press).

RISKIN, D. (1988). 'Reform: Where is China Going?' mimeographed, Queens University, New York, and East Asia Center, Columbia University.

ROBBINS, L. (1932). *An Essay on the Nature and Significance of Economic Science* (London: Allen & Unwin).

—— (1938). 'Interpersonal Comparisons of Utility', *Economic Journal*, 48.

ROBERTS, K. W. S. (1980*a*). 'Interpersonal Comparability and Social Choice Theory', *Review of Economic Studies*, 47.

—— (1980*b*). 'Price Independent Welfare Prescriptions', *Journal of Public Economics*, 13.

ROCHFORD, S. C. (1981). 'Nash-Bargained Household Decision Making in a Peasant Economy', mimeographed.

—— (1982). 'General Results of Stable Pairwise-Bargained Allocations in a Marriage Market', mimeographed.

ROEMER, J. (1982). *A General Theory of Exploitation and Class* (Cambridge, Mass.: Harvard University Press).

—— (1985). 'Equality of Talent', *Economics and Philosophy*, 1.

—— (1986*a*). 'An Historical Materialist Alternative to Welfarism', in Elster and Hylland (1986).

—— (1986*b*). 'Equality of Resources Implies Equality of Welfare', *Quarterly Journal of Economics*, 101.

—— (1988). *Free to Lose: An Introduction to Marxist Economic Philosophy* (Cambridge, Mass.: Harvard University Press).

—— (1990). 'Welfarism and Axiomatic Bargaining Theory', *Recherches économiques de Louvain*, 56.

—— (1992). 'Distributing Health: The Allocation of Resources by an International Agency', in Nussbaum and Sen (1992).

ROGERS, B. (1980). *The Domestication of Women* (London: Tavistock).

ROSENZWEIG, M. R., and SCHULTZ, T. P. (1982). 'Market Opportunities, Genetic Endowments, and Intra-Family Resource Distribution: Child Survival in Rural India', *American Economic Review*, 72.

ROSS, D. (1980) (ed.). *Aristotle: The Nicomachean Ethics* (Oxford: Clarendon Press).

ROTBERG, R. I., and RABB, T. K. (1985). *Hunger and History* (Cambridge: Cambridge University Press).

ROTH, A. E. (1979). *Axiomatic Models of Bargaining* (Berlin: Springer-Verlag).

ROTHSCHILD, M., and STIGLITZ, J. (1973). 'Some Further Results in the Measurement of Inequality', *Journal of Economic Theory*, 6.

ROWNTREE, B. S. (1901). *Poverty: A Study of Town Life* (London: Longmans).

—— (1941). *Poverty and Progress* (London: Longmans).

RYAN, A. (1979) (ed.). *The Idea of Freedom: Essays in Honour of Isaiah Berlin* (Oxford: Clarendon Press).

SADKA, E. (1977). 'On Progressive Income Taxation', *American Economic Review*, 67.

SAMUELSON, P. A. (1938). 'A Note on the Pure Theory of Consumer Behaviour', *Economica*, 5.

—— (1947). *Foundations of Economic Analysis* (Cambridge, Mass.: Harvard University Press).

—— (1956). 'Social Indifference Curves', *Quarterly Journal of Economics*, 70.

SASTRY, S. A. R. (1977). 'Poverty, Inequality and Development: A Study of Rural Andhra Pradesh', *Anvesak*, 7.

—— (1980a). 'A Survey of Literature on Poverty Income Distribution and Development', *Artha Vijnana*, 22.

—— (1980b). 'Poverty: Concepts and Measurement', *Indian Journal of Economics*, 61.

SAWHILL, I. V. (1988). 'Poverty in the U.S.: Why is it so Persistent?', *Journal of Economic Literature*, 26.

SCANLON, T. M. (1975). 'Preference and Urgency', *Journal of Philosophy*, 72.

—— (1982). 'Contractualism and Utilitarianism', in Sen and Williams (1982).

—— (1988a). 'The Significance of Choice', in *Tanner Lectures on Human Values*, viii (Salt Lake City: University of Utah Press).

—— (1988b). 'Notes on Equality', mimeographed, Harvard University.

—— (1990). 'The Moral Basis of Interpersonal Comparisons', mimeographed, forthcoming in J. Elster and J. Roemer (eds.), *Interpersonal Comparability*.

—— (1992). 'Value, Desire and Quality of Life', in Nussbaum and Sen (1992).

SCHEFFLER, S. (1982). *The Rejection of Consequentialism* (Oxford: Clarendon Press).

—— (1988) (ed.). *Consequentialism and Its Critics* (Oxford: Oxford University Press).

SCHELLING, T. C. (1960). *The Strategy of Conflict* (Cambridge, Mass.: Harvard University Press).

SCHELLING, T. (1984). *Choice and Consequences* (Cambridge, MA: Harvard University Press).

SCHOKKAERT, E., and VAN OOTEGEM, L. (1990). 'Sen's Concept of the Living Standard Applied to the Belgian Unemployed', *Recherches économiques de Louvain*, 56.

School of Public Health, Harvard University (1985). *Hunger in America: The Growing Epidemic* (Cambridge, Mass.: School of Public Health, Harvard University).

SCHOTTER, A. (1985). *Free Market Economics: A Critical Appraisal* (New York: St Martin's Press).

SCHWARTZ, T. (1981). 'The Universal Instability Theorem', *Public Choice*, 37.

—— (1986). *The Logic of Collective Choice* (New York: Columbia University Press).

SCRIMSHAW, N. (1987). 'Biological Adaptation in the Maintenance of Nutrition and Health', mimeographed, MIT.

—— TAYLOR, C. E., and GOPALAN, J. E. (1968). *Interactions of Nutrition and Infection* (Geneva: World Health Organization).

SEABRIGHT, P. (1989). 'Social Choice and Social Theories', *Philosophy and Public Affairs*, 18.

—— (1992). 'Pluralism and the Standard of Living', in Nussbaum and Sen (1992).

SEADE, J. (1977). 'On the Shape of Optimal Tax Schedules', *Journal of Public Economics*, 7.

SEASTRAND, F., and DIWAN, R. (1975). 'Measurement and Comparison of Poverty and Inequality in the United States', presented at the Third World Econometric Congress, Toronto.

SEIDL, C. (1975). 'On Liberal Values', *Zeitschrift für Nationalökonomie*, 35.

—— (1986a). 'Poverty Measures: A Survey', in Bos, Rose, and Seidl (1986).

—— (1986b). 'The Impossibility of Nondictatorial Tolerance', *Journal of Economics: Zeitschrift für Nationalökonomie*, 46.

—— (1990). 'On the Impossibility of a Generalization of the Libertarian Resolution of the Liberal Paradox', *Journal of Economics*, 51.

SEN, A. K. (1970a). *Collective Choice and Social Welfare* (San Francisco: Holden-Day). (Republished Amsterdam: North-Holland, 1979.)

—— (1970b). 'Interpersonal Aggregation and Partial Comparability', *Econometrica*, 38. (Repr. in Sen 1982a.) ('A Correction', *Econometrica*, 40, 1972.)

—— (1970c). 'The Impossibility of a Paretian Liberal' *Journal of Political Economy*, 78. (Repr. in Hahn and Hollis 1979 and Sen 1982a.)

—— (1973a). *On Economic Inequality* (Oxford: Clarendon Press and New York: Norton). (Also referred to in the text as *OEI*.)

—— (1973b). 'Behaviour and the Concept of Preference', *Economica*, 40. (Repr. in Sen 1982a.)

—— (1973c). 'Poverty, Inequality and Unemployment: Some Conceptual Issues in Measurement', *Economic and Political Weekly*, 8.

—— (1973d). 'On the Development of Basic Economic Indicators to Supplement GNP Measures', *United Nations Economic Bulletin for Asia and the Far East*, 24.

—— (1974). 'Informational Bases of Alternative Welfare Approaches: Aggregation and Income Distribution', *Journal of Public Economics*, 4.

—— (1976a). 'Poverty: An Ordinal Approach to Measurements', *Econometrica*, 44. (Repr. in Sen 1982a.)

—— (1976*b*). 'Real National Income', *Review of Economic Studies*, 43. (Repr. in Sen 1982*a*.)

—— (1976*c*). 'Liberty, Unanimity and Rights', *Economica*, 43. (Repr. in Sen 1982*a*.)

—— (1977*a*). 'Social Choice Theory: A Re-Examination', *Econometrica*, 45. (Repr. in Sen 1982*a*.)

—— (1977*b*). 'On Weights and Measures: Informational Constraints in Social Welfare Analysis', *Econometrica*, 45. (Repr. in Sen 1982*a*.)

—— (1977*c*). 'Rational Fools: A Critique of the Behavioural Foundations of Economic Theory', *Philosophy and Public Affairs*, 6. (Repr. in Sen 1982*a*.)

—— (1978*a*). 'On the Labour Theory of Value: Some Methodological Issues', *Cambridge Journal of Economics*, 2.

—— (1978*b*). 'Ethical Measurement of Inequality: Some Difficulties', in Krelle and Shorrocks (1978). (Repr. in Sen 1982*a*.)

—— (1979*a*). 'Personal Utilities and Public Judgements: or What's Wrong with Welfare Economics?' *Economic Journal*, 89. (Repr. in Sen 1982*a*.)

—— (1979*b*). 'Utilitarianism and Welfarism', *Journal of Philosophy*, 76.

—— (1979*c*). 'The Welfare Basis of Real Income Comparisons', *Journal of Economic Literature*, 1. (Repr. in Sen 1984.)

—— (1979*d*). 'Informational Analysis of Moral Principles', in R. Harrison (ed.), *Rational Action* (Cambridge: Cambridge University Press).

—— (1979*e*). 'Issues in the Measurement of Poverty', *Scandinavian Journal of Economics*, 81.

—— (1980*a*). 'Equality of What?' in McMurrin (1980). (Repr. in Sen 1982*a*; and in Rawls *et al.* 1987.)

—— (1980*b*). 'Description as Choice', *Oxford Economic Papers*, 32. (Repr. in Sen 1982*a*.)

—— (1980–81). 'Plural Utility', *Proceedings of the Aristotelian Society*, 80.

—— (1981*a*). *Poverty and Famines: An Essay on Entitlement and Deprivation* (Oxford: Clarendon Press).

—— (1981*b*). 'Public Action and the Quality of Life in Developing Countries', *Oxford Bulletin of Economics and Statistics*, 43.

—— (1982*a*). *Choice, Welfare and Measurement* (Oxford: Blackwell and Cambridge, Mass.: MIT Press).

—— (1982*b*). 'Rights and Agency', *Philosophy and Public Affairs*, 11. (Repr. in Scheffler 1988.)

—— (1982*c*). 'Liberty as Control: An Appraisal', *Midwest Studies in Philosophy*, 7.

—— (1983*a*). 'Liberty and Social Choice', *Journal of Philosophy*, 80.

—— (1983*b*). 'Evaluator Relativity and Consequential Evaluation', *Philosophy and Public Affairs*, 12.

—— (1983*c*). 'Development: Which Way Now', *Economic Journal*, 93.

—— (1983*d*). 'Poor, Relatively Speaking', *Oxford Economic Papers*, 35.

—— (1984). *Resources, Values and Development* (Oxford: Blackwell and Cambridge, Mass.: Harvard University Press).

—— (1985*a*). 'Well-being, Agency and Freedom: The Dewey Lectures 1984', *Journal of Philosophy*, 82.

—— (1985*b*). *Commodities and Capabilities* (Amsterdam: North-Holland).

—— (1985*c*). 'A Reply to Professor Townsend', *Oxford Economic Papers*, 37.

—— (1985*d*). 'Women, Technology and Sexual Divisions', *Trade and Development*, 6.

—— (1985*e*). 'The Moral Standing of the Market', *Social Philosophy and Policy*, 2.

—— (1986*a*). 'Social Choice Theory', in Arrow and Intriligator (1986).

—— (1986*b*). 'Information and Invariance in Normative Choice', in Heller, Starr, and Starrett (1986).

—— (1987). *On Ethics and Economics* (Oxford: Blackwell).

—— (1988*a*). 'Freedom of Choice: Concept and Content', *European Economic Review*, 32.

—— (1988*b*). 'The Concept of Development', in Chenery and Srinivasan (1988), vol. 1.

—— (1988*c*). 'Africa and India: What do we have to Learn from Each Other?' C. N. Vakil Memorial Lecture, 8th World Congress of the International Economic Association; published in K. J. Arrow (ed.), *The Balance between Industry and Agriculture in Economic Development* (London: Macmillan).

—— (1989*a*). 'Women's Survival as a Development Problem', *Bulletin of the American Academy of Arts and Sciences*, 43 (Nov.). (A revised version published in *New York Review of Books*, Christmas Number, 1990.)

—— (1989*b*). 'Economic Methodology: Heterogeneity and Relevance', *Social Research*, 56.

—— (1990*a*). 'Welfare, Freedom and Social Choice: A Reply', *Recherches économiques de Louvain*, 56.

—— (1990*b*). 'Justice: Means versus Freedoms', *Philosophy and Public Affairs*, 19.

—— (1990*c*). 'Gender and Cooperative Conflicts', in Tinker (1990*a*).

—— (1991*a*). 'Welfare, Preference and Freedom', forthcoming in *Journal of Econometrics*.

—— (1991*b*). 'Well-Being and Capability', forthcoming in Nussbaum and Sen (1992).

—— (1991*c*). 'The Nature of Inequality', in Arrow (1991).

—— (1992*a*). 'Minimal Liberty', forthcoming in *Economica*.

—— (1992*b*). 'Markets and Freedoms', text of John Hicks Lecture, forthcoming in *Oxford Economic Papers*.

—— (1992c). 'On Indexing Primary Goods and Capabilities', mimeographed, Harvard University.

—— and SENGUPTA, S. (1983). 'Malnutrition of Rural Indian Children and the Sex Bias', *Economic and Political Weekly*, 19 (Annual Number).

—— and WILLIAMS, B. (1982) (eds.). *Utilitarianism and Beyond* (Cambridge: Cambridge University Press).

—— MUELLBAUER, J., KANBUR, R., HART, K., and WILLIAMS, B. (1987). *The Standard of Living* (Cambridge: Cambridge University Press).

SEN, P. K. (1986). 'The Gini Coefficient and Poverty Indexes: Some Reconciliations', *Journal of the American Statistical Association*, 81.

SERAGELDIN, I. (1989). *Poverty, Adjustment and Growth in Africa* (Washington, DC: The World Bank).

SHARMA, U. (1980). *Women, Work and Property in North-West India* (London: Tavistock).

SHESHINSKI, E. (1972). 'Relation between a Social Welfare Function and the Gini Index of Inequality', *Journal of Economic Theory*, 4.

SHKLAR, J. (1990). *The Faces of Injustice* (New Haven: Yale University Press).

SHORROCKS, A. F. (1980). 'The Class of Additively Decomposable Inequality Measures', *Econometrica*, 48.

—— (1982). 'Inequality Decomposition by Factor Components', *Econometrica*, 50.

—— (1983). 'Ranking Income Distributions', *Economica*, 50.

—— (1984). 'Inequality Decomposition by Population Subgroups', *Econometrica*, 52.

—— (1988). 'Aggregation Issues in Inequality Measurement', in Eichhorn (1988a).

—— and FOSTER, J. E. (1987). 'Transfer Sensitive Inequality Measures', *Review of Economic Studies*, 54.

SIDGWICK, H. (1874). *The Method of Ethics* (London: Macmillan).

SILBER, J. (1983). 'ELL (Equivalent Length of Life) or Another Attempt at Measuring Development', *World Development*, 11.

SLOTTJE, D. J. (1984). 'An Analysis of the Impact of Relative Price Changes on Inequality in Size Distribution of Various Components of Income: A Multidimensional Approach', Southern Methodist University, Dallas.

SMART, J. J. C., and WILLIAMS, B. (1973). *Utilitarianism: For and Against* (Cambridge: Cambridge University Press).

SMEEDING, T., RAINWATER, L., and O'HIGGINS, M. (1988). *Poverty, Inequality, and the Distribution of Income in an International Context* (Brighton: Wheatsheaf).

SMITH, ADAM, (1776). *An Inquiry into the Nature and Causes of the Wealth of Nations.* (Republished London: Home University, 1910.)

—— (1790). *The Theory of Moral Sentiments*, revised edn. (Republished Oxford: Clarendon Press, 1975.)

SOLOW, R. M. (1984). 'Relative Deprivation?' *Partisan Review*, 51.

SONSTEGAARD, M. (1987). 'A Reply to Perelli-Minetti', *Theory and Decision*, 22: 3.

SPARROW, J. (1977). *Too Much of a Good Thing* (Chicago: University of Chicago Press).

SRINIVAS, M. S. (1962). *Caste in Modern India and Other Essays* (Bombay: Asia Publishing House).

SRINIVASAN, T. N. (1981). 'Malnutrition: Some Measurement and Policy Issues', *Journal of Development Economics*, 8.

—— (1992). 'Undernutrition: Concepts, Measurements, and Policy Implications', in Osmani (1992*a*).

—— and BARDHAN, P. (1974) (eds.). *Poverty and Income Distribution in India* (Calcutta: Statistical Publishing Society).

————— (1988) (eds.). *Rural Poverty in South Asia* (New York: Columbia University Press).

STARRETT, D. A. (1988). *Foundations of Public Economics* (Cambridge: Cambridge University Press).

STEINER, H. (1982). 'Individual Liberty', *Proceedings of the Aristotelian Society*, 82.

—— (1990). 'Putting Rights in their Place', *Recherches économiques de Louvain*, 56.

STERN, N. H. (1976). 'On the Specification of Models of Optimum Income Taxation', *Journal of Public Economics*, 6.

STEVENS, D., and FOSTER, J. (1978). 'The Possibility of Democratic Pluralism', *Economica*, 45.

STEWART, F. (1985). *Planning to Meet Basic Needs* (London: Macmillan).

—— (1988). 'Basic Needs Strategies, Human Rights and the Right to Development', Development Studies Working Paper No. 2, Queen Elizabeth House.

STIGLITZ, J. E. (1982). 'Utilitarianism and Horizontal Equity: The Case for Random Taxation', *Journal of Public Economics*, 18.

STOCKER, M. (1990). *Plural and Conflicting Values* (Oxford: Clarendon Press).

STRASNICK, S. (1976). 'Social Choice Theory and the Derivation of Rawls' Difference Principle', *Journal of Philosophy*, 73.

STREETEN, P. (1981). *Development Perspectives* (London: Macmillan).

—— (1984). 'Basic Needs: Some Unsettled Questions', *World Development*, 12.

—— with BURKI, S. J., HAQ, MAHBUBQUL, HICKS, N., and STEWART, F. (1981). *First Things First: Meeting Basic Needs in Developing Countries* (London: Oxford University Press).

SUBRAMANIAN, S. (1987). 'The Liberal Paradox with Fuzzy Preferences', *Social Choice and Welfare*, 4.

SUGDEN, R. (1981). *The Political Economy of Public Choice* (Oxford: Martin Robertson).

—— (1985). 'Liberty, Preference and Choice', *Economics and Philosophy*, 1.

—— (1986). 'Review of *Commodities and Capabilities*', *Economic Journal*, 96.

—— (1989). 'Maximizing Social Welfare. Is it the Government's Business?' in A. Hamlin and Pettit (1989).

SUKHATME, P. V. (1977). *Nutrition and Poverty* (New Delhi: Indian Agricultural Research Institute).

—— (1982). 'Autoregulatory Homeostatic Nature of Energy Balance', *American Journal of Clinical Nutrition*, 35.

SUNDARAM, K., and TENDULKAR, S. D. (1981). 'Poverty Reduction in the Sixth Plan', Working Paper 233, Delhi School of Economics.

SUPPES, P. (1966). 'Some Formal Models of Grading Principles', *Synthese*, 6.

—— (1977). 'The Distributive Justice of Income Inequality', *Erkenntnis*, 11.

—— (1987). 'Maximizing Freedom of Decision: An Axiomatic Analysis', in Feiwel (1987).

—— (1988). 'Lorenz Curves for Various Processes: A Pluralistic Approach to Equity', *Social Choice and Welfare*, 5.

SUZUMURA, K. (1978). 'On the Consistency of Libertarian Claims', *Review of Economic Studies*, 45. ('A Correction', 46.)

—— (1980). 'Liberal Paradox and the Voluntary Exchange of Rights-Exercising', *Journal of Economic Theory*, 22.

—— (1983). *Rational Choice, Collective Decisions and Social Welfare* (Cambridge: Cambridge University Press).

—— (1988). 'Introduction' to the Japanese trans. of *Commodities and Capabilities* (Tokyo: Iwanami).

—— (1991). 'Alternative Approaches to Libertarian Rights', in Arrow (1991).

SVEDBERG, P. (1988). 'Undernutrition in Sub-Saharan Africa: Is there a Sex Bias?' Working Paper 46, WIDER, Helsinki.

—— (1990). 'Undernutrition in Sub-Saharan Africa: A Critical Assessment of the Evidence', in Drèze and Sen (1990), vol. 3.

SWAMINATHAN, M. (1988). 'Inequality and Economic Mobility', D.Phil. dissertation, Oxford University.

SZAL, R. J. (1977). 'Poverty Measurement and Analysis', ILO Working Paper WEP 2–23/WP60.

SZPIRO, G. G. (1987). 'Hirschman versus Herfindahl: Some Topological Properties for the Use of Concentration Indexes', *Mathematical Social Sciences*, 14.

SZRETER, S. (1986). 'The Importance of Social Intervention in Britain's Mortality Decline *c*.1850–1914: A Reinterpretation', Discussion Paper 121, Centre for Economic Policy Research, London.

TAKAYAMA, N. (1979). 'Poverty, Income Inequality and their Measures: Professor Sen's Axiomatic Approach Reconsidered', *Econometrica*, 47.

TAWNEY, R. H. (1931). *Equality* (London: Allen & Unwin).

TAYLOR, C. (1979). 'What's Wrong with Negative Liberty?', in Ryan (1979).

—— (1982). 'The Diversity of Goods', in Sen and Williams (1982).

TAYLOR, L. (1977). 'Research Directions in Income Distribution, Nutrition and the Economics of Food', *Food Research Institute Studies*, 15.

TEMKIN, L. S. (1986). 'Inequality', *Philosophy and Public Affairs*, 15.

—— (1989). 'Inequality', D.Phil. thesis (Oxford); revised version to be published by Clarendon Press, Oxford.

THEIL, H. (1967). *Economics and Information Theory* (Amsterdam: North-Holland).

THOMSON, W., and VARIAN, H. (1985). 'Theories of Justice Based on Symmetry', in Hurwicz, Schmeidler, and Sonnenschein (1985).

THON, D. (1979). 'On Measuring Poverty', *Review of Income and Wealth*, 25.

THON, D. (1982). 'An Axiomatization of the Gini Coefficient', *Mathematical Social Sciences*, 2.

THUROW, L. D. (1975). *Generating Inequality* (New York: Basic Books).

—— (1987). 'A Surge in Inequality', *Scientific American*, 256.

TILLY, L. A. (1983). 'Food Entitlement, Famine and Conflict', in Rotberg and Rabb (1985).

—— (1985). 'Sex and Occupation in Comparative Perspectives', mimeographed, New School for Social Research, New York.

TINBERGEN, J. (1970). 'A Positive and Normative Theory of Income Distribution', *Review of Income and Wealth*, 16.

TINKER, I. (1990*a*) (ed.). *Persistent Inequalities* (New York: Oxford University Press).

—— (1990*b*). 'A Context for the Field and for the Book', in Tinker (1990*a*).

—— and BRAMSEN, M. B. (1976). *Women and World Development* (Washington, DC: Overseas Development Council).

TOWNSEND, P. (1979). *Poverty in the United Kingdom* (Harmondsworth: Penguin).

—— (1985). 'A Sociological Approach to the Measurement of Poverty: A Rejoinder to Prof. Amartya Sen', *Oxford Economic Papers*, 37.

TSAKLOGLOU, P. (1988). 'A Family of Decomposable Poverty Indices', unpub. manuscript, University of Bristol.

TUOMALA, M. (1984). 'On the Optimal Income Taxation: Some Further Numerical Results', *Journal of Public Economics*, 17.

—— (1990). *Optimal Income Tax and Redistribution* (Oxford: Clarendon Press).

UNDP (1990). *The Human Development Report 1990* (New York: United Nations Development Programme).

—— (1991). *The Human Development Report 1991* (New York: United Nations Development Programme).

UNICEF (1987). *The State of the World's Children 1987* (Oxford: Oxford University Press).

UNICEF (1992). *The State of the World's Children 1992* (Oxford: Oxford University Press).

USHER, D. (1968). *The Price Mechanism and the Meaning of National Income Statistics* (Oxford: Clarendon Press).

VAIDYANATHAN, A. (1985). 'Food Consumption and the Size of People: Some Indian Evidence', *Economic and Political Weekly*, 20.

—— (1987). 'Poverty and Economy: The Regional Dimension', mimeographed, paper presented at the Workshop on Poverty in India, Queen Elizabeth House, Oxford.

VALLENTYNE, P. (1989). 'How to Combine Pareto Optimality with Liberty Considerations', *Theory and Decision*, 27.

VAN GINNEKEN, W. (1980). 'Some Methods of Poverty Analysis: An Application to Iranian Data 1975–76', *World Development*, 8.

VAN PARIJS, P. (1990a). 'Equal Endowments as Undominated Diversity', *Recherches économiques de Louvain*, 56.

—— (1990b). 'The Second Marriage of Justice and Efficiency', *Journal of Social Policy*, 19.

—— (1991). 'Why Surfers should be Fed: The Liberal Case for an Unconditional Basic Income', *Philosophy and Public Affairs*, 20.

VAN PRAAG, B. M. S. (1968). *Individual Welfare Functions and Consumer Behaviour* (Amsterdam: North-Holland).

—— (1978). 'The Perception of Welfare Inequality', *European Economic Review*, 10.

—— (1992). 'The Relativity of the Welfare Concept', in Nussbaum and Sen (1992).

—— HAGENAARS, A. J. M., and VAN WEEREN, H. (1982). 'Poverty in Europe', *Journal of Income and Wealth*, 28.

VARIAN, H. (1974). 'Equity, Envy and Efficiency', *Journal of Economic Theory*, 9.

—— (1975). 'Distributive Justice, Welfare Economics and the Theory of Fairness', *Philosophy and Public Affairs*, 4.

VAUGHAN, M. (1985). 'Famine Analysis and Family Relations', *Past and Present*, 108.

—— (1987). *The Story of an African Famine: Gender and Famine in Twentieth Century Malawi* (Cambridge: Cambridge University Press).

VAUGHAN, R. N. (1987). 'Welfare Approaches to the Measurement of Poverty', *Economic Journal*, 97.

VERBA, S., et al. (1987). *Elites and the Idea of Equality* (Cambridge, Mass.: Harvard University Press).

VISARIA, P. (1961). *The Sex Ratio of the Population of India*, Monograph 10, Census of India 1961 (New Delhi: Office of the Registrar General).

WAAL, A. DE (1989). *Famine that Kills* (Oxford: Clarendon Press).

WALDRON, I. (1976). 'Why do Women Live Longer than Men?' *Social Science and Medicine*, 10.

—— (1983). 'The Role of Genetic and Biological Factors in Sex Differences in Mortality', in Lopez and Ruzicka (1983).

WALDRON, J. (1984) (ed.). *Theories of Rights* (Oxford: Oxford University Press).

WALSH, V. (1964). 'Discussion: The Status of Welfare Comparisons', *Philosophy of Science*, 31.

—— (1987). 'Philosophy and Economics', in J. Eatwell, M. Milgate, and P. Newman (eds.), *The New Palgrave: A Dictionary of Economics*, iii (London: Macmillan).

—— (1991). 'Rationality, Allocation and Reproduction: Some Key Concepts of Microtheory', mimeographed.

WALZER, M. (1983). *Spheres of Justice: A Defence of Pluralism and Equality* (Oxford: Blackwell).

—— (1992). 'Objectivity and Social Meaning', in Nussbaum and Sen (1992).

WEALE, A. (1980). 'The Impossibility of Liberal Egalitarianism', *Analysis*, 40.

WEBSTER, M. (1986). 'Liberals and Information', *Theory and Decisions*, 20.

WEDDERBURN, D. (1961). *The Aged in the Welfare State* (London: Bell).

WESTEN, P. (1982). 'The Empty Idea of Equality', *Harvard Law Review*, 95.

WEYMARK, J. (1981). 'Generalized Gini Inequality Indices', *Mathematical Social Sciences*, 1.

WHITEHEAD, A. (1985). 'Gender and Famine in West Africa', *Review of African Political Economy*.

—— (1990). 'Rural Women and Food Production in Sub-Saharan Africa', in Drèze and Sen (1990), vol. 1.

WIGGINS, D. (1985). 'Claims of Need', in Honderich (1985).

—— (1987). *Needs, Values, Truth* (Oxford: Blackwell).

WILLIAMS, A. (1985). 'Economics of Coronary Bypass Grafting', *British Medical Journal*, 291 (3 Aug.).

—— (1991). 'What is Wealth and Who Creates It?', in J. Hutton, S. Hutton, T. Pinch, and A. Shiell (eds.), *Dependency to Enterprise* (London: Routledge).

WILLIAMS, B. (1962). 'The Idea of Equality', in P. Laslett and W. G. Runisman (eds.), *Philosophy, Politics and Society*, Second Series (Oxford: Blackwell).

—— (1972). *Morality: An Introduction to Ethics* (New York: Harper & Row).

—— (1973a). *Problems of the Self* (Cambridge: Cambridge University Press).

—— (1973b). 'A Critique of Utilitarianism', in Smart and Williams (1973).

—— (1981). *Moral Luck* (Cambridge: Cambridge University Press).

—— (1985). *Ethics and the Limits of Philosophy* (London: Fontana and Cambridge, Mass.: Harvard University Press).

—— (1987). 'The Standard of Living: Interests and Capabilities', in Sen *et al.* (1987).

WILSON, G. (1987). *Money in the Family* (Aldershot: Avebury).

WOLF, M. (1987). *Revolution Postponed: Women in Contemporary China* (Stanford, Calif.: Stanford University Press).

WOLFSON, M. C. (1974). *Strength of Transfers, Stochastic Dominance, and the Measurement of Economic Inequality* (Ottawa: Statistics Canada).

WOLLHEIM, R. (1955–6). 'Equality and Equal Rights', *Proceedings of the Aristotelian Society*, 56.

WORLD BANK (1984). *China: The Health Sector* (Washington, DC: The World Bank).

—— (1990). *The World Development Report 1990* (Oxford: Oxford University Press).

—— (1991). *The World Development Report 1991* (Oxford: Oxford University Press).

WRIGLESWORTH, J. (1982). 'The Possibility of Democratic Pluralism: A Comment', *Economica*, 49.

—— (1985). *Libertarian Conflicts in Social Choice* (Cambridge: Cambridge University Press).

WYON, J. B., and GORDON, J. E. (1971). *The Khanna Study* (Cambridge, Mass.: Harvard University Press).

XU, Y. (1990). 'The Liberal Paradox: Some Further Observations', *Social Choice and Welfare*, 7.

—— (1991). 'Urgency and Freedom', mimeographed, Murphy Institute, Tulane University.

YAARI, M. E., and BAR-HILLEL, M. (1984). 'On Dividing Justly', *Social Choice and Welfare*, 1.

YITZHAKI, S. (1979). 'Relative Deprivation: A New Approach to the Social Welfare Function', *Quarterly Journal of Economics*, 93.

YOUNG, H. P. (1986) (ed.). *Fair Allocation*, American Mathematical Society, Symposia in Applied Mathematics; forthcoming.

YOUNG, K., WOLKOWITZ, C., and McCULLAGH, R. (1981) (eds.). *On Marriage and the Market: Women's Subordination in International Perspective* (London: CSE Books).

YSANDER, B. (1992). 'Comment on Erikson', in Nussbaum and Sen (1992).

ZADEH, L. A. (1965). 'Fuzzy Sets', *Information and Control*, 8.

ZAMAGNI, S. (1986). 'Introduzione', in A. K. Sen, *Scelta, Benessere, Equita* (Bologna: Il Mulinao).

ZEUTHEN, F. (1930). *Problems of Monopoly and Economic Welfare* (London: Routledge).

Name Index

Subject Index